Praise for
Spark by Frank Koller

"Striking . . . against the backdrop of the layoff mania that has claimed more than eight million American jobs since late 2007." —*Wall Street Journal*

"A fascinating depiction of a rare human resource practice in a company with a long and hearty track record—food for thought for the rest of us." —*Harvard Business Review*

"Clear, vivid and compelling."
—*Cleveland Plain Dealer*

"Fascinating. . . . Instructive and heartening."
—*Publishers Weekly*

"A valuable perspective for evaluating our employment system in a time of crisis . . . an eminently readable narrative about one company's journey through the landscape of American capitalism." —*CHOICE Library Review*

"A fascinating story."
—MICHAEL ENRIGHT on
The Sunday Edition, CBC Radio One

"A fascinating insight into a singular operation that may be an alternative for layoff-plagued America."
—*Akron Beacon Journal*

"Highly recommended, extremely well-written and impeccably documented."
—JIM STANFORD, Chief Economist,
Canadian Autoworkers Union

"Remarkable story of the best side of US capitalism . . . required reading for everyone from the president and his economic advisors to business leaders and employees everywhere." —RICHARD FREEMAN, Harvard University

"Never worry about losing your job in a down economy? The stuff of fairy tales . . . but for workers at Lincoln Electric, it's reality." —MARKETPLACE/American Public Radio

"A compelling read . . . fascinating . . . good storytelling . . . and well-researched." —*Ottawa Business Journal*

"Timely. . . . Well-researched and well-written." —THOMAS KOCHAN, MIT/Sloan School of Management

"Remarkable. . . . Excellent." —NORMAN BERG, Harvard Business School

"What the 200-page book does best is drive home the fact that the approach the Lincolns designed for 19th-century factory workers fits as well today as it did then: Be good to your people, and they'll be good to you." —*Inside Business Magazine*

SPARK

SPARK

How Old-Fashioned Values
Drive a Twenty-First-Century Corporation:
Lessons from Lincoln Electric's Unique
Guaranteed Employment Program

Frank Koller

PublicAffairs | New York

Hardcover first published in the United States in 2010 by PublicAffairs™, a member of the Perseus Books Group.
Paperback first published in the United States in 2011.

PublicAffairs books are available at special discounts for bulk purchases in the U.S. by corporations, institutions, and other organizations. For more information, please contact the Special Markets Department at the Perseus Books Group, 2300 Chestnut Street, Suite 200, Philadelphia, PA 19103, call (800) 810-4145, ext. 5000, or e-mail special.markets@perseusbooks.com.

Designed by Jeff Williams

Text set in Electra LH

The Library of Congress has catalogued the hardcover edition as follows:

Koller, Frank.
    Spark : how old-fashioned values drive a twenty-first century corporation : lessons from Lincoln Electric's unique guaranteed employment program / Frank Koller. — 1st ed.
        p. cm.
    Includes bibliographical references and index.
    ISBN 978-1-58648-795-9 (alk. paper)
    1. Lincoln Electric Company—Management. 2. Welding equipment industry—Ohio—Management. I. Title.
    HD9697.W434L565 2010
    338.7'62197709771—dc22

                                                2009050853
Paperback ISBN 978-1-61039-053-8
E-book ISBN 978-1-58648-868-0

10 9 8 7 6 5 4 3 2 1

The Actual Is Limited: The Possible Is Immense.

CONTENTS

PREFACE

THE MAINTENANCE STAFF began clearing away the tables in the cafeteria right after lunch on December 12, 2008. At one end of the huge windowless room, technicians hustled to put the finishing cosmetic touches on a small stage, attaching the company logo, testing the sound system and the big-screen TVs. At three o'clock, at least 1,000 employees of the Lincoln Electric Company would try to squeeze in for a ritual dating back to the Great Depression: the annual announcement of the profit-sharing bonus by the chairman of the board. Those who couldn't get into the cafeteria, which is located off a pedestrian tunnel running under the main factory of Lincoln Electric in suburban Cleveland, would watch the ceremony on huge video screens set up in the several other company buildings located next door and across St. Clair Avenue. More screens were being installed in a second factory complex in Mentor, Ohio, twenty miles to the east, and in sales offices across the country, employees would be able to watch the ceremony streamed live onto their computers. In all, the vast majority of Lincoln Electric's 3,300 employees in the United States were planning to stop work early, anxious to hear what 2008 would mean to both their pocketbooks and their futures.

For most Americans on that December afternoon, the verdict on 2008 was already in. It was a lousy year, and 2009 was guaranteed to be worse. The stock market had taken a nosedive, taking their 401(k)s down with it. Housing prices were falling, imperiling the millions of people who had borrowed with subprime mortgages. Commodity prices, car sales, and job numbers were following suit. It seemed as if the whole economy was poised to fall right off a cliff. Even the national euphoria over the election of Barack Obama that November was starting to wane as the enormity of the crisis he would soon face in the Oval Office began to dawn on supporters and opponents alike.

The Lincoln Electric Company is the world's largest manufacturer of electric arc welding machinery and products, a market position it has held for many decades. Apart from its American workers, the company employs more than 6,000 people in nineteen other countries, including Canada, Mexico, France, China, Brazil, and Indonesia. Since the 1930s the company has been widely regarded as the technological leader in many sectors of the global welding industry. The company regularly appears in *Forbes* magazine's listing of the 400 Best Big Companies in America and on the Fortune 1000 list as well.

Of course, by late 2008, an impressive historical résumé and a balance sheet solidly in the black hardly constituted an insurance policy against the carnage being inflicted by a deepening economic crisis. Many, if not most, of the other successful companies on those "best of" lists were already in serious trouble, and tens of thousands of their employees were paying the price: more than 500,000 jobs had disappeared just in November.

Lincoln Electric was founded in Cleveland in 1895, at a time when the city was one of the most important industrial centers in the United States. But starting at the end of World War II, Cleveland's big manufacturing companies deserted this quintessential

Rust Belt hub in a steady stream, hollowing out the once-healthy local economy and relentlessly inflating the ranks of the unemployed year after year. The pain continues to this day. In 2006–2007 Cleveland suffered the largest decline in population of any city in the United States. As the mortgage crisis grew through 2007 and 2008, Cleveland's housing foreclosure rates regularly topped many national listings of the worst of the worst. Yet Lincoln Electric has stayed put, expanding its footprint in the community year after year by buying up the neighboring deserted properties of those who fled, as well as investing heavily in a new research center for robotic welding and expanding operations abroad.

As a manufacturer of welding machinery, Lincoln Electric is precisely the type of "sunset industry" in which, according to many international trade experts, America simply can't (and, it's often suggested by those experts, shouldn't) compete. Low labor costs grant emerging economies such as China, India, and Brazil a comparative advantage. Well before the latest financial maelstrom spilled out from Wall Street, American manufacturing companies had already been among the hardest hit by the intense competitive pressure of globalization.

None of the 3,300 American employees preparing to listen to the annual bonus announcement had any illusions that their company was immune from the economic chaos affecting the global economy. The global welding market was in trouble just like virtually every other part of the economy. But unlike millions of other American workers, those at Lincoln Electric could look back over their company's long history for reassurance that they could survive the hard times ahead. Two indisputable facts provided comfort. First, for more than sixty years, no permanent employee of the Lincoln Electric Company in Cleveland who meets the firm's performance standards had ever been laid off due to lack of work. It's a promise, a company policy enshrined in the

Employee's Handbook and in the *Form 10-K Annual Report* that is submitted each year to the Securities and Exchange Commission in Washington. Second, for seventy-four uninterrupted years starting in 1934, the company had paid out a profit-sharing bonus just before Christmas. Based on an annual merit-rating program, the bonus had almost always exceeded 60 percent of an employee's basic earnings. In a number of those years, it had exceeded 100 percent.

When John Stropki, the chairman, president, and CEO of the company, took the stage at three o'clock, the cafeteria was completely packed. Latecomers who found themselves stuck behind the many red concrete support pillars eagerly peered around to see the boss. Toward the end of the thirty-minute presentation in which he reviewed the year just ending and then looked ahead to 2009, Stropki quoted Charles Dickens's "best of times, worst of times" line, adding, "No one is certain as to how long the current recession will last or how severe it will be. In anticipation of a long, deep recession, we will continue to look for ways to reduce our overall costs and do it in a way that protects our long-term financial viability and preserves our long-standing and very successful Guaranteed Employment Policy."

Then, before every employee in the cafeteria—and across the United States—was handed a personalized white envelope, Stropki announced that the check inside represented roughly 61 percent of each employee's base earnings: The average bonus being handed out was $28,873. Furthermore, no permanent Lincoln Electric employees in the United States were laid off for economic reasons in 2008.

HOW IS IT THAT what most Americans would call an old-fashioned business in an old-fashioned industry, based in the wounded heartland of the economically beleaguered Midwest, has been able to survive two world wars, the Depression, and other economic crises, expand internationally, and consistently succeed at avoiding the kind of mass layoffs that devastate communities and local economies?

It's not as if Lincoln Electric operates in secret. In fact, a case study written in 1975 for MBA students at Harvard Business School remains to this day the best-selling case study in Harvard's history. The case is widely taught, year after year, in almost every business administration school in the United States and in countless others around the world. Yet very few people in the business world have ever heard of Lincoln Electric. More troubling, the very existence of a profitable company that is able to keep a long-standing promise to its employees to guarantee steady work is widely dismissed as, at best, an admirable but probably irrelevant one-of-a-kind oddity.

This recession, and especially Wall Street's role in creating it, has produced a widespread cynicism about corporate America's motives that sours almost every public discussion about possible economic recovery strategies. At the same time, deep down, most people in the United States —whether in their roles as citizens, as workers, as managers, as owners of businesses—surely want to believe that the first response of a profitable business when economic troubles loom should not be, and need not be, to start laying off its employees.

The day before the 2008 bonus was announced, I asked John Stropki, Lincoln Electric's current CEO and a thirty-six-year veteran of the company, why his firm had stuck for so long with a promise to place the interests of its employees on par with those of its customers and its shareholders. "I don't think of this as a social responsibility," Stropki answered as we sat in his office overlooking the vast parking lot at the Cleveland factory. "I think my philosophy and that of my predecessors is that we can perform in an economically challenging environment, and we can spread

that pain in a way that long term will better represent our shareholders' interests without crucifying our employee base, and we
think it is good business, not bad business, to do that."

Corporate executives say this kind of thing all the time, of
course. What's different is that for nearly a century, through thick
and thin, Stropki, his predecessors, and the company's employees
have been able to sustain their unusual and beneficial relationship. The company's perennially robust profit margins (driven by
consistently innovative technology), the dramatically heightened
job security and quality of life enjoyed by its employees, and the
benefits that accrue to the local Cleveland economy should give
the rest of the American business world pause.

Is Lincoln Electric an anomaly, as its critics contend? An
anachronism that has somehow survived from a bygone era? Or
are there lessons to be learned from this company's unique management system—lessons that can help American industry get
back on course?

chapter one

"TOSSED OUT ON THE STREET LIKE WORTHLESS SCRAP"

In the summer of 1895, John C. Lincoln, a twenty-nine-year-old family man with a wife and two young children, was laid off from his job at a small Cleveland, Ohio, manufacturing company that made electric motors.

A financial panic that had erupted in New York City two years before had brought the economy of the United States to a near standstill. Banks were failing. Foreign investors, fearful about those insolvent financial institutions and worried about many of their other ventures, began pulling their money out to take back across the Atlantic. The resulting credit crunch served to dry up badly needed investment in most sectors of the economy, particularly in the railroads that were so important to the nation's economic health in those days. Agricultural prices were falling, forcing farmers into bankruptcy. Millions of people were out of work. Washington seemed unable to help.

Lincoln's partners in Cleveland, who had recruited him several years earlier, concluded that with sales rapidly falling off, they could no longer afford to pay the young inventor's salary, even though he had recently designed the firm's most successful product to date. And so Lincoln was "frozen out," as he called it years later.[1]

Rather than scramble to take the first job he could find by working for somebody else, Lincoln decided to gamble by striking out on his own: He opened up the Lincoln Electric Company, a business dedicated to designing and manufacturing electric motors, in the basement of his small home.

As a high school student in the 1880s, John Lincoln had fallen in love with the new and rapidly evolving science of electricity. His desire to explore the untapped potential of this new form of energy led him to enroll in engineering at Ohio State University in 1885. Three years later, he quit, sensing he'd learn more through practical experience than from out-of-date college lectures.

Lincoln got all the experience he wanted in spades in his first full-time job with the Brush Electric Company, where he earned ten cents an hour as a trainee.[2] Charles F. Brush, a contemporary of Thomas Edison and George Westinghouse, had devoted his life to developing practical uses for electricity. A few years before Lincoln joined the company, Brush had caused a national sensation by illuminating Cleveland's central square at night with twelve of his electric-arc lamps, a first for the country. In 1884 the first electric streetcar line in the United States opened in Cleveland. Soon, dynamos (an early type of electric motor) made by Brush Electric were powering streetcars in many U.S. cities. In 1891, after being loaned out to work for a colleague of Brush's, Lincoln found himself in charge of planning and building a complete transit system for Rochester, New York.[3]

Like any small-scale entrepreneur, Lincoln did everything and anything to grow his new business. He designed small custom-order electric motors, wrote and sold an instructional manual on the principles of electricity, and even began experimenting with electric automobiles, no doubt inspired by his experience with the Brush Electric streetcars.

In 1904 Lincoln's first electric vehicle hit the streets of Cleveland with a top speed of fifteen miles an hour.[4] The inventor soon figured out that achieving higher speeds over longer distances would require both a lighter engine and a longer-lasting battery. His search for a better power source led Lincoln to begin designing and selling battery chargers, which quickly became a new source of profit for his company. A battery charger comprised an electric motor (made by Lincoln, of course) plugged into a wall socket—a relative novelty in those days and rarely available in private homes—that powered a generator to charge a car battery overnight.

Given our current environmental calamities, it's unfortunate that well before the First World War began in 1914, the electric car in the United States was already losing its battle against the gasoline engine and was soon on its way to becoming a curiosity (at least for another eighty years or so).

But as the electric automobile market withered away, Lincoln realized he was still holding a winning hand in a promising new field: The powerful electrical current produced by his motor-generator unit could do much more than charge a car battery—it could also create an arc of electricity hot enough to melt steel.

WELDING 101

There is nothing mysterious about the process. The edges of the parts to be joined are brought to the proper welding temperature and fused together. The heat required to fuse the metal is developed by an electric arc. An electric arc is nothing more than a sustained spark between two terminals or electrodes. In arc welding, the arc is formed between the work to be welded and an electrode usually held in the operator's hand.

ARC WELDING, The Lincoln Electric Company, 1926

You know you're laying down a good arc weld when it sounds like bacon frying in a pan.

MARK BOWEN, welding instructor, Ottawa, 2008

Human beings have been joining pieces of metal together for at least 5,000 years. Sumerians and Egyptians heated iron over a charcoal fire until it became soft and then hammered two or more pieces together (known as forging). Soldering—thought to be almost as old—involves heating a metal alloy (usually a mixture of tin and lead that melts at a relatively low temperature) and pouring the molten liquid over the joint between two pieces of metal. When cool, the solder acts as glue, although the resulting joint is very brittle. It was not a good way to make swords that needed to withstand a lot of heavy action. Welding involves heating the actual pieces of metal being joined until they melt, which requires much higher temperatures. The liquid metal from both pieces flows together and, once cooled, hardens to create a much stronger joint.

In 1801 Sir Humphrey Davy created the first electric arc (a long-lasting spark) between two plates of a primitive battery. Eighty years later, in France, Auguste de Meritens used the heat of an electric arc to melt and join two metal plates of a battery. He received the first known patent for arc welding. In 1890 an American, C. L. Coffin, received a patent for a process that used the heat of an arc of electricity to melt a metal electrode held by a welder. The molten electrode metal (called "flux") then "crossed" the arc (in essence, dropped down due to gravity) to help fuse the joint between two pieces of metal below, which were also in a liquid state from the intense heat.[5]

John Lincoln was convinced that welding would soon become a key technology, and market, for American industry.

CLEVELAND, OHIO, in 1895 was the right place to be for a talented inventor and entrepreneur like Lincoln, despite the severe economic recession. Over the previous century, what started as a small trading post on the southern shores of Lake Erie had mushroomed into one of the biggest cities in the country and an important driver in the transformation of the United States into a global manufacturing powerhouse. A critical hub for the nation's iron and steel industry, Cleveland was also the headquarters for hometown magnate John D. Rockefeller's Standard Oil and home to the second-largest shipbuilding port in the world, after the Clyde River yards in Scotland.[6] Most important for John Lincoln, Cleveland was filled with eager inventors who shared his passion to exploit the untapped commercial potential of electricity, whether through lighting, transportation, or communications.

In recent years historians have compared Cleveland at the end of the nineteenth century to California's Silicon Valley at the end of the twentieth, first for the astonishing level of technological innovation on display by local inventors but also for the fact that the economies of both communities were driven by start-up businesses funded by venture capitalists. Whenever experimenters like John Lincoln achieved technological breakthroughs—and over his lifetime he was granted fifty-five patents—they raced to form their own companies to commercially exploit their ideas rather than let already established firms reap the potential benefits.[7]

Cleveland was just one of many American cities undergoing an economic transformation toward the end of the nineteenth century. Mark Twain was the first to call this period the Gilded Age, an era when larger-than-life industrialists and financiers such as Rockefeller, Andrew Carnegie, J. P. Morgan, and Cornelius

Vanderbilt presided over the explosive growth of their various business empires. These new ventures—in banking, transportation, and manufacturing—were bigger than anything the country had ever seen, spanning the nation from coast to coast and requiring vast numbers of employees: It was the birth of the modern industrial workforce. In the process, these shamelessly extravagant entrepreneurs also set a very public example for others who aspired to the lives of power and excess that they enjoyed.

Men like Carnegie took the job of making money seriously—and ruthlessly. But he and his fellow titans of industry also harbored a sense of responsibility to the society that nurtured their great fortunes, albeit a responsibility they themselves defined. In 1889 Carnegie published *The Gospel of Wealth*, in which he argued that the immense power accumulated and wielded by this small elite group of Americans was an unavoidable outcome of industrialization. Equally unavoidable but actually integral to the efficient functioning of the system, Carnegie believed, was the inability of the vast majority of the population to share in the benefits of a growing economy. Yet while the mighty grew richer and richer, they nevertheless had an obligation to use their riches to help those less fortunate, he argued. In Carnegie's case, it was the impetus to begin funding public libraries in his name across the world.

With immense financial resources at their command, these arch-capitalists were able to sculpt a rapidly industrializing national economy to their own advantage. They were seldom hesitant to react forcefully whenever they felt that their commercial ambitions were being threatened. Moreover, they had little to fear from the federal government of the day: Washington's influence over the national economy in the last decades of the nineteenth century was incomparably weaker than at present, and as a result, the nation's political leaders were severely limited in their ability to influence the course of economic and social developments. (Just as in our day, however, Washington was highly susceptible to the influence of "special interests" eager to use the huge sums of money at their disposal to ensure legislators made the "right" decisions.)

There was a dark side to the relentless change. The owners of these industrial empires, very often aided and abetted by all levels of government, exhibited an "exceptional hostility" toward the growing labor movement in the United States.[8] Outright violence against workers of all sorts became a regular occurrence whenever they organized to create unions or struck to demand better working conditions. The Haymarket bombing in 1886 of a labor rally for an eight-hour day that killed at least ten people, the Homestead strike against Carnegie Steel in 1892 that resulted in seven workers dying, and the Pullman strike of 1894 that stopped the nation's railroads until federal troops intervened were just a few of the most notable conflicts.

In John Lincoln's Cleveland, a streetcar strike in 1899 led to ten days of chaos across the city, burned-out vehicles blocking roads, and a call from a local newspaper for police to shoot rioters. Rockefeller and his fellow business leaders were quick to call upon private guards armed with nightsticks and guns to keep their factories and mines in operation during periods of labor unrest. Protecting factories from angry strikers, while ensuring the buildings also stayed open so that strikebreakers could take up the slack, was a profitable business; in the last decade of the century, the Pinkerton detective agency was widely reported to have had more employees at its beck and call than the entire U.S. Army.

Fear is not a word that is heard very often these days when management gurus expound on how to increase motivation and raise productivity. Now we "incentivize" employees, much to the horror of anyone who loves the English language. But fear was a powerful and prevalent motivator in many if not most American industrial workplaces toward the end of the nineteenth century

and well into the twentieth. Few readers in 1906 of *The Jungle*,
Upton Sinclair's best-selling novel that exposed the horrors of life
inside Chicago's meatpacking industry, would have thought it
was fiction.

In the final years of his life, Frederick Winslow Taylor, the
man who is often blamed for doing more than anyone to dehu-
manize industrial work a century ago with his *Principles of Scientific Management*, became very worried about the state of the
American workplace. "There is no question," he wrote in 1911,
"that a large part of the organization of employers, as well as employees, is for war rather than for peace."[9]

For more than thirty years, Taylor had been monitoring and
measuring and timing workers in brickyards, mines, and factories
from coast to coast. His goal was to analyze the operational mechanics of industries of all kinds, based on his belief that "every
single act of every workman can be reduced to a science." While
Taylor's focus on efficiency at the near-microscopic level of work
had unquestionably helped to make some industrial procedures
more economically productive overall, it had more often served
to support what was then called "the drive system" of industrial
management.

Managing with the drive system was relatively easy: Workers
were given an ultimatum to work harder, or else—the "or else"
consisting of verbal and physical abuse, often horrific work environments, wage cuts, longer hours, no time off, more dangerous
assignments, or, most critically, simply being fired on the spot.
Under those conditions, it was no surprise that workers commonly quit jobs in unbelievable numbers. Many companies, from
mining to manufacturing, suffered employee-turnover rates of 200
to 300 percent each year. When Henry Ford introduced his first
moving automobile assembly line at Highland Park near Detroit
in 1913, the turnover at the massive facility soared as high as 400
percent a year![10] At first, employers could generally find replace-

ments fairly quickly, hiring from the massive flood of new immigrants that poured into the United States from the 1890s to the start of World War I. Eventually, however, some factory owners began to realize how incredibly costly it was to lose and then replace so many workers on an ongoing basis. With their factories often shut down by picket lines, even those employers who regularly resorted to calling in scab labor could see that overall productivity was being severely reduced and that the quality of production was falling, with dire economic consequences.

The American public also knew that something was desperately wrong in the world of work. Social reformers began to demand action from governments, insisting that at a minimum, some semblance of peace and stability be restored in industry and in the streets. Most businessmen probably didn't really care much about what happened beyond the doors of their factories, but they too began to realize that for their economic self-interest alone, such high levels of unrest were too costly and the public scrutiny both unwanted and ultimately dangerous. Teddy Roosevelt captured this unsettled mood in his first State of the Union address in 1901. Although he was nervous about the more strident calls to radically overhaul the basic structure of the nation's economy, Roosevelt was clearly concerned about the overt violence in the streets and worried about so many voting citizens being hurt by economic hard times: "The tremendous and highly complex industrial development which went on with ever accelerated rapidity during the latter half of the nineteenth century brings us face to face, at the beginning of the twentieth, with very serious social problems. The old laws . . . are no longer sufficient. . . . Disaster to great business enterprises . . . is worst for those furthest down. The capitalist may be shorn of his luxuries but the wage-worker may be deprived of even bare necessities."[11]

Gradually, those capitalists, whether shorn or not, grudgingly accepted that industrial calm needed to be restored for the economic health of the country. Their solution was to embrace what has come to be termed *welfare capitalism*: a set of employment policies based on the belief that it was in every corporation's long-term financial interest to protect its workers from the worst and seemingly inevitable ravages of the industrialization process. Thus began a period of economic history in which a great many Americans—both employers and workers—would look to the world of business as a source of social stability.

IT WAS INTO THIS heady environment that John Lincoln launched his newly formed company in 1895. By 1907, as he contemplated how to expand his electric motor business into the new market for welding machinery, Lincoln began to ponder his own role in the coming transition. He was starting to realize that his passion was for invention, not management, and he suspected that running a rapidly expanding business was not the life he wanted to live. Nonetheless, his growing company, which by then had more than thirty paid employees, clearly needed a firm hand in the front office. Lincoln found the answer to his dilemma in his younger brother, James, who had just agreed to join the company after dropping out of engineering at Ohio State (without earning a degree, like his sibling). Almost instantly, it became clear to both men that James was much better suited to the day-to-day challenges of the business world.

With James on the payroll, the Lincolns began to seriously explore the commercial potential of electric arc welding. Within two years they had designed, built, and sold their first welding machine, a behemoth that weighed more than 1,500 pounds. Over the next few years, John devoted more and more of his time to tinkering and inventing. He was soon granted several groundbreaking patents that ensured Lincoln Electric's early technological lead in the new industry. (John Lincoln's inventing instincts were catholic: He once received a patent for using electricity to cure meat.) Those successes in the laboratory, a growing confidence in his younger brother's business skills, and a series of health problems convinced him that it was time to relinquish the never-ending responsibilities of a company president to someone more suited to the task, and in 1914 he appointed James F. Lincoln, then thirty-one, as general manager.[12]

By all accounts from those who knew him as a young man and right up to the end of his life in 1965, the younger Lincoln brother was a natural in the business world, an inspiring and charismatic leader who from the start was determined to earn the loyalty of every employee. At Ohio State, Lincoln had been a star fullback as well as captain of the football team. Archival pictures from his early days at the company suggest he was a big man with a powerful physical presence. Some people describe him as intimidating. Donald Hastings, who was hired by James Lincoln in 1952 and later became president and then chairman of the company in the 1990s, recalling his first boss with a smile, said, "He was certainly a man who was comfortable saying 'no' to anyone."[13]

Under James's leadership, Lincoln Electric commenced its steady ascent over the next few decades to its prominent position in the global welding industry, and it was James who created a high performance workplace a half century before that term was invented. Virtually everyone remembers that he had an immense respect for people who worked hard, whether they were welding on a Lincoln Electric assembly line, sweeping out a warehouse, or living on the road for months on end as a sales executive. Bob Maffit, who retired in 2006 after forty-three years in the plant, recalled that when he started in the early 1960s, Lincoln would still walk the floor almost every day, always in a shirt and tie, stopping to talk with his employees. On one occasion as he chatted with Maffit, the aging patriarch noticed that his own grandson, working at a summer job, was struggling on the assembly line a few yards away in the suffocating heat of the unventilated, windowless building; Maffit remembered Lincoln whispering to him, "It's beautiful to watch that young fellow work up a sweat like that."[14]

TREAT WORKERS AS WE WOULD LIKE TO BE TREATED

The deep respect that the Lincoln brothers shared for hard work most probably grew out of their early years spent as the sons of a peripatetic and impoverished midwestern preacher. As a young man in London, England, in the 1850s, their father, William, had been captivated by the sermons of a well-respected antislavery preacher visiting from Ohio. Determined to follow in his footsteps, William emigrated just before the Civil War to the United States, where he enrolled in theology at Oberlin College in Ohio. Soon afterward, he married a fellow student, and in 1866 their first son, John, was born. James came along in 1883.

The elder Lincoln seems to have been an extremely devout and outspoken man, quick to judge the moral failures of his various congregations and then share his verdict with them. Years later John remembered that his father "would first find out what his parishioners were fond of and then attack it."[15] Unsurprisingly, the family moved regularly.

In later life both brothers were quite comfortable in openly expressing a deeply held belief that Christianity offered a foolproof blueprint for a good life here on earth. John became increasingly passionate about the relationship between religion and public morality. In a 1948 book about Christianity, he stressed that "Christ's object in life was to replace the bad elements in society by good . . . and a greatly improved society would have been the result." James, his younger brother, was equally familiar with the Bible and able to provide quotations at the drop of a hat; he was even more explicit in extolling the Good Book's contemporary importance. James drew a straight line from the Sermon on the Mount to the profitable management of a modern business: "The program that Christ announced, 'as ye would that others would do to you do ye even so to them' is the complete answer to all problems that can arise between people. . . . The first change in industry that would occur if we were to accept the Christian philosophy would be the elimination of present labor-management friction." Several years after guaranteed employment had become a promise at Lincoln Electric, James summed up his conviction that providing workers with steady employment was both an expression of true Christian values and an absolutely essential management policy to ensure any company's continuing profitability: "If we follow the philosophy of Christ . . . we shall have the proper answer to the problem of lay-offs. When we treat the worker as we would like to be treated, the answer is plain. Continuous employment is needed to secure the cooperation of the worker. It is also basically sound."[16]

Despite being prolific writers and lecturers on the subject of Christianity's place in the executive office, the Lincoln brothers seem to have led their employees by example, not through efforts at conversion. None of the many retirees whom I have interviewed who are old enough to have met James before his death in 1965 recall any discussion of religion in their dealings with him. Former CEO Don Hastings believes that over the years, the Lincolns' inclination to heed the Bible's call to respect every person regardless of status simply became deeply imbedded in their company's DNA: "It is ingrained that people are important as people and jobs are important to their families' well-being, and that's important for the long-term success of the company."

WELFARE CAPITALISM AND THE BUSINESS OF BENEVOLENCE

Employers in the very early years of the twentieth century may have sensed that some improvement in the generally deplorable conditions of the average American workplace was necessary, even inevitable.[17] But why did some, including Lincoln Electric, voluntarily decide to so significantly raise pay and improve working conditions (in some cases by including a no-layoff promise) for their employees beyond the basic financial terms that had been settled when those workers were first hired?

The standard answers offered by most scholars of the period demonstrate a common suspicion of big business of the time: Owners wanted desperately to keep unions at bay by any means, they wanted to buff up their public image, they wanted to run their businesses more profitably, and on and on. Only in a few instances do historians suggest that employers primarily wanted to do what they genuinely believed was right. In reality, of course, almost every employer had a number of motives for engaging in "the business of benevolence," as McGill University historian Andrea Tone has called it.

Even during the tumultuous last decades of the nineteenth century, there were a few firms that demonstrated a more enlightened interest in the well-being of their workers. Some built company towns in an effort to provide virtually everything imaginable for their employees. Pullman, Illinois, created by the Pullman railroad car company in 1880, was regarded as a model community for its first few years, until a violent strike at the company forever tarnished its reputation. Procter and Gamble offered its employees a profit-sharing plan in 1886. In the 1890s the founder of Yale Locks also began to share profits with his workers while working hard to establish a sense of teamwork in the factory.

The great heyday of welfare capitalism was the period from roughly 1910 until 1929. It was particularly strong in the decade after the First World War when Americans were able to focus once again on the challenges at home. David Brody, the distinguished labor historian at the University of California, suggests that the horrors of that overseas conflict—given that the decision to send U.S. troops to war in Europe had been extremely controversial—probably contributed to the growth of welfare capitalism back here. Once the fighting ended, there was a sense at many levels of society that the widespread brutality, coercion, and insecurity experienced by so many ordinary workers in the United States were a domestic evil that simply couldn't—and shouldn't—be allowed to continue.[18] A growing fear of a workers' revolution, fed by the success of the Bolsheviks in Russia in 1917, no doubt played a role in the decision by employers to offer a variety of new benefits to their employees.

These benevolent employers tended to be among the biggest in the country in those days, including firms such as General Electric, Eastman Kodak, Sears Roebuck, and Procter and Gamble. Certainly, it was more cost-effective for large firms than for smaller enterprises to upgrade working conditions for their employees. These were also the companies that by virtue of their great size were much more likely to find themselves targeted by social reformers outraged by bad labor practices, which in turn meant facing the glare of public opprobrium. Finally, because the larger employers were generally nonunion firms, they were potentially rich targets for organized labor to expand their membership rolls. So owners had a lot of reasons to take defensive action.

Welfare capitalism in practice, according to Harvard labor historian Lizabeth Cohen, comprised five basic elements: a desire to heal the generally atrocious relationship between employers and employees, the use of financial incentives and rewards to raise productivity, experiments with shop-floor democracy (as long as it didn't include unions), programs to help the lives of workers outside of work, and shouldering greater civic responsibilities.[19]

Inside factories and offices, employers experimented with a variety of approaches, involving both financial incentives and better working conditions, to encourage their employees to, at a minimum, stay on the job for a decent amount of time and, if possible, perhaps even work a bit harder. Eastman Kodak's profit-sharing plan could augment a worker's base pay by more than 10 percent. Other welfare benefits commonly included pensions and rudimentary life insurance: General Electric offered both just before World War I. Employees were often offered financial support to buy their company's stock, and in many firms, such as International Harvester and Procter and Gamble, workers often held a majority of outstanding shares. Metropolitan Life Insurance provided free, hot, "nourishing" lunches to as many as 16,000 of its employees every day.[20] Finally, some firms, such as Sears Roebuck, went to great lengths to avoid layoffs whenever sales fell. Job security in the form of no-layoff promises was sometimes offered as both inducement and reward for employee efforts to continuously increase the overall efficiency of the business.

Welfare capitalism did unquestionably change the way work was organized inside some American companies in the 1920s. The drive system of industrial management, so hated at the birth of the last century, was largely administered out on the factory floor by plant or office foremen who were granted near-absolute power by their bosses. It was a system rampant with such abuse that unions were particularly dedicated to destroying it.

The alternative to the drive system offered by welfare-capitalist employers was to involve ordinary workers in day-to-day decision making (which, with luck, might neutralize any nascent union-organizing campaign). Many different approaches to cooperation, consultation, and delegation, almost revolutionary given the times, began to appear around the turn of the century. They grew rapidly in practice after 1914, following the Ludlow massacre, where a dozen women and children were killed by Colorado state militia trying to oust strikers at one of John D. Rockefeller's mining companies. He quickly ordered the company to find some way to reform labor relations at the mine. The result was a joint committee of workers and managers that was granted the power to make often quite substantial decisions about the workplace. Because of Rockefeller's prominence, this novelty served as a powerful example for other employers nationwide, and soon similar committees were created, with varying degrees of enthusiasm, by companies such as U.S. Rubber, Standard Oil of New Jersey, and Bethlehem Steel. General Electric was one of the most aggressive in creating these so-called employee representation plans (ERPs).

The best of these programs embraced ideas about reforming the structure of a company's actual work processes and about improving communications between employees to defuse shop-floor tensions before serious problems arose. In many companies, the committees operated in remarkably similar fashion to independent labor unions by first challenging and then convincing senior management to develop better factory safety programs, better medical facilities, and even to help workers with legal problems. Often described as "company unions," employee representation programs were eventually declared illegal by Congress under the National Labor Relations Act (also known as the Wagner Act) in 1935. The argument advanced at the time was that workers in these programs had no real "freedom of choice" to push an agenda they felt to be important—that is, lacking the power of an independent and externally organized union, they remained completely vulnerable to management retaliation in times of disagreement. As a result, it was argued that the ERPs were inherently a coercive tool for the company in question. In recent years, many labor experts have been rethinking the legal

ban on company unions. Lincoln Electric's experience with its
Advisory Board, discussed in the next chapter, offers persuasive
evidence that reconsideration might be appropriate.[21]

LOOKING BEYOND the walls of their factories and mills, welfare-
capitalist employers endeavored to upgrade the living situations
of workers and their families in both their homes and their wider
communities, again for a variety of motives. These programs were
generally much more visible to the public at large (and hence
good public relations fodder) than whatever benefits were offered
to workers laboring deep inside a company. For example, Westinghouse, widely regarded as one of the most progressive welfare-
capitalist firms, began organizing baseball leagues and other
sports programs, sponsoring dances and family picnics, supporting local libraries, and even offering financial help for workers to
obtain mortgages.[22]

Welfare-capitalist programs were unquestionably often quite
paternalistic. In some cases, they were decidedly intrusive into a
worker's family life. Henry Ford, for example, regularly disquali-
fied employees from participating in some components of his
company's profit-sharing plan because of their poor moral character, as assessed in regular—and compulsory—home visits by
company representatives.

Of course, no discussion of welfare capitalism can avoid dealing with perhaps the most contentious assertion, that it was really
nothing more than a sophisticated strategy to keep labor unions
at bay. Historians have come down on all sides of that question.
There is no doubt that many industrial leaders in the early days
of the last century were terrified by the growing power of unions
and embraced some of the trappings of "benevolence" with the
explicit hope that their employees could be bought off and thus
kept out of the clutches of union organizers. At the same time,

there also seems little doubt that union organizers often dogmat-
ically refused to accept that nonunionized workers in welfare-
capitalist firms were actually enjoying what many of their own
rank-and-file members were being consistently, and sometimes
violently, denied: relatively steady work with good pay earned in
workplaces that were steadily becoming safer and less abusive. In
the words of John Commons, an economist sometimes called the
"spiritual father" of the New Deal, the best welfare-capitalist firms
in the 1920s were "so far ahead of the game that trade unions cannot reach them. Conditions are better, wages are better, security
is better, than unions can actually deliver to their members. The
other(s) are backward, either on account of inefficiency, competition, or greed."[23]

Other inducements for employers to adopt welfare-capitalist
policies came out of the then new science of industrial psychology. It was not unusual at the dawn of the last century for employers to genuinely believe—if they cared at all—that the
attitude of their workers had no impact at all on the quality of
the work they performed. They either did as they were told or
were fired. But, gradually, experts in this new discipline came to
the near-revolutionary conclusion that what workers felt about
their work, on the job and off, actually mattered to the financial
future of a company. It was not an easy sell, however. The propo-
sition that a happier worker was a more productive worker was a
radical concept in the early 1900s for many employers. Even
harder for them to accept was the suggestion that it would be
profitable to invest in a variety of workplace improvements to
recognize that reality.

Although some employers did slowly institute changes, it
would be naive and historically dangerous to assume they had un-
dergone religious conversions. Many who became interested in
industrial psychology's insights and then acted on them still shared
the feelings of this Sears Roebuck executive: "Don't imagine that

anything we do for our people . . . is done for philanthropic motives—not in the least. Whatever we do for our employees we do
because we think it pays, because it is good business."[24]

Ultimately, for an employer in those times, there were three
ways to gauge whether adopting welfare-capitalist policies was
working. Did the previously exorbitant rates of employee turnover
and absenteeism fall? Did the overall productivity of the company rise? Was there a discernible reduction in the level of strife
in the workplace?

Probably no more than 20 percent of American companies
in the 1920s would have embraced a wide portfolio of welfare-
capitalist policies, although many more introduced one or two
of the strategies into their work environments. Even among that
roughly 20 percent, there was a significant variation in how well
welfare capitalism worked, measured against the three questions
of the preceding paragraph. On paper, for example, GE and GM
were both exemplary welfare-capitalist employers. In reality,
GM—much more so than GE—never really seemed to have
bought into the idea of sharing information and decision making
with its workers, and from the start GM's motives seemed to have
been significantly more about the *capitalism* and less about the
welfare of its employees.[25] Nevertheless, between 1910 and 1929,
the idea that a corporation could and should play a role in providing some kinds of security for its workers, even if for its own
self-interested financial reasons, became almost commonplace.

JAMES LINCOLN was intrigued by the question of why people work
and why some people worker harder than others from the moment he took over the day-to-day management of Lincoln Electric. Many years later, he recalled the challenge he faced when he
assumed that responsibility: "I knew that if I could get the people

in the company to want the company to succeed as badly as I did, there would be no problems we could not solve together."[26]

Within a few years of taking the helm of Lincoln Electric, James had introduced three of the four major components of the management system that has proved enduringly successful: a company-wide "open-door" policy of internal communications, the use of piece rates to pay workers in the factory, and an annual merit-based bonus system. The fourth—the promise of guaranteed employment—took longer to become reality, but was part of his plan from the early days.

Lincoln was no revolutionary. Progress in America was the responsibility of those in charge of the nation's industries, he wrote in many of his books, and throughout his life he expressed disdain for what he saw as the ever-expanding power of the federal government into American business and public life. For James Lincoln, Franklin Roosevelt's New Deal placed dangerous limits on the freedoms of American society; by nature it was a "glorious larceny," its impact "vicious." Yet he was harder still on those business leaders who through their shortsightedness, greed, and arrogance stood in the way of material progress. Lincoln believed most business executives refused to recognize that their employees were human beings first and workers second, and as a result they failed to understand how to motivate people to work both hard and creatively.

At his core, James Lincoln believed every company had to earn the right to expect hard work from its employees, but at the same time he was absolutely convinced that no employer could expect to motivate his employees to work hard just by paying money. He would argue, passionately, that first and foremost employees wanted to be respected as human beings who were engaged in a process of creating a worthwhile product. It was the job of leadership—and Lincoln believed it was a hard job—both to demonstrate and to earn that respect every day. Once employees came to believe that they were truly valued as individuals — in other words, that respect was the everyday currency of the workplace — Lincoln was convinced working hard would become the norm, not a rarity. Respect also required an employer to shoulder a sense of responsibility for the well-being of each employee in the firm, particularly to allay what Lincoln believed was the worst fear of every working man: "He has learned from bitter experience [that] when business was slack, he was tossed out on the street, often with no more thought for his future than was given to any other worthless scrap." From there, it was a relatively short step, for Lincoln at least, to his conclusion that the fundamentals of most management systems of the time were self-defeating: "The idea that Free Enterprise [is a system] where fear of losing your job is the incentive which causes a man to work . . . is outmoded . . . because of the fact that you [do not get] results. I do not believe [in] that idea of fear with its relatively small productivity, relatively small profits and relatively small satisfaction."[27]

A TIME OF TESTING APPROACHES

When James assumed the role of general manager in 1914, Lincoln Electric was still primarily engaged in the electric motor business, with electric arc welding just a growing sideline. Up until the First World War, American industry considered welding to be an interesting technology, but one with very limited uses. It was seen as an acceptable method of repairing cracks in cast iron, but riveting remained the overwhelmingly favored technique when the job was to join together large pieces of metal for a new structure, whether in shipping, heavy industry, or construction.

The Lincoln brothers believed with a near-religious fervor in the overwhelming technological advantages of arc welding pieces of lightweight steel over banging hot rivets through heavy sections of cast iron or steel. They were convinced that the skeptics would eventually agree, and during the 1920s Lincoln and the heads of several other companies looking to expand the market for arc welding joined forces on a number of national advertising and promotional campaigns.

Meanwhile, John Lincoln's decision to return to the lab had quickly turned out to be a very smart strategic move. The elder Lincoln's stream of inventions (particularly the Fleetweld 5 coated electrode) helped advance welding technology and soon gave the company a significant competitive advantage over its rivals. His brother, James, was able to quickly exploit these new ideas commercially, propelling the company to the forefront of a growing national industry, ahead of competitors such as General Electric and Westinghouse.

In Cleveland, under James's direction, the company became focused on a simply stated goal: making better and better welding products at lower and lower prices to sell to more and more customers. Within little more than a decade, welding had begun to displace riveting in construction of all kinds in the United States, and as October 1929 approached, Lincoln Electric had carved out roughly 30 percent of the business.

Comparing the stock market crash of 1929 to that of 2008–2009 has become a grim parlor game for economists, politicians, business leaders, and ordinary Americans watching their 401(k)s shrink; many experts worry that the psychological effect of so much gloom trumps the actual erosion of business fundamentals. There are historical parallels for Lincoln Electric as well. The year 1929 was the company's best ever in its 34-year history; the same was true for 2008 after 113 years, when gross sales exceeded $2.5 billion worldwide.

During the Great Depression, when so many companies that had been considered welfare capitalists abandoned their promises and their workers, Lincoln Electric and its employees survived and even thrived. And at the absolute lowest point of the economic carnage, Lincoln Electric and its workers took a gamble: Collectively, they agreed to share the pain of what they hoped would be the short term, in order to share in the gain when good times returned. The gamble paid off.

chapter two

"IF WE TRIED HARDER, COULD
THE COMPANY PAY US MORE?"

For the vast majority of Americans, Black Tuesday—October 29, 1929—was just a normal working day. In Gloucester, Massachusetts, fishermen would have headed out to sea well before dawn. In Chicago, seamstresses in clothing factories would have been hard at work. Outside Albuquerque, New Mexico, farm families along Route 66 would have been preparing for winter. And in Cleveland, Lincoln Electric employees were struggling to keep up with the demand for their latest product, a new coated welding electrode called the Fleetweld 5. Few Americans back then had any interest in what was happening on Wall Street, and even if they did, they had no way to monitor the growing panic, minute by minute, as the markets imploded.

By 1933 the Great Depression that we now mark as starting on that Tuesday had wrought terrible changes both in the United States and in the rest of the world. The few Chicago seamstresses

lucky enough to be still working at their sewing machines probably ate lard sandwiches for lunch. Route 66 on many days was
clogged with dispossessed farm families from Oklahoma and
Kansas heading west to California. Nationally, economic production had dropped by 40 percent, and roughly one out of every four
Americans who wanted to work couldn't find a job of any kind. In
Cleveland, then the fifth-biggest city in the country, the unemployment rate was even higher, probably one in three.

The Great Depression had an enormous impact on the operations of most companies that during the 1910s and 1920s had
adopted welfare-capitalist policies. Some employers were able to
delay abandoning their various commitments to employees
longer than others: Eastman Kodak, widely regarded as one of
the best, remained "an island of security in the midst of a turbu-
lent sea" for much of the 1930s, while Sears Roebuck, another
company later described as a "vanguard" welfare-capitalist firm
and the virtual inventor of catalog sales, actually hired new retail
staff during much of the Depression.[1]

But the majority of companies that had tried during the previous decade to carve out new types of relationships between management and workers found themselves laying off employees like
so many others, pleading no alternative, just like the rest. Their
relatively recent strategies of stable employment, joint decision
making, and profit sharing with workers on the factory floor—
strategies often proudly defended at the time as cost-effective and
certainly never justified as charity—went out the window when
owners of those businesses faced imminent disaster.

Historians still debate the reasons welfare capitalism proved to
be so vulnerable in the 1930s, if by the middle of the 1920s it had
demonstrated its strength as a profitable alternative business strategy. Many, of course, point to the glaringly obvious answer: The
Great Depression earned its name honestly, because it was an eco-

nomic calamity of unprecedented scale that swept aside almost every social and economic institution in its path. Why should welfare capitalism have been an exception? Others suggest that the welfare-capitalist model was just too new. Most of its adherents had never been sufficiently stress-tested by weathering smaller economic storms. Further, welfare-capitalist policies require time to grow sufficiently resilient such that the people involved—workers and senior managers—are willing to gamble on each other for their mutual long-term survival. A deep reservoir of trust between employer and employees is absolutely essential if alternative strategies such as welfare capitalism are to survive large-scale economic challenges. (This didn't mean that these workers always shared the same goals as managers and owners, or that they believed the companies were operating in the workers' best interests. But given the available options in non-welfare-capitalist firms, working for an employer who offered steady employment, profit sharing, some degree of joint decision making, and sometimes literally a free lunch represented a logical choice.)[2]

Nonetheless, trust at the profound level that has operated at Lincoln Electric for so many decades was definitely a minority commodity even among welfare-capitalist companies during the 1920s. And so when the economy collapsed after 1929, in many cases the bonds forged between comparatively enlightened employers and their comparatively satisfied employees were not yet strong enough to allow them to work together to survive the crisis.

As the 1930s unfolded, tens of millions of workers across the United States lost their jobs. Toward the end of the decade, when an economic recovery seemed possible, many formerly unorganized workers (including those in welfare-capitalist companies) became interested in what unions had to offer, convinced that through collective power they would never again be so victimized

by the titans of industry. Between 1930 and 1940, union membership in the United States nearly tripled, from 3 to 9 million, and
it looked as if welfare capitalism's time had largely passed.

Lincoln Electric, however, was just hitting its stride.

GAMBLING IN HARD TIMES

When the Depression began, Lincoln Electric had changed significantly from the small company James had taken over in 1914.
Under his leadership during the 1920s, the main focus of the firm
had formally shifted, as arc welding became professionally acceptable and commercially profitable in the United States. Lincoln Electric was now in the business of manufacturing welding
machinery and producing the huge volumes of consumable products, such as flux-coated electrodes, that arc welding required in
its growing variety of day-to-day industrial uses; electric motors
were now almost a sideline product for the company. (Many years
later, Professor Norman Berg of the Harvard Business School
compared the welding industry to shaving: Welding machines
were akin to the razor; the consumable rods and wire were the
blades.)

In the early years of the Depression, few of Lincoln Electric's
regular customers (sticking with Berg's shaving analogy) had the
money to buy expensive new razors. But most could still afford to
purchase new and relatively inexpensive razor blades that they
needed to stay in business, and so the sale of its consumable products kept Lincoln Electric alive.[3]

By 1933, however, the economy of the United States had
slowed so much that even the sale of welding rods was falling off.
Fifty percent of industrial workers in Cleveland were out of work,
and some believed the city was the worst afflicted of any in the
country. Lincoln Electric had been able to avoid layoffs, but only
by steadily cutting hours and wages. Finally, in late 1933, one

brave factory worker summoned up the courage to ask Lincoln: "If we did more, tried harder and worked together as a real team, could the company pay us more?"[4]

The question fell on receptive ears. Lincoln had recently heard one of Franklin Roosevelt's radio broadcasts in which the president spoke about American workers deserving a "more abundant life."[5] Roosevelt said that "Church and State" had an obligation to collaborate to achieve this important goal. Although never a great fan of President Roosevelt and his New Deal, Lincoln later admitted he was touched by that appeal, and so he agreed to a one-year experiment, promising that any increase in profits would be shared with every one of Lincoln Electric's employees.[6] At the worst of times, it was a gamble everyone in the company agreed to take together.

MR. TOLAND: Isn't it a fact that you distribute these bonuses to evade paying the corporate taxes to the government of the United States?

MR. LINCOLN: That is not true.

House of Representatives Naval Committee, May 27, 1942

Nine years later, in May 1942, James Lincoln found himself being roughly interrogated in a wood-paneled hearing room on Capitol Hill in Washington, the subject of considerable national notoriety.[7] The president of what had become the world's largest maker of arc welding equipment was forced to defend himself and his company against accusations that the annual bonus paid to Lincoln Electric's employees constituted nothing more than an accounting scam designed to avoid paying corporate income taxes. Much worse than that, said his accusers, it constituted a disgraceful act of war profiteering, just six months after the attack on Pearl Harbor.

Over and over, Edmund Toland, the chief counsel of the House of Representatives Naval Committee and a well-known lawyer described by *Time* as "cobra-cold," tried to force Lincoln to admit that paying a factory worker an annual bonus worth 100 percent or more of his basic wages couldn't possibly be justified under normal accounting procedures. At times, Chairman Carl Vinson of Georgia reined in the committee's aggressive lawyer, but Vinson himself was suspicious of Lincoln's testimony: "It just looks to the average man as if something is wrong somewhere. . . . It is just a reckless expenditure."[8] News stories of the day suggest that James Lincoln, the ex-football player, looked as if he was about to explode in the hearing room.

As a long afternoon of questioning continued, the only thing Lincoln ever admitted was that back in 1934, he'd been unprepared to believe that the bonus system would actually work. He said, "You have questioned the size of these bonuses. I don't blame you. If you had come to me in 1934 . . . and said 'Here, Lincoln, in 1941 you are going to be paying these men pretty nearly 100% of their wages [in a bonus] and it is going to reduce the cost of your commodity,' I would not have believed it either."[9]

Facts—and profits—had changed Lincoln's mind. Once he had agreed to try a new incentive system, the employees did work together as "a real team," as they had promised. Over the next year, they achieved a dramatic reduction in the manufacturing costs of welding products in virtually every division of the factory. As a result, in the middle of the Depression, the company was able to cut prices, which led to a near tripling in sales. Just before Christmas 1934, Lincoln Electric's employees were called into the company cafeteria, where they received a cash bonus averaging 22 percent of their earnings for the year; they were reportedly stunned.[10] "We paid the bonus with our tongue in our cheek," Lincoln told the congressional committee, but the next year it rose to 30 percent of base pay, then 51 percent, and by 1941 it was 111 percent.

As the members of Congress struggled to understand how the bonus system worked at Lincoln Electric, many seemed fixated on what they felt were the exorbitant earnings of blue-collar factory workers (as much as $5,000 a year, nearly three times the national average for all kinds of employees) and outraged by the corporate taxes allegedly being ducked (more than $3 million, a huge amount in the 1940s). In his testimony, Lincoln kept trying to refocus his interrogators on what his firm was actually doing for the war effort: Lincoln Electric technology was widely known to be the best in the world, he explained with growing impatience; its welding products were the lowest cost (and steadily falling) of any available to the U.S. government to build its Liberty ships, tanks, and airframes; and Lincoln Electric was sharing its technological expertise with many of its higher-priced competitors (including Westinghouse and General Electric) by helping to train their engineers for free.

He also stressed to the committee that because Lincoln Electric's workforce was so much more productive than those of its competitors, his company actually spent proportionally much less on total labor costs than any of the other major welding manufacturers in the country, even after factoring in the 110 percent bonuses. The subsequent increase in productivity, an outcome that everyone at the company believed was due to the incentive of a huge bonus, allowed the firm to sell its products for less. By his calculations, Lincoln's lower prices were saving the U.S. government $35 million annually. (As in our own time, "productivity" remains a difficult economic concept to explain—even with its most simple definition of "doing more with less"—and most of the congressmen didn't seem to get it.)

Finally, Lincoln challenged the legislators to recognize that their professed concerns about the alleged evasion of taxes—all the more offensive during wartime—were nothing more than proof of their snobbishness toward the kinds of people who worked in his factory. His words read today as powerfully as they must have sounded in that committee room in 1942, as a definitive statement from a successful American businessman who believed that company profits and employee satisfaction are not mutually exclusive concepts: "I want to say one more thing because I think it is important with the present attitude. . . . Here is something which is making it possible for those men to be home owners, to be self-respecting, to have the feeling that they are men among men, who have the feeling that they are going to send their children to college, that they are going to be just as good as anybody else, and what is more, they are."[11]

It took nearly a decade of further legal battles before Lincoln was finally able to convince Congress that his company had not been illegally profiteering during the Second World War. The company faced additional skirmishes during the 1940s with both the Internal Revenue Service and the Federal Trade Commission, the latter charging that the firm was selling its products below their cost of production in order to eliminate its competition (called "dumping" in our day). During the IRS dispute, Lincoln testified that a senior tax official had once complained to him that "no man who worked with his hands should receive as much as $5,000 a year." In the end, the company prevailed over the government in every case.

THESE DAYS, no one believes that Lincoln Electric regularly cooks its books to avoid paying corporate income taxes. But there is most definitely a pervasive belief in the American business community that Lincoln Electric's structure of incentives and guaranteed employment simply won't work in a modern global economy. On top of that, argue the doubters, the concepts are surely too complex and internally costly to bother trying to emulate in the first place.

What makes the Lincoln Electric story so fascinating is that the company did not invent a unique system for managing its employees. Many other welfare-capitalist companies offered similar financial incentives to their employees and, in most cases, also offered much more generous nonfinancial benefits. Lincoln Electric was most definitely a no-frills employer. What *is* unique about Lincoln Electric is that its management system survived the many challenges of the past hundred years largely intact, while most other similarly structured employers were unable to sustain their policies anywhere near as long.

Now, let's be clear. Lincoln Electric's system of managing its employees is complicated. There is no single magic bullet. One thing Lincoln employees from top to bottom all agree on is that it has taken a long time to develop an incentive system that works and for new employees to trust it. Nevertheless, it is possible to understand what Lincoln Electric has been doing and to suggest that others can profit from its experience.

Four key elements make up Lincoln Electric's incentive management system. Three of those four were already in place by the 1940s: the Advisory Board and the open-door policy, the use of piecework, and the merit-based bonus system. The fourth, a believable promise of guaranteed employment, had yet to become official company policy, but was already in operation de facto. All four of these policies were introduced by James F. Lincoln during his five decades at the helm of the firm: They constitute the heart of how Lincoln Electric functions for the benefit of its customers, its workers, and its investors. As Lincoln tried to explain to his interrogators in 1942, the four policies powerfully reinforced each other out on the factory floor then and continue to do so today. This chapter explains the first three in action. Guaranteed employment is the policy that has the greatest impact on the world outside Lincoln Electric—financially and socially—and is the subject of the next chapter.

THE ADVISORY BOARD AND THE OPEN-DOOR POLICY

The worker who asked James Lincoln in the depths of the Depression about the possibility of sharing company profits more equitably didn't confront his boss as he walked by the assembly line. Their conversation took place at a session of the Lincoln Electric Advisory Board, which has met roughly every two weeks since 1914.

On his first day as general manager, Lincoln was smart enough to understand that simply wanting his company to succeed wasn't a strategic business plan: He seemed well aware that he didn't know enough about electric arc welding or manufacturing to guide the company's progress without a lot of help from its workers. The challenge he faced was how best to involve them in building a future together. Lincoln worried that "military management"—in other words, a dictatorial command structure—would simply kill any possibility of initiative emerging from below. Yet a union in his company would make workers stagnant and resistant to new ideas, whether his or theirs. In a unionized factory, he believed, a worker would "always be a clod like every other clod in the same group."[12]

To carve out what he hoped would be a useful middle ground, Lincoln convened what he called the Advisory Board, made up of representatives elected from the various divisions throughout the factory. They would meet every two weeks "for discussion conducive to the mutual interests and welfare of the employees and management." The Advisory Board has continued to meet with the president on a regular basis ever since, without interruption.[13]

The board was never designed to operate as a democratic institution, and it doesn't now: Lincoln was adamant about that point from its inception, and the word of the company president has remained the final authority. But in 1946, Lincoln wrote that in the first thirty years of the board's existence, he had never used his veto to overrule one of its recommendations, and the track record since then suggests things haven't changed all that much.

As mentioned in Chapter 1, these kinds of joint management-employee gatherings—most decidedly nonunion!—were common in the early decades of the last century. If you ask modern labor economists and historians whether Lincoln Electric's Advisory Board is in essence a company union—and, as a result, the kind of in-house gathering of workers and managers that was declared illegal by Washington in 1935 in order to safeguard workers' rights to freely determine their future—most tend to respond with something along the lines of "Sure, but so what?" In these experts' eyes, regardless of Congress's worries in the 1930s, the good wages and job security enjoyed by Lincoln employees for decades constitute proof that the Advisory Board has not been a forum for worker exploitation or abuse. Their verdict stands despite the limitation laid down in federal labor law that the Advisory Board cannot discuss wages and other forms of financial compensation.

Of course, skeptics have argued that as the charismatic and physically imposing owner of a privately held nonunion company, James Lincoln held absolute economic power over his workers, which was more than sufficient to ensure that Advisory Board meetings ran smoothly—his way! In other words, the fear of being fired is a strong incentive for any employee not to stand up to the boss, regardless of how important an issue might be to that employee.

History suggests otherwise. As a result of discussions begun at Advisory Board meetings, Lincoln Electric introduced many progressive workplace policies that have been, in some cases, groundbreaking for laborers in the American economy: group life insurance (1915), an employees' association (1919), paid vacations (1923), employee stock ownership (1925), a suggestion system with cash payouts (1929), the annual cash bonus (1934), annuities for retired employees (1936), the merit-rating system (1947), and guaranteed continuous employment (1958).[14]

More recently, the Advisory Board has continued to shape and influence company policy. During tough economic times in the early 1990s, then CEO Don Hastings imposed a 25 percent lower pay scale for newly hired employees in order to cut labor costs (two-tier pay structures were then becoming popular in many sectors of the American economy, unionized and not). New employees were also excluded from health care coverage for their first six months on the job. Lincoln Electric's established workers, who had no personal reasons to fear the new lower wage scale, would have none of it. Their representatives on the Advisory Board spoke out forcefully against the policy, arguing that it was inherently unfair and a violation of company tradition. Hastings soon rescinded his decisions.[15]

Skeptics again—and by this point, you may be noticing that there are a lot when it comes to Lincoln Electric—have pointed out that Hastings's reversal in policy came during one of the extremely rare periods in Lincoln Electric's history when some workers were openly discussing the need for a union at the company. The critics argue that Hastings's retreat on the two-tier wage system was a management sop designed to defuse a much more threatening union-organizing effort. It is true that those discussions about a union petered out over the next few months. But the reality remains that for nearly a hundred years, the Advisory Board has been an extremely effective mechanism to enhance communications within the company about important production and technological issues. It has also helped to foster a company-wide consensus on significant policy decisions that are important to management, workers, and shareholders.

Take the meeting of August 4, 2008, which took place just before the financial meltdown began in earnest. The issues under discussion that day covered a lot of territory: how to ensure a fairer distribution of overtime hours among workers, a discussion about whether jobs in Cleveland were being "exported" to Lincoln Electric's subsidiary in China, how to resolve computer problems with company ID and health-record swipe cards, questions about Lincoln's role in a growing nationwide public discussion on energy self-sufficiency, and clarification of whether older Lincoln Electric shirts that were not of the current approved corporate colors could be worn on the shop floor. (The answer on the shirt controversy, delivered several weeks later, was "no, please.")

Dwight Rorabaugh served on the Advisory Board four times during his thirty-six years with Lincoln. He was first elected as a representative (with a one-year term) from the factory floor where he had started wielding a pick and shovel, returning later on behalf of the quality-assurance division and, most recently, representing a team of calibration inspectors. Over the years, he's had the responsibility for communicating the concerns of his fellow workers directly to five different CEOs, an experience Rorabaugh said he has enjoyed immensely: "This is the only thing we have. We don't have a union, so if we don't use the Advisory Board to the best of our ability, it's our own fault. You have to bring things up because if people hold things back, they're going to blow up and there will be unrest out on the floor."[16]

Rorabaugh admitted he cringed during those meetings when someone at the table raised "trivial issues" such as a problem with vending machines in the cafeteria or acceptable shirt colors, but he accepted that as part of the process of open discussion. Overall, he said, meetings deal, in sometimes heated fashion, with serious problems such as workplace safety, medical insurance, or the future of the pension plan's financial surplus. The burly fifty-five-year-old father of three grown children has never worried that challenging the company's CEO could be dangerous: "You have to be tactful, you do not always get the answer you want, but I've always felt comfortable that they won't do anything to me. After one hundred years, they'd blow the system right out of the water to hurt me, and I just don't think they would do that."

Another indication of James Lincoln's commitment to ensure a free flow of information throughout his company—also introduced soon after he took over—was an open-door policy to the boss's office that survives to this day. In many interviews in the factory, virtually everyone told me that either they have or someone they know has turned up unannounced at the chairman's or president's door to discuss an important issue of one sort or another. Obviously, employees try to resolve problems further down the chain of command, but there is no personal cost for going straight to the top. "I'd probably meet with ten employees in my office on an average week," former CEO Don Hastings told me, "and while my secretary would try to be a gatekeeper, an employee would say that 'I want to talk to the president,' and we simply allow that."

PIECEWORK

Of all Lincoln Electric's long-standing management policies, the use of piecework as a compensation system has remained the most controversial—at least outside of the company, where it has been an incendiary issue in labor relations in North America for more than 150 years. The very word still calls up images of Dickensian sweatshops where overworked and underpaid laborers struggle under appalling conditions. In the fall of 2008, at a community picnic in suburban Cleveland, I was regaled with the most wonderfully lurid tales of pressure and brutality on Lincoln Electric's assembly lines—told with absolute certainty by the neighbors of Lincoln Electric workers who had never actually been to the factory. Inside Lincoln Electric, piecework's reputation is quite different: It is almost universally regarded as a source of great strength for the company, ever since it was introduced around 1915, soon after James created the Advisory Board.

Paying a worker a fixed amount of money for each task that she or he completes—a *piece rate*—had been in widespread use in the United States for more than a century by 1915. It was especially prominent in the garment industry in New York City (and in Cleveland, another important center for clothing). Piecework was championed by Frederick Winslow Taylor, who was convinced that virtually any kind of work could be broken down into a series of small measurable physical movements and that a worker should be paid a fixed amount for each separate action he completed. In the last decades of the nineteenth century, piecework spread rapidly into manufacturing across the United States.

For James Lincoln, piecework—as a theory—constituted an accurate and fair system to pay his workers for their efforts. He was also convinced it created a powerful incentive to encourage employees to work together for the good of a firm and everyone in it: "Piecework is basically for the purpose of inspiring and training the worker to do his best. It is not primarily for the purpose of getting him to do the work for less."[17]

That said, Lincoln was acutely aware that a wide swath of American society—laborers, union leaders, social reformers, and much of the general public—believed wholeheartedly that the whole purpose of piecework *was* to squeeze workers to produce more for less, through the application of relentlessly increasing pressure by management. He knew that many Americans were convinced that piecework, by its very nature, too easily allowed and, in many forms, actually encouraged employers to treat workers unfairly.

Lincoln agreed with them: He believed strongly that piecework's poor reputation was well deserved, because of the behavior of inept managers. He also argued that the system's weaknesses could be quite easily overcome, for the mutual benefit of employers and workers. "Piecework has had a bad name," he wrote, "not because of the worker, but because of management. The great difficulty was that as soon as a man really started to increase his earnings, [the piecework rate] was renegotiated and his earnings reduced. We feel it is essential that that sort of thing should not occur. Once we set a price on a job, that price is guaranteed forever; regardless of how much a man makes, it will stand. Only if a new method or a new machine, one that would make a real change in the job itself, is introduced is a new price set. And that price is [also] guaranteed forever."[18] Lincoln employees were given the right to challenge every new piece rate if they felt it was set unfairly low.

Finally, Lincoln announced an unusual departure from common piecework practice of the time, one that remains in place to this day. There would be no upper cap on a worker's potential wages: "There [is] literally no limit . . . on the earnings that a worker can get, except the worker's own limitations."[19]

Roughly a third of Lincoln's 3,000 employees in Cleveland are paid through the piece-rate system. Most of those work in the various factories. The rest of the workforce is equally split between hourly and salaried compensation. Everyone participates in the other elements of the system: the Advisory Board, the merit-based annual bonus, and the guaranteed employment program.

Because Lincoln Electric still relies on piecework, it's common to hear the argument that the company has few lessons to offer in the twenty-first century. Certainly, piecework, strictly defined, is nowhere near as common in the American economy as it was a century ago; probably fewer than one in twenty workers is now paid through piecework.[20] In our service and information economy, it is generally much harder to accurately measure the discrete bits of what we do in a working day, compared with someone who works on an assembly line (unless, of course, you work in a call center!). However, many more Americans do receive part of their pay based on various kinds of financial incentive systems, and it's important to understand how incentives work — or don't.

Take the story of Safelite Glass, the folks who can quickly replace your car's front window after it's cracked by a flying stone on the interstate. In the mid-1990s, Safelite introduced piecework into its nationwide chain of drive-in repair shops and allowed researchers from Stanford University to monitor the results, which were dramatic.[21] Productivity across the company rose by 44 percent, which resulted in a significant increase in profits. Ninety percent of Safelite's workers saw their wages increase by at least 10 percent compared to the old hourly pay system. Quality increased (according to external insurance company reports). And, finally, management felt it was able to attract better-quality workers who were more inclined to stay on the job.

But echoing what virtually every employee of Lincoln Electric has ever told me, Garen Staglin, the CEO of Safelite at the time, cautioned that piecework by itself was really not the key to transforming Safelite into a more profitable company: "It requires a fundamental change in the business culture," he stressed, based on trust.

AS NOTED EARLIER in the evolution of the Advisory Board, continuity has been a hallmark of Lincoln Electric's overall management system, and the company's reliance on piecework is no exception. A formal explanation in 2008 of how piecework operates in practice is almost identical to the wording first introduced almost a century ago, although the specific procedures employed to calculate piece rates and the options available to employees to challenge those rates are now spelled out in greater detail. Everyone in the company understands exactly what the system is all about: "The piecework system rewards the employee for what is done rather than how much time is spent on the job."[22]

Melissa Latessa introduced me to the mechanics and complicated mathematics of piece rates at her workstation in Cleveland. A friendly blonde woman of forty, she comes from a Lincoln Electric family with seven relatives working for the company. In 2007, after fourteen years on the job, Latessa was Employee of the Year. My mention of that elicits a quick smile, a blush, and a shrug.

Latessa's job was to assemble several slightly different models of the "innershield nozzle 6," the part that sits on the business end of a variety of arc welding guns. As we talked, she continued to work, grabbing (without looking) a small brass tube from a plastic bin with her left hand, inserting a spring liner with her right, and then setting it down near a baking oven before repeating the sequence. The pile of brass tubes grew steadily on her incredibly ancient wooden workbench. "You think that's old?" she laughed when I mentioned the bench. Pointing to an electric motor on another table nearby, she said, "This is a LincolnWeld motor with a date plate of 1927! It's run perfectly as long as I've been here."[23]

Assembling a nozzle consists of four separate tasks—sleeving, painting, buffing, and testing—and each job has been assigned its own separate piece rate. The actual pricing calculations are arcane—even for new employees, let alone outsiders—but if Latessa was to just concentrate on "sleeving" at a rate of 100 tubes per hour, her hourly pay would be about $21. In the end, it's up to her to organize her shift to manufacture as many completed nozzles as possible: "Normally, in an eight-hour day, I try to do 150 to 175, taking each through all four steps. The most I've ever done is probably 200, but I have bad days too—they're few and far between—when it's maybe only 100 or 125." With overtime (and from 2001 until the late fall of 2008 there was a lot of compulsory overtime) and the annual bonus, Latessa made upwards of $90,000.[24]

Calculating piece rates is serious business, because once published, they are virtually set in stone, as James Lincoln promised ninety years ago. "It's critical," says Doug Lance, general manager of the consumables division, "because if we set [a piece rate] too low, employees have the right to challenge it. If we set it too high, where the company is losing money, we're stuck with it. We can't retime it."[25]

A piece rate (for a new machine or process being introduced into the factory, or for an old machine that has been modernized) is calculated by a time-study expert (usually a former factory employee) who spends many hours watching a fellow worker, and sometimes a series of workers, perform the assigned task over and over. Every bend of an elbow, every turn of the body, every twist of a wrist is documented and timed. The end result is a numerical estimate of how many operations an average employee could complete over the course of a normal eight-hour working day, working at an average rate of effort. Finally, a monetary piece rate is calculated "to allow an employee of normal productivity" to earn a competitive wage for that job (compared to similar jobs elsewhere in the Cleveland labor market).[26]

Lance stressed that out on the factory floor, changing piece rates is so fraught with controversy that even when he realizes a mistake has been made in setting a new piece rate, he often makes a judgment call to just let things stand. "I'd lose my long-term credibility just to start retiming things when we make a mistake. You just can't go in there and make workers feel like they're being screwed. We do retime things, but I do not spend the time or money on a small amount of people who may be making too much. It's not worth it." Jeff Iannini, the manufacturing manager who reports to Lance, agrees that the extreme reluctance of management to tinker needlessly with piece rates pays off for the company whenever new technologies are introduced: "In the past couple of years, we have made about twenty changes on our production lines in various places, but there have been no challenges" by employees on the resulting recalculated pay scales.[27]

There is no question that piecework creates pressure on the job. Some of it arises from the challenge of meeting minimum performance standards that are clearly established and enforced (more rigorously in tough economic times). A lot of the pressure arises from the demands employees put on themselves to make the most out of a system that places no limits on their potential earnings. "Your stomach turns in knots every day, and mine certainly did up until about ten years before I retired," remembered Steve Simcak, who spent most of his thirty-eight years working on the electrode assembly lines before retiring in 2002. "It's definitely a pressure-filled place because you know you're going to be put through everything under the sun once you're in there. And a slacker will get found out quickly."[28]

Joe Latessa Sr., Melissa's father-in-law, told me virtually the same story. "I used to get nauseous in the morning before I went to work because the pace was so intense," said Latessa, a forty-year veteran before he retired in 2002. A crane operator, his responsibility was to ensure workers on the assembly lines never ran out of raw materials: "There was so much pressure to give them what they needed until I finally had the confidence to realize that what was fastest for me was what is fastest for all the pieceworkers, and it made all our paychecks possible."[29] (Four generations of his extended family have worked at Lincoln Electric, a story told in Chapter 5.)

Robert Clapp worried a lot about the pressure Lincoln Electric workers faced in the factories. For many years, he was pastor of the Boulevard Presbyterian Church of Euclid, where many workers attended Sunday services. Now retired, Clapp said Lincoln Electric employees were "very much involved in their community and their church and the church school," which he believed was due to the steady work and good wages they earned. But "the weakness" with piecework, he recalled, "was that it created a spy system because if I worked beside you and you were not doing your work, that cost me . . . and people always talked about that."[30]

Piecework at Lincoln Electric, as far as I was able to discern, has earned overall acceptance by those who have profited from it over the generations because it has always held fast to one important principle: It is a system committed to avoiding surprises and capricious decision making by managers. It displays what Raymond Hogler, an expert on labor law and history at Colorado State University, calls "complete transparency," and that's what continues to make it an indispensable component of the company's management strategy.[31]

THE MERIT-BASED BONUS

The dollar amount of Lincoln's annual bonus—an average of $28,873 in 2008—has been an object of amazement and a subject for controversy from the day it was first paid out in 1934. Over the decades, the bonus has ranged from more than 120 percent of base pay to (exceedingly rare) as low as 25 percent; since 1955, it has averaged 77 percent.

In recent years, the total pool of money set aside each December for distribution among employees has been set by the Board of Directors at 32 percent of the annual profit earned before paying the interest on debt obligations, corporate taxes, and the bonus itself (it's called EBITB in the accounting world). In other words, no profits, no bonus. But there is also no upper limit placed on the dollar value of the bonus pool, even in good years.

Initially, James Lincoln believed that in a workplace where trust flows both ways, "the amount is of secondary importance, since the essential thing is that the man should know he is getting a fair share of what he has helped earn." But during the 1950s, the company's balance sheet showed that workers at all levels of the company were clearly responding to the extraordinary scale of the bonus by working both harder and more creatively. The bonus was regularly approaching (and some years exceeding) 100 percent of an employee's base wage, and Lincoln became convinced that, in fact, size did matter: "Under conditions of maximum desire for efficiency, the bonus should average more than wages."[32]

"Every December [when the bonus is announced and quickly reported in the Cleveland media], our neighbor used to get mad at us and wouldn't talk to us for a month," laughed Fred Wells, a recently retired tool-and-die maker at Lincoln. "He was a pipe fitter, and he made good money too, but he just didn't think I really earned that kind of money."[33] The perennial public amazement about the Lincoln bonus arises from the fact that it is proportionally so much bigger than virtually any other type of year-end bonus in the country, apart from those of now largely discredited Wall Street financiers.

Given that the company has paid its annual bonus for seventy-five years without interruption, Lincoln employees have become accustomed to receiving a large financial reward for working hard, although most try hard to guard against becoming complacent about it. Yet while the amazingly large dollar value of the publicly announced average bonus receives the bulk of attention outside the company, the merit rating is what drives intense interest inside the firm, because it is the merit rating that determines whether each individual employee receives a larger, or smaller, bonus than the average. A small example: In 2008, an *average* Lincoln employee (one who earned 100 merit points) received a bonus worth 61 percent of his or her base wage. For someone on the assembly line, a welding-lab technician or a junior engineer earning $50,000 in basic wages last year, that meant a bonus of $30,500, for a total pay of $80,500. An employee who earned the same $50,000 in base wages but received a higher merit rating of 120 points (perhaps because she was rated as more of a team player in the factory, or someone who made profitable cost-saving suggestions and produced higher-quality work) would see her bonus increased by a further 20 percent: The bonus would be worth $36,600, resulting in total pay of almost $87,000. In similar fashion, a merit rating of just 80 points would result in lower overall earnings of just over $74,000. The merit rating also identifies employees who are failing to meet the company's demanding performance standards. Persistent merit ratings below 80 lead, first of all, to discussions between management and an employee about his or her future with Lincoln Electric and, ultimately, may be used in an evaluation process leading to dismissal. "We never tell anyone, because nothing good can come of it," replied Joe Latessa Jr. when I asked him about his most recent merit rating.[34] I knew that his wife, Melissa, had earned one of the highest ratings in the company the previous year, but when I asked her how high, she just said, "Oh, I wouldn't want anyone to know. You're pretty much competing against other people."

In the early days of the bonus, Lincoln Electric was small enough and James F. Lincoln was confident enough about his managerial judgment that he personally reviewed and compared the performance of every worker in his company. But after World War II, reportedly prompted by the IRS's breathing down the company's neck during the lawsuit mentioned earlier, merit rating evolved into a much more sophisticated process. Yet as with so much at Lincoln, the merit-rating system of 2008 is remarkably similar to that in place a half century ago.

Several times during a year, every employee on piecework is rated by his supervisors on five different performance attributes, each measured on a 20-point scale: overall *productivity*, overall *quality* of the work performed, the extent to which the worker demonstrates *adaptability and flexibility* on the job, her *dependability* and sense of *teamwork*, and, finally, the employee's awareness and compliance with the company's *environmental, health, and safety* priorities. (The first four were in place in the 1940s; the environmental merit scale is obviously a product of changing social priorities in the past decade or so.) An employee can be awarded more than 20 points on a particular scale for clearly superior performance, but only if someone else in the same work group being evaluated by that supervisor receives less. In other words, there is a limited number of points to be distributed among any group of workers, and so Latessa's comment that she's always competing against her colleagues is true: "Whenever people come in late, I always say, 'Hey, thanks for the points.'"

Lincoln Electric's hourly and salaried employees are rated on a slightly different set of metrics. Obviously, the *quantity* or *quality* of work performed by a factory worker winding transformer coils is easier to measure than the work performed by a design engineer or an accounting technician. The "Performance Development System" used for these employees draws on a more modern management lexicon of *goals* and *core competencies*, designed to measure and rank attributes such as decision-making ability and judgment, customer focus, and innovation. In the end, however, the overall evaluation structure and its financial implications for individuals are similar for every employee in the company.

MERIT RATING is about much more than determining the relative size of an employee's year-end bonus at Lincoln. The company, its workers, and the many management experts who have studied the firm over the years regard it as a powerful mechanism for curing many of the common failings of piece-rate manufacturing (problems that were identified as far back as the nineteenth century) and, more important, for motivating employees at every level of the company to work together for a common goal.

Take Melissa Latessa as she assembles welding-gun nozzles. The quicker she works to build those parts, the more she earns — first, because she is paid a fixed amount for every completed nozzle, and second, because a higher-than-average production level will raise the *productivity* merit rating she receives at the end of the year. But the natural rush to produce more in piecework manufacturing has always been a major roadblock to maintaining high-quality work. In other words, what's to stop Latessa from cutting corners as she smoothes a wire sleeve onto each brass tube?

The answer to that lies in the *quality* scale of her annual merit rating. In many manufacturing environments, it's become the role of near armies of quality-control inspectors to closely monitor employees to ensure quality is not sacrificed to speed. And in recent decades, a flood of management techniques has swept through the nation's factories (Japanese factory organization systems such as Theory Z, Six Sigma tools — it's a long list), designed in part to instill a greater sense of personal responsibility and teamwork among employees.

At Lincoln Electric, the solution is straightforward and financially direct: A consistent pattern of on-the-job production mistakes will lead directly to a lower merit rating on that employee's quality scale, which will significantly reduce the bonus at the end of the year and, in extreme cases of substandard work, lead to disciplinary procedures for poor performance. It's in Latessa's direct financial interest that every item she produces pass her self-administered quality inspection. (For many years, the system has tracked individual production quality, although this is more difficult now, given the increasing complexity of modern manufacturing with teams and cell organization. In the machine division, for example, an employee would "sign" for each completed task on each machine, in the early days by putting his initials on a small label that was glued inside the chassis, and more recently, where possible, by the use of bar codes. A production error discovered in a machine after it had been sold—whether across Cleveland or in the mountains of Montana—could be traced back to a specific worker. If the fault was due to human error. rather than defective materials or a machine malfunction, that worker would be docked the equivalent amount of time necessary to repair the problem. "It's not uncommon for a major mistake to cost an employee between $500 and $1,000," said Doug Lance.)

Delegating the ultimate responsibility for quality control to those who actually make the product creates an additional cost-saving advantage. The supervisor-to-employee ratio at Lincoln Electric—on the factory floor, but also throughout the entire administrative structure—is significantly lower than in other similar industries. One floor supervisor managing up to sixty to seventy line workers in Cleveland is a common occurrence, whereas the U.S. manufacturing-industry average can easily be as high as one to ten. This leaner management structure saves a lot of money without compromising quality, and similar savings occur in the salaried divisions of the company.

Another persistent challenge with piecework has always been how to instill a sense of cooperation and teamwork among a group of employees. In other words, if your job pays you to work fast and accurately, why should you care how well or how quickly someone else works?

There are a number of reasons to work as a team at Lincoln Electric. First, if a coworker on an assembly line is supplying you with poor-quality parts, your ability to subsequently turn out quality work will be limited, which will directly reduce your ability to "earn good points," as Lincoln workers describe it. So it is clearly in your financial interest to help a coworker to improve the quality of his or her production and vice versa. Second, developing ways to reorganize the work environment for yourself and others around you—ideas that may result in higher overall production levels at lower production costs—can also increase the points you earn on the scale that rates every employee for *ideas and cooperation*. It's a suggestion-box system that really pays off. It also strengthens the company's bottom line, and that means a larger bonus pool to be distributed at year's end.

As a result, virtually every employee at Lincoln Electric can describe situations on the factory floor, in research labs, or in the front offices, where workers have voluntarily collaborated to solve production and administration problems. "It's a competitive environment, definitely, where the more you make, the more money's in your pocket," said Yonatan Necoechea, an engineer in charge of production quality for flux-core welding wire. "But each guy knows that the other guys depend on him to make good-quality products, so when challenges come up, they know they need to work in a team environment. There is a natural incentive."[35]

Merit rating at Lincoln Electric involves both the subjective and the objective evaluation of every employee's performance. Many years ago, Harvard University economist Michael Jensen, a leading expert on the role of incentives in the workplace, explained why most employers are loath to adopt these policies, especially when large amounts of money are at stake, as at Lincoln Electric. Jensen argued that, on the one hand, "the lack of trust between employees and supervisors and their distaste for conflict" kept companies away from subjective evaluation methods, while, on the other hand, the significant difficulties of accurately measuring performance and "the dysfunctional behavior" of employees being evaluated drove them away from objective evaluation systems.[36] His analysis was essentially a much more complicated version of what the CEO of Safelite Glass said about his company's successful experience with piecework: For most companies, it demands a fundamental change in a firm's business culture to make incentive systems work well.

The merit-rating and bonus programs work at Lincoln Electric precisely because there *is* an extraordinarily high level of trust flowing through the organization. Most employees understand that this system of evaluating their work isn't perfect, but the majority seem to accept its shortcomings because the process has proved to be so beneficial for so many workers for so many decades. "A lot of [merit rating] is subjective," agreed Joe Latessa Sr., father of Joe and father-in-law of Melissa, who worked at Lincoln for forty years as both a pieceworker and an hourly paid supervisor. "It's not just about numbers, and, yes, it is somebody else's idea of who you are. But the thing is that because it's spread out, the impact of one guy thinking 'Joe Latessa is worthless' is not going to have a huge effect. There have been times I felt I'd been treated unfairly, but I'm a realist; it was going to happen sometimes. As a foreman, I had to rate people too, and not everyone was happy." Latessa also remembered that when he joined in the 1950s, management "made life unbearable for people if they didn't perform. If [your merit rating] fell into the 70s, even the low 80s, you were given warnings, and if something didn't change, you would be let go."

His second son, Michael, a welding technologist who has been with the company for twenty years, feels that the rating system encourages him to see his job as part of a larger manufacturing process. "It's very important to me because it lets me know that someone appreciates what I did," said the younger Latessa in the busy welding-research lab. "I know I'm doing a good job if I seldom see my manager, I'm working hard, I'm taking pride in my work, I don't need to be managed, and that is part of merit rating, how well you work without supervision. It makes his job easier, and, in turn, he rewards me."[37]

The merit system also has its detractors, of a sort. Richard Siktberg, an electrical engineer who worked at Lincoln Electric for thirty-nine years, sounded very much like Winston Churchill evaluating democracy's virtues when I asked him about merit ratings. "No one liked the hated merit system, but no one could ever figure out a better way. You always had people who were 'above average' and others who were 'below average,'" recalled Siktberg, "but when you come down to it, it's a system which forces the company to evaluate people whether you want to or not and to compare employees to everyone else, which is a good thing."[38]

Some employees—and some of their spouses as well—called the bonus and merit system "a trap"; some saw it as an inducement to toe the line in order to ensure a good rating before the next December's check, while others felt that after a year when the bonus had been relatively small, workers reluctantly stuck around in the hope that the coming year would make up the difference. "I never met anyone who really liked their job," said John Konich, who worked on information systems from 2000 to 2003, but "with the bonuses coming down, you're trapped."[39]

Bill Sass was one of the few employees who spoke openly about the abuse of the merit rating. In the mid-1990s, Sass was involved in an attempt to organize a union at Lincoln Electric (see Chapter 4). The campaign failed, and Sass said he paid a price: "If you spoke up against the company, they'd cut your merit rating, which then affected your bonus. People were afraid. They cut mine, and it affected my livelihood."[40] Sass retired in 2002 after thirty-eight years of work.

But for Tony Zalar, an executive in Lincoln Electric's corporate credit department, the merit system was a revelation when he arrived in 2005 after working for other manufacturing firms, including Continental Tire and Avery Dennison, the maker of self-adhesive labels. "The bonus and the merit system reminds you every day of how you are accountable to each other," said Zalar, and "it affects the decisions you make. Other companies talk about it, but you can't feel it there, and you don't open the door for a guy working on the plant floor at other companies."[41]

People open doors for each other for another reason at Lincoln Electric. There is only one entrance to the huge factory building located in the Cleveland suburb of Euclid. Virtually everyone from Zalar to Latessa to Chairman John Stropki walks through it with coworkers every day, coming to work and heading home.

IN 1945, as President Harry Truman prepared to host a postwar reconstruction conference of national business and labor leaders, James Lincoln wrote an open letter to the president in which he offered his advice on how best to refocus the U.S. economy on the nation's domestic priorities.

From my understanding of Lincoln, he would have recoiled from ever hearing the word *welfare* applied to the form of capitalism he used to manage Lincoln Electric. Yet his letter to Truman, detailing the principles underlying his company's economic success for so many years, reads almost like a welfare capitalist's manifesto. Lincoln wrote about cooperation in the workplace, financial stability, increasing dividends for investors, steadily rising wages, an ever-expanding workforce hired to satisfy growing consumer demand—and, finally, the promise of continuous employment, all of which were part of the Lincoln Electric experience. He told Truman that "no person in the last twenty years has been laid off because of lack of work."[42]

A little more than a decade later, guaranteed employment was finally enshrined as a formal company policy at Lincoln Electric.

chapter three

"UNDERSTANDING WHAT THE END GAME IS ALL ABOUT"

This is our AC-225. It was in the movie *Home Alone* where the little kid uses it to shock the burglar." Lee Seufer rested his right hand on a bright-red and black welding machine, about the size of a large portable beer cooler. The machine had just passed its final quality check on the assembly line. "We thought, boy, that's not exactly a great way to showcase the product, especially because it actually wouldn't work the way he used it. But it sure looked good," he laughed.[1] In recent years, the AC-225 also had a recurring role in Tim Allen's *Home Improvement* television series and starred in cameo performances in other feature films. As director of manufacturing for Lincoln Electric, Seufer is responsible for overseeing production of the machines that have kept the company at the forefront of the global welding industry for more than seventy-five years.

If you're a hobby welder in North America, working on a favorite old car on weekends, you can pick up an AC-225 for a few hundred dollars at Home Depot or Lowe's to repair a rusting underbody. "It's probably a forty-year-old design," says Seufer fondly, "and every time we look at it and try to shrink it or add functions to it, customers come back and say, 'We don't need it. My grandfather had one for twenty-five years, and that's all I want too.'"

If you're an automobile manufacturer looking to modernize your out-of-date assembly lines, an oil company building a drill rig in the Gulf of Mexico, or a construction firm laying down a pipeline in Asia or Alaska, Lincoln Electric has welding machines for those jobs as well, though at a much higher price.[2] (Many of Lincoln Electric's heavy-industrial customers around the world are in the "infrastructure" business, and they have been praying that government stimulus packages everywhere can resuscitate the global economy. It's a prayer Lincoln Electric shares.)

At fifty-two, Seufer has been with the company for twenty-eight years. It's a family tradition: His father joined in the 1940s, when James Lincoln was still running the company hands-on, where he started off in maintenance and later worked in the offices. His brother retired in 2008 after forty-two years with the company.

Lee Seufer grew up in the 1960s in a small town east of Cleveland. Like many children of Lincoln employees, he held summer jobs at the company when he was studying mechanical engineering at Ohio State. "The neat thing was that I could earn enough here during the summer that my parents didn't have to pay for my education, and when I graduated, I only had a few hundred dollars of debt," he recalled.

Once college was over, Seufer had job interviews with Lincoln Electric as well as with GM and several other large manufacturing companies. In the end, familiarity won out. "What was neat [a word Lee Seufer uses a lot in conversation] was that I knew this company, I knew the work ethic, I knew what was expected of me, I knew the responsibility the company gives its people, and I knew how cautious and careful it was with its employees."

After nearly three decades, exercising caution and care with employees is as much a part of Seufer's job as it is to ensure the quality of the company's latest welding machines.

LINCOLN ELECTRIC'S global headquarters and major U.S. manufacturing complex stretches for three-quarters of a mile along the north side of St. Clair Avenue in Euclid. A ten-story white water tower sporting the company's red and black logo is visible from miles away when you're driving along nearby Interstate 90.

Fronted by a huge parking lot, the massive main building is a long, unadorned light-gray two-story corrugated-steel structure, windowless except for a glassed-in section around the front entrance. To the east and across the street at the west end are more company buildings, mostly redbrick, bought over the years from other once-thriving Cleveland manufacturing firms that were forced into bankruptcy or moved their production out of the United States. The neighborhood, like much of Cleveland, has seen better days: An abandoned shopping mall sits wasting away directly to the east, and a string of auto-body shops surrounds Stingers Bar and Grill—with its one barred, cracked window— just across 222nd Street to the west.

It's a completely different story inside the machine division, Lee Seufer's turf, which occupies the western half of the plant (the other section is devoted to production of welding electrode rods and wire, the so-called consumables). The factory is about as clean and bright as a manufacturing plant in North America could be yet still wear the label "heavy industry." It is cavernous, about 800,000 square feet overall, and so spacious that at many locations, it's impossible to see the far walls through a thickening blur of yellow ceiling lights, gray roof trusses and ventilation ducts, red warning

signs, and tall gunmetal fans circulating fresh air. It's pleasantly
warm inside, noisy, but not overpowering.[3] "We make everything
in this building," said Seufer, waving his arm over the expanse as
we walked along glistening sealed concrete, "all the electrical-
grade lamination steel welded together for the coil cores, all the
copper and aluminum that goes in here, the wiring harnesses, the
rectifier assemblies, and the printed circuit boards."

As we stopped in front of a bank of brand-new highly automated metal stamping presses, I asked what had happened to the
people who had operated the old manual stamping presses. Were
they just shown the door along with the obsolete mechanical
equipment? No, said Seufer. "I know we always have lots of good
work under this roof for people to do, and my goal is always to
take people and put them working on something more interesting that we can't mechanize." And in the tough times? "We are
not going to lay you off because things are slow, and you are not
going to lose your job!"

But there is one absolute prerequisite for employees looking to
benefit from Lincoln Electric's guaranteed employment program,
stressed Seufer: "The guaranteed employment promise depends on
everyone—from management to the employees—understanding
what the end game is all about."

THE "END GAME" is to ensure the continuous profitability of a tech-
nologically savvy manufacturing firm in an exceedingly competitive global marketplace. That was John C. Lincoln's goal in 1895,
his brother James's goal when he took over in 1914, and it has remained the goal of every CEO ever since. It is also the game plan
for every other private business in the country. But what sets Lincoln Electric apart is that the company has shown that it can
achieve its goals while demonstrating a degree of respect for its
workers that is exceedingly rare in the United States.

James Lincoln always said that only the firm's satisfied customers, not its management, could really guarantee employment
for its workers. But during the 1950s, once the idea of formalizing
a guarantee had been raised at an Advisory Board meeting and
Lincoln had agreed to make it a priority, senior executives began
to analyze how a formal promise could survive the regular ups and
downs of normal business cycles. (By that point in the company's
history, there had apparently been no layoffs for several decades,
which must have been encouraging for everyone involved.)

Two recessions, in 1954 and again in 1957, tested management's
evolving strategies to keep people at work without threatening
long-term growth. George Willis, then in charge of the electrode
division and later chairman during the 1980s, told me that during
those years, he and others regularly met with Lincoln to review
the progress toward adopting guaranteed employment. A key concern for Willis was how to ensure that the required reassignment
of employees from one division to another during economic
downturns didn't compromise production quality. A worker unfa-
miliar with the machinery or processes being used in a distant part
of the factory was a potential risk to profitability when he was para-
chuted in with little advance notice, said Willis.[4]

Gradually, Lincoln grew confident that a no-layoff policy
could work, and in 1958, the board voted to adopt the Guaranteed
Continuous Employment Plan. It remains in place, essentially
unchanged, to this day.

Guaranteed employment, as people inside the company call
it, is not about jobs for life. It is a contract that describes in quite
precise detail the obligations of workers and management on a
day-to-day basis and the penalties that ensue when the obligations
aren't met. New employees are introduced to the policy as soon
as they are hired, and in dozens of interviews over many years, I
have never run across anyone who doesn't understand the terms
of the plan and what it means for them.

GUARANTEED CONTINUOUS EMPLOYMENT AT LINCOLN ELECTRIC

- It is seen as a competitive advantage for the company.
- It provides covered workers with security against layoffs due to lack of work when the economy slows down.
- The plan covers permanent employees in Cleveland (95 percent of the U.S. workforce) who have completed three years of service.[5]
- Employees are guaranteed at least thirty hours of work per week.
- Employees are required to work overtime whenever scheduled.
- Workers are not guaranteed a particular job or rate of pay.
- Every employee must be willing to accept transfer from one job to another.
- The plan only covers workers who uphold Lincoln Electric's well-defined performance standards.
- Finally, if the company's survival is threatened by conditions beyond its control—from recessions to natural disasters—the guarantee does not hold.

"IF DAD ANSWERS THE PHONE AND IT'S LINCOLN, HE'S GOING IN"

A normal workweek in Ohio, according to state labor law, is forty hours. Work more than that, and your employer is legally bound to pay you overtime. At Lincoln Electric, employees are contractually bound to work overtime whenever they're asked. Of course, they're paid time and a half and other premiums, according to state regulations.

In 2007, Mark Wells logged more than five hundred hours of overtime as a skilled tool-and-die maker at Lincoln Electric. So did a lot of other people in the company, as orders poured in from across the United States and overseas. Fifty-five-hour workweeks were common, and many people were working half a day or more on Saturday.

In December 2008, a couple of days before the annual bonus was announced, Wells and I shared a beer at Ruby Tuesdays in Mentor, twenty miles east of Cleveland, close to Lincoln Electric's second big plant. The TVs above the bar were broadcasting the latest market reports from Wall Street, while Washington struggled with its bailout proposals. A burly and very friendly man, Wells is thirty-seven years old, married, with three children. "This year, I stopped working overtime in March because things just began slowing up, slowing up, and then the bottom fell out," he said. "Now I'm on thirty-two hours a week; it's kind of a nice break."[6]

By early 2009, with the recession well over a year old, almost every pieceworker and hourly paid employee at Lincoln Electric was down to thirty-two hours; some were working only thirty hours, the minimum under the policy. Though hardly welcomed as a desirable situation, the reductions were nonetheless accepted as business as usual, especially by people like Wells, who joined the company in 1992. "It's not news. It's laid out this way, and they sit you down on your first day and tell you that," said Wells, making it all sound quite normal. "And if it lasts a year, it lasts a year." Wells had been down to thirty-two hours once before, in 2003 for about three months, but his normal working life at Lincoln Electric has meant years of service with a lot of overtime.

It all happens by design, not through poor manpower planning. "We typically staff this place to run at about forty-five to forty-six hours a week when things are normally busy," said George Blankenship, the president of the firm's Cleveland operations. In some parts of the company, such as the electrode division, fifty hours and more each week can be normal for years on end.[7]

But when business starts to slow, reducing hours from forty-five down to forty hours a week for the vast proportion of employees has the same impact as laying off 11 percent of the workers. Take it down to thirty hours when the bottom drops out—as it did in the fall of 2008—and it's equivalent to Lincoln

Electric slashing its workforce by 33 percent without having to
send anyone out the front door and off to the unemployment office. (Nonetheless, some people from Lincoln Electric have still
headed for the unemployment office in the past year, a point we'll
return to later.)

Blankenship regards the ability to adjust hours as a tremen-
dously powerful tool, given how volatile consumer demand can
be. By late 2008, when it was becoming clear that the global economy was severely contracting, he said the company would have
been "stressed financially" if it hadn't been able to reduce hours.
"In such chaotic times, the year's financial outcome would have
been totally different" without the built-in adjustments permissi-
ble under guaranteed employment, according to Blankenship.

Not everyone working at Lincoln Electric is paid through
piecework or on an hourly basis. For the engineers, the sales executives, the research scientists, administration staff, and managers
who are on salary, their world under guaranteed employment
changes in a different fashion when customer orders stop pouring
in. "We have more cars in the parking lot on Saturdays than we do
on Fridays," said chairman John Stropki, "because we told our
salaried people that 'you are responsible for putting the piecework
and hourly people back to work.'"[8]

Stropki had been a full-time employee of Lincoln Electric for
thirty-six years—he also worked three summers as a summer student in college—which has been long enough to see a number
of recessions come and go. He said that the company's unusual
HR policies put heavy demands on salaried workers as well as
those out on the assembly lines: "I don't care where you work—
engineering, finance—find ways to get new products out the
door, cut costs in how we produce, sell more, because you guys,"
he raised his hand pointing out the door of his office, "are not
getting your hours cut like those people [on piecework] are. You

are benefiting from guaranteed employment, so get out and get the job done for them."

The spirit of *we're all in this together* is reinforced by the fact that when sacrifices are required, the pain seems to be widely and equitably shared. Even Bill Sass, the leader of the failed campaign to bring a union to Lincoln Electric in the 1990s, is adamant that people are treated equally when hours need to be cut: "They did not keep older employees working forty hours a week and get rid of the newer people. They reduced everybody fairly, which is really a compliment to the older guys. They were the ones who were really making money, but never had time to enjoy it!"

When business is booming, under the terms of guaranteed employment, scheduled overtime is mandatory. Yet the system can deliver even more when needed. In 1991, coming out of a relatively short recession, Lincoln Electric found itself facing severe production bottlenecks when orders increased unexpectedly quickly. Cautiously, the company began to hire new employees, but it was soon apparent that they couldn't be trained fast enough to satisfy the demand. To fill the gap, management asked for help from its seasoned employees, who responded in dramatic fashion—or perhaps for this company, just as normally expected. More than 400 workers voluntarily gave up weekends, holidays (including the Fourth of July, Labor Day, and Thanksgiving), and 614 weeks of vacation time until the fresh recruits were finally able to take their place.

In an era when company loyalty has become rare, for all too obvious reasons, Lincoln Electric benefits from a management policy that has been clearly defined and honored for decades. Rebecca Wells, Mark's wife, believes her family has benefited as well, and not just from the financial stability they have enjoyed. "Our kids know that if the phone rings and Dad answers and it's Lincoln, then he's going in," says Wells, who is also a trained tool-and-die maker (she met Mark when they were both enrolled in the same technical college). "The one thing that Lincoln Electric has taught our family is the work ethic, especially the kids. If work needs you, you go, and then you will be rewarded for it."[9]

A LEOPARD CAN CHANGE ITS SPOTS

"When business drops off nearly 50 percent over eighteen months, what do you do with our people?" In 1982, when former CEO Don Hastings was then vice president of sales, he found himself asking that question, knowing the answer could not involve layoffs. The full impact of competition from Japanese and other foreign steel and auto producers had brought many American manufacturers almost to their knees, and many of them were Lincoln Electric's major customers. Unemployment soared to 10.8 percent nationwide, the highest since the Great Depression.

Hours of work for the majority of employees had already been slashed to thirty-two per week, but Hastings thought he still had a little room left in his department. The company was poised to launch a new line of small welding machines designed specifically for auto-body shops and small sheet-metal fabricating businesses. Hastings asked to borrow some of the idled production workers who had experience building the new machines on the assembly lines so that he could send them out into the field as sales representatives. They were the people who knew exactly what the product could do, Hastings reasoned, and with a little training, they would be a formidable sales force. These leopards would change their spots, hence the name of the experiment, Operation Leopard.

Hastings could have simply requested that the executive in charge of the assembly lines reassign workers to his program: It's common procedure under the terms of the guaranteed employment plan, and more than 15 percent of workers had already changed jobs as the recession worsened. Instead, he asked for volunteers, gambling that he'd get more enthusiastic recruits. Leopard volunteers were told they would have to pay their own moving expenses to various parts of the country as well as their basic living costs while they stayed there.

Terry Dattilio, a university-educated accountant working on the welding-machine line in Cleveland, jumped at the opportunity. After two intense weeks of sales training, Dattilio found himself living in Pittsburgh and demonstrating the new welders to "body shops, small steel mills, and pottery plants in West Virginia."[10] Dattilio remembered thinking that the "incredible breadth of knowledge" of the fifty-one new employees who transferred to Hastings's sales department was a particularly powerful marketing tool: The company said at the time that, on average, each "leopard" generated more than $200,000 in new sales.

More than a quarter century later, Hastings wasn't really sure the program was quite that financially successful, but he had no doubts about its overall importance to the company's survival in a very challenging economic time. By doing something "so dramatic," he argued, it had a significant impact on morale throughout the company: "Here were people willing to move to everywhere from Maine to San Diego to be part of this program, all so we wouldn't have to lay people off." Plus, when these former factory workers eventually returned to the assembly line, Hastings believed that they brought back a new appreciation for the role of others in the company; these were factory workers who now knew firsthand that the sales guys did not live on "three martini" lunches, remembered Hastings.

Dattilio spent three and a half years in Pittsburgh. "It was very stressful on my family, who stayed in Cleveland, but it was a great career opportunity," he recalled.

✧   ✧   ✧

LINCOLN ELECTRIC'S employees don't just change their spots during crises. Under the terms of the guaranteed employment plan, it happens on a regular basis in good times as well. Once they've been with the company for a few years, almost every employee, at every level, has had "the tap"—the visit from a supervisor announced by a tap on the shoulder to say that starting the next day or the next week, they'll have a new job in a different division of the company. "You're there as an employee to fill the customers' needs," said James Maffit, a twenty-year employee who currently tracks and manages the diverse streams of waste materials at the company's electrode plant in Mentor. Maffit has been tapped a number of times since he started on the welding assembly line in 1989. "It is hard at first because you don't ever grow comfortable in your position," he said matter-of-factly, "but you might be working in a department when all of a sudden the bottom falls out of that product, and there is just no demand for what you're doing. You gotta go and help out where there is demand."[11]

Mike Latessa, the welding technician, was similarly relaxed about having to shift his job at a moment's notice. "You have to be willing to accept any change," he stressed, "and if they came right now and grabbed me out of the applications lab, I would have no question, because I have always had a job, and my responsibility is that if they need me, I have to go."

Starting a new job at a moment's notice is understandably difficult at times. But much more challenging is the fact that employees can find themselves working on a lower-paying assignment for many months. In some situations, the financial hit they suffer is relatively minor. But in the case of pieceworkers, a reassignment can have serious implications for their pocketbooks if they're shifted to a workstation in a new assembly cell that pays less per hour. During several economic downturns in his thirty-eight years with Lincoln Electric, Steve Simcak even found himself pulled off the electrode production lines to paint walls for three or four months. "I didn't make much money," said Simcak, "but at least I was working, and that's pretty important for my family." After those downturns ended, he returned to his former higher-paying positions.

I have met employees who felt that over the years, they've been shifted unfairly, due to the personal whims of a supervisor or manager. Those workers admitted that they were often reticent to protest their reassignment because that same supervisor was in charge of their all-important merit rating at the end of the year. They seem few and far between, though, and overall Lincoln employees quite evidently do believe the system treats them fairly over the long term.

There is no question that being able to get help quickly makes life easier for senior managers, according to Richard Siktberg, for many years the head of engineering in the machine division. "We would always be able to get extra people in the labs when we needed them to help us build and test projects," he said, and as a result, it created a great competitive advantage. During our conversation, Siktberg warned me not to overromanticize Lincoln Electric's employment promise, saying that it is still a company with all the normal problems that occur when human beings work together. Still, he stressed, "one of the strengths compared to the automobile companies, say, is the flexibility of being able to assign workers where they are actually needed." Union contracts in the auto industry (and many others) traditionally place strict limits on the ability of management to reassign employees quickly.

Damian Kotecki, a widely respected expert on welding who worked in engineering research institutions and other manufacturing companies before joining Lincoln Electric in 1989, was also a great fan of the flexibility that guaranteed employment affords. "It was the most stunning thing to me in my early years there," said the now retired executive, "the cooperation you got from anybody. It really worked."[12] Especially in the last week of August 2005, while Lincoln Electric's production lines hummed along at near-peak capacity in Cleveland, and 1,000 miles to the south, Hurricane Katrina was destroying New Orleans.

Soon after the storm had passed, calls from the disaster-reconstruction administration and many local businesses across the Gulf region began pouring into Lincoln Electric's sales department asking for help to quickly replace thousands of welding machines that had been damaged or lost during the flooding. "Shipyards, manufacturing companies, oil companies—they were sending us pictures of hundreds of our welding machines with 'scrap' stenciled on them," recalled Lee Seufer.

Immediately, Ron Nelson, the vice president of the machine division, began pulling in employees "from all over, the labs, everywhere," and within days seventy employees from other divisions of the Cleveland complex were working 24/7 to rush production of new welding machines for shipment to Louisiana. What made the process so efficient was that many of these workers already had experience in machine assembly because they'd been reassigned on previous occasions. Nelson and virtually everyone in the company are convinced that "the payback" of a workforce ever ready to change jobs is huge.

THIS IS NOT A "BE-KIND-TO-THE-EMPLOYEE" PLAN

Interest in Lincoln Electric's guaranteed employment plan from those outside the company ebbs and flows in inverse proportion to the health of the American economy. It's no surprise that during this latest recession, there have been many more references to the company in the national media than over the previous decade. But the commitment to keeping good people at work is much more than a defensive strategy during downturns; it is a powerful competitive advantage in normal economic times as well. "I see this in our competition all the time," said John Stropki as we sat in the chairman's office. He leaned forward to stress the word *all*. "You see new faces turning up all the time in critical areas, and while they may be very bright people, they do not understand the business, and they may not even know how to make the products."

Stropki was hired after graduating from Purdue with an industrial engineering degree and an MBA from Indiana University. He has worked in virtually every division of the company. Relaxed in conversation, Stropki becomes animated in discussing the economic advantages of a workforce with so many years of experience.

Does guaranteeing employment help encourage technical innovation and the development of new products? "There is no question in my mind," he said, "because with very few exceptions everyone here understands welding. The guys on the shop floor who understand an arc, the welding engineers who understand consumables, these are all people who have been associated with welding all their working lives!"

Stropki has heard the warnings of many economists and management consultants who caution that a guaranteed employment promise can be very dangerous for a firm's long-term survival prospects. The experts argue that by retaining such a large proportion of its workforce for long periods of time, a company like Lincoln Electric risks finding itself badly out of touch with cutting-edge—and rapidly changing—technologies. A steady stream of new employees, in contrast, regularly injects fresh ideas into the company and thus reduces the chances of the firm's being blindsided by its competition, as Kodak was by the advent of digital photography. (Or Addressograph-Multigraph, the mechanical duplicating-machine manufacturer once located next

door, which ignored the risk to its business posed by Xerox pho-
tocopiers and was ultimately forced into bankruptcy. Lincoln
Electric later bought the empty factory.)

Those arguments have some validity, agreed Stropki, yet he is
convinced that a critical mass of experience—in a company that,
he emphasized, is continually testing itself out in the real world—
is sufficient protection from the dangers of isolation. He also believes that because Lincoln Electric employees don't spend time
worrying about losing their jobs, they are far more willing—at all
levels of the firm—to take greater risks through experimentation
than in competing companies. That comfort level with risk taking ensures the firm stays on the innovative edge of new technology and production methods.

Tom Matthews, the company's head of new product development, took a slightly different tack from his boss on the competitive advantage of guaranteed employment and the resulting
stability of the workforce. A mechanical engineer by training with
twenty years under his belt at Lincoln Electric, Matthews believes
that the dangers of failing to ensure the transmission from generation to generation of the firm's vast store of practical and theo-
retical knowledge are immense. That danger can be minimized
only through the workforce longevity achievable with a no-layoff
promise. New ideas are great, said Matthews, but of little use if
they fail to become part of what he calls a company's *tribal knowledge*. "I hate to say this, but even after five years on the job, an engineer here may know *how* to design something, but he won't
know *what* to design. That takes until about year ten," according
to Matthews. If that engineer then decides to leave—or, worse, is
laid off unnecessarily—a decade of expertise walks out the door.
"All companies do a very poor job of documenting tribal knowledge, and those of our competitors who claim they do it are very
naive," said Matthews. He added that all the management-speak
about the importance of "knowledge databases" tends to ignore

the overwhelming significance of those with experience sharing it face-to-face with younger employees over time. Companies need to "keep their people around" to preserve that knowledge base.[13]

Thomas Eagar is one of those who aren't sure that is always such a good thing for a company. Eagar is an internationally acknowledged expert on welding technology who teaches in MIT's Department of Materials Science. He has worked as a consultant for Lincoln Electric as well as for others in the industry. Eagar has immense respect for the tenacity and determination and hard work that have made Lincoln Electric such a success throughout the past century. Yet he also believes that over the years, the guaranteed employment policy (and the resulting low turnover of employees) — as well as Lincoln's marketplace dominance — has helped to nurture a potentially dangerous conservatism, especially in the areas of scientific innovation. "For garden-variety bridges and buildings, they know more empirically about welding than *anyone*," Eagar told me, "but when you get into new areas — aluminum or high-strength steels or robotics — well, I don't admire them for their lack of intellectual curiosity. As an academic, that is not my favorite thing. The dark side of all this hard work, the guaranteed employment, is that they become insular."[14]

I put that worry to Tom Matthews, the head of new product research, asking about the challenge of staying at the front end of the innovation curve. Matthews said that a lot has changed since he started at Lincoln Electric twenty years ago: "It was really bizarre. Engineering research was in a cage, doors were locked, we were not allowed to talk to salesmen, much less customers, and the assumption was that we'd just come up with stuff and it would sell. We made a big change in all that in the mid-'90s, and we've gotten a lot better in trying to understand our customers." (I also asked Matthews about the chances of being sucker punched by some new technology out of the blue that might threaten Lincoln Electric's whole business, the way digital technology undermined Kodak's monopoly. "A bit of a stretch, but, yes, I'm thinking about glues" was his answer, referring to the nightmare scenario of a for now impossible method of joining pieces of metal that wouldn't require the intense heat and power of electric arc welding. "Will the laser guys ever figure it out?" It is an area the company is exploring.)

Another advantage of not using layoffs to solve financial problems is that an employer is able to avoid paying the often hidden costs when trained workers—assets for Lincoln Electric managers—are pushed out the door. Dick Sabo, a retired Lincoln Electric executive who was for many years the chief public face of the company, remembered once being assured that it cost the company only $4,000 to replace a pieceworker on the electrode assembly lines. (Guaranteed employment notwithstanding, people do leave Lincoln Electric of their own volition from time to time before they have worked for decades!) Sabo, who has a master's degree in industrial technology, was suspicious of that number and so decided to find out for himself. After several weeks of investigation, he became convinced that once factors such as severance payments, recruiting expenses, training (which required another skilled employee being pulled off his or her job), and the learning curve (which inevitably, in manufacturing, involved a lot of expensive mistakes) were all accounted for, the real cost of replacing a pieceworker was closer to $100,000. It was powerful ammunition, said Sabo, which he used on the rare vice president ("usually one hired from outside the company") who doubted the financial payoff of guaranteed employment.[15]

KEEP THINKING AHEAD TO THE BAD TIMES

"My Excel spreadsheet skills are really, really good," joked Gretchen Farrell, vice president of human relations, when I asked her about working in a company that makes underhiring a priority. "We never have enough people to do all the things you want to do in the good times," she said as we talked in her office, one of the handful in the whole building with a window.[16]

From its earliest days, Lincoln Electric has always relied on the flexibility of its workforce—in pay, hours, and assignments—to act as a buffer against the unpredictable ups and downs of the business cycle. Being thinly staffed is almost a corporate virtue, said Farrell, and essential to maintain the commitment to guaranteed employment.

No one in the company ever indicated to me that there were specific targets for keeping hiring under capacity. Given that the normal legal workweek under Ohio labor law is forty hours, while Lincoln generally operates at forty-five to fifty, that does imply an approximate underhiring target of 12 to 25 percent. "We don't think of it in those formal terms," Farrell replied to my question about targets. "At this point it's more of a feeling." A lawyer by training, she worked as a consultant with Ernst and Young before joining Lincoln Electric twelve years ago. "We're not as systematic as you might think, given our size in the U.S. economy, and that's part of not having tons of people."

Bruce Cable was in charge of hiring in the factories—where the majority of employees work—for several decades. (A few months after we met in Cleveland, he retired after thirty-seven years on the job.) Cable reiterated that there is no formula for running a company "a little understaffed and sometimes more than a little." He described it as a process of constantly working with division heads—who by their longevity on the job have seen business soar and crater—to anticipate the future. "It just causes you to be prudent," said the psychology graduate who started as a factory worker himself, because the company simply can't— and won't—"hire five hundred people and then decide you don't need them in six months."[17]

CEO John Stropki described the process of establishing an appropriate staffing level—again, with no mention of numerical targets—as a feedback loop, shaped by decades of experience. "We have a workforce that understands that if we need to work fifty-four hours a week, we will do that," says Stropki, "because if we don't, the company is liable to hire a lot of [extra] people, and then, because of guaranteed employment, that could put us all at an increased risk of a reduced number of working hours when economic conditions weaken."

THERE ARE TWO THINGS that a visitor to Lincoln Electric finds striking about the makeup of its workforce. The first is that people stay around for a long time. After several interviews, I simply began guessing people's ages and then subtracting twenty years: Invariably, it was a very close approximation of their tenure in the company, even when my age estimates rose into the fifties and sixties! Guaranteed employment seems to work by that measure. The second notable discovery is that there are an extraordinary number of multigenerational employee families in the company. It is still not unusual for a father, a son, a daughter, or an uncle to meet in the lunch line in the cafeteria—an age-old tradition in American manufacturing that is fading fast.

Piecework in a factory setting, long the heart of production at Lincoln Electric, is hard, physical work in a competitive industrial environment. The stories are legion inside the company of how much harder it used to be in the years before Congress passed the 1970 Occupational Safety and Health Act (OSHA), which eventually led to more rigorous safety inspections, significantly better ventilation, and other workplace and environmental improvements.

Two generations ago, the workplace was a much rougher place in human terms as well, according to those who were there. One retired employee who still has children at the company told me that in the 1960s, when he started, "it was a lot more ruthless in terms of what foremen expected of you. There were no mincing words, and they didn't have to be politically correct or polite. It was 'If you don't do this, we're going to find the worst job in the place for you.'" For many people in the Cleveland metropolitan region, working for Lincoln Electric is the stuff of urban legends, such as the absolute conviction that horribly unsafe physical working conditions persist to this day and that rampant personal abuses—"backstabbing" is commonly mentioned—are part and parcel of life under a nasty and brutal piece-rate pay system. One story that I heard repeated several times is that there is a small office in the underground tunnel where workers can go to "squeal" on shirkers in their area of the plant and receive a cash reward in return.

The inherent demands of working in heavy industry may indeed self-select for type-A personalities as a survival mechanism. There is no question that working at Lincoln Electric is a far cry from laboring in the Internet economy; it is tough work. A hundred years ago, most employees were recruited from Cleveland's huge base of Slovenian, Polish, Croatian, and other eastern European ethnic communities. Sons joined fathers at their piece-work stations in the plant, where they learned not just the mechanics of the assembly lines but about the premium placed on hard work and the good pay earned for doing it. For generations, there was no better recommendation for getting a job at Lincoln Electric than having a family member already at the plant put in a good word with a supervisor. Once on the job, the presence of an uncle working just across the corridor created a powerful social-control mechanism to encourage a new employee to do his best: Upholding a family's reputation was important.

Family referrals still play a role in hiring, according to Cable. But with a recruiting priority now being placed on hiring employees with up-to-date technical skills and experience, it is not as common as it was when he started in the 1970s. Lincoln Electric has also always placed a premium on hiring from within the company. Again, according to Cable, while that is still a company goal whenever possible, the technical demands of a rapidly changing industry have meant more recruiting outside the firm.

For generations, most hiring was done through personal interviews, and it led to very high early quit rates. "Over the past thirty years and more, we often lost 30 to 50 percent of our new hires in the first three months," said Cable. Most recently, another hiring challenge has been the fact that fewer and fewer people who apply for a job at Lincoln Electric have any familiarity with factory work. A country that sees its manufacturing base erode as deeply as the United States has pays this price.

In 2006, however, the company began using an interactive online recruitment program designed to filter out potential candidates who lack some degree of experience. That has resulted in the ninety-day quit rate dropping to just over 10 percent. (It's always been much lower in professional positions, Cable stressed.) Of those who survive their first ninety days in the factory, "90 to 95 percent make it to three years," the point when they become covered by the guaranteed employment policy. Lincoln Electric's overall average employee turnover rate these days is less than 6 percent annually, which is roughly one-fifth the average for American manufacturing companies. In fact, since the 1930s, the company's annual turnover rates have always been a very small fraction of the average American manufacturing firm's. The guaranteed employment promise not only protects this company from the significant costs of layoffs but is also a powerful incentive to keep valued employees from quitting to find greener pastures.

THE EXPECTATION THAT PEAK PERFORMANCE IS NORMAL

"People misunderstand guaranteed employment as a job for life, and it just doesn't say that," George Blankenship told me. "What it means is that we won't lay people off for economic reasons, but when the economic climate changes, we will eliminate people based on performance standards."

Lincoln Electric does have one more lever it can use—beyond the flexibility to change work hours, pay, and assignments—to adjust the size of its effective workforce that does not break the promise of guaranteed continuous employment: termination for poor performance on the job. The company has never been shy about exercising that authority, yet, according to virtually everyone I've interviewed, both retired and current employees, it is rarely used with unnecessary force. As mentioned earlier, employees who receive several consecutive annual merit ratings less than 80 fully expect to come under the microscope of their supervisors, whether they work on the factory floor, in a research laboratory, or with the accounting department. Each division is replete with spreadsheets charting over time the performance metrics of every employee, the standard deviations of performance, and the outliers, both top and bottom.

"When we have been very busy, we are tolerant of people who may not be performing as well as they should, because we need the warm bodies," said Blankenship, the head of operations in Cleveland, adding that "the bar does move up and down" depending on the economic pressures on the company. "As long as things are good, we will move those people through the system by training them, pushing on them, or if they are really poor, we will drop them."

His boss, John Stropki, was equally uncompromising about the standards of work at Lincoln Electric: "I make it very clear to the managers that if you have low-performing people who are taking up space and costing money, get rid of them. We're pretty clear about what our expectations are, and you do see people stepping up their game" in difficult times. Yet in the same breath,

Stropki took special care to emphasize that ultimately, a worker who isn't performing represents a failure of management. He tells those who report to him that they have the responsibility to make sure they "put every ounce of energy you have into making that person better, because you chose to spend money to hire that person and train them." (Even the most senior managers are subject to regular evaluations at Lincoln Electric: A pattern of poor employee performance in their department reflects poorly on their merit rating, which then results in a lower share of the annual bonus come December's meeting in the cafeteria.)

When sales start to fall as a recession approaches, said Stropki, the first priority is to bring work back into the company that may have been contracted out to external suppliers or performed by temporary employees. Like any large American company, Lincoln Electric does look outside the firm for help with relatively small short-term staffing challenges that don't warrant an expansion of its permanent employee base.

As economic pressures increase, poor performance ratings drive termination decisions. First to be asked to leave for performance reasons are workers with less than three years' tenure (not subject to the guaranteed employment promise), then those above the three-year line if they have recorded a consistently low merit rating. Finally, if Lincoln Electric were to suffer such a precipitous and sustained fall in consumer demand that its very future was in doubt, the company would reluctantly begin layoffs among its permanent employees, regardless of their successful performance ratings and the no-layoff policy. In that case, the first to go would likely be those with less than three years on the job, and then layoffs would begin among those over the three-year line. It's the nightmare scenario that has never materialized since the policy was adopted in 1958 nor, given very vague memories, as far back as 1948. And possibly even longer.

SLUMPS ARE USEFUL

Continuously prosperous operation is very dangerous to progress, since prosperity develops wasteful habits. Progress in cost reduction takes place most rapidly in time of slump. They should be anticipated and so used.

—James F. Lincoln, *A New Approach to Industrial Economics*

George Blankenship and I were walking down a hallway near the company's research labs when I noticed some masking tape covering up a few paint cracks on the walls. "If things really slow down as the recession gets worse, isn't this what guaranteed employment gives you," I asked, "the ability to pull some factory workers in here just to do some painting?" (It is part of company lore that at its most extreme, guaranteed employment means putting people to work with paintbrushes rather than laying anyone off.) "We are already painting walls, and it's not because we want to keep people busy," he fired back. "The next business cycle starts now, and these are the times when we can take business away from others."

Blankenship said that with so many of its customers under tremendous financial pressure to cut costs and reduce expenditures, Lincoln Electric's challenge is to seize those opportunities by promoting its latest energy-saving welding technologies. In times like these, he argued, guaranteed employment is always regarded as an advantage rather than a liability: The ability to quickly reassign workers allows the company to redirect normally scarce resources to address new challenges.

In a recession, Blankenship said, "think about what salespeople are usually taught: Stay home and cut your sales budget. Not us. This is the perfect time to reach end users who are under pressure and now have the time to listen to us. We bring them here to the factory and sell them. We are The Welding Experts [the company's corporate motto], and we have to present this facility well. They come away believers." Hence the need for a rare touch of cosmetic repairs to the company's exceedingly spartan facilities.

While most people in business outside of Lincoln Electric tend to see a rule against laying people off as an unnecessary restriction, Blankenship and his colleagues in senior management believe that the demands of its guaranteed employment policy actually drive good strategic decision making. Ron Nelson, the vice president of the machine division, explained that because guaranteed employment has been tested by economic downturns so many times before, there is now a near-automatic shift in corporate priorities that takes place gradually but systematically as demand starts to fall off. "We'll focus now on more cost reductions, more quality improvements, more scrap reductions, more new products," said Nelson, because the normal demand for product volume simply isn't there. The overall operating structure of the company — production, research, sales, and administration — self-adjusts, he said, precisely because there *is* a prohibition on quickly letting people go.

An update on the AC-225: Despite the fact that customers have repeatedly "warned" Lincoln Electric in no uncertain terms not to play with its classic welding machine (movie star of *Home Alone*), Lee Seufer admitted that in early 2009, with the recession in full force, a small change to the inside mounting of a front-panel control switch was made to the AC-225.[18] Seufer said that because his staff remained at full strength despite the tremendous decline in new orders, he was able to reassign people to revisit the machine's basic design. By eliminating one metal part and changing a bend in the interior front panel — which he said with a chuckle that loyal customers will never see — the company will save "thousands of dollars" in production costs in coming years.

Both former CEO Don Hastings and Gretchen Farrell, the VP of human resources, told me that there is a natural tendency to adopt a dangerously cautious style of management in a company with a guaranteed employment plan. "We may not make them as fast as in other companies, but we are incredibly conservative about making good decisions," laughed Farrell as we discussed managing with a no-layoff policy. "It is, yes, in some sense, dangerous," she said, because it requires a constant balancing act between ensuring the promise is kept while ensuring the company is still able to take all the risks necessary to survive and expand in a dynamic market. "It is sustainability versus growth all the time."

Fighting the inclination to be overly conservative was a prime motivation for increasing the probation period for new employees from two to three years in 1991, remembered Hastings. "Everyone from senior managers to foremen to floor supervisors had become so concerned about having to lay off people [who were covered by the guarantee after two years] that they weren't hiring anyone. We were working people too long at fifty to sixty hours a week before taking on additional workers." Lengthening the probation period by one year created a larger "escape hatch," said Hastings, by expanding the number of employees with less than three years' experience who, in theory, could be let go without violating the promise extended to those above the magic three-year mark.

By the spring of 2009, Lincoln Electric had ordered layoffs for reasons of poor performance in its U.S. operations, but according to Farrell, no one below or above the three-year probation line had been let go for lack of work. I haven't found a worker at Lincoln Electric who disagrees with that.

TRUST OR INTELLIGENT SELFISHNESS?

"I've seen it play out time and time again the way it's promised," said James Maffit when I asked why he and his fellow workers at Lincoln Electric seem to have such faith that the promise of guaranteed employment will survive intact. "My father worked at the company for forty-two years, so did my uncle, and my dad was a very loyal employee. Every place you go, you have that bell curve of disgruntled to fully engaged employees. My father was definitely not at the disgruntled end of the curve, and I just followed suit."[19] We were meeting at the Branding Iron Cook House, near the electrode plant, a few days after the company had canceled contracts with many of its outside suppliers (a decision taken to bring that work back inside) as well as with temporary agencies who were providing support in several departments. A few permanent employees, all with less than three years of service, had also been let go for performance reasons, according to information released by the HR department. Maffit does not believe that those terminations constituted an end run on the promise of guaranteed employment. "You have got to work up to Lincoln's standards every day. I don't see the company making tricky excuses," he said.

There is a fascinating tension throughout James Lincoln's writings between his belief in the importance of getting people to work together for a common goal and in the importance of motivating people to work hard to better themselves as individuals. On the one hand, building trust was essential, in Lincoln's view, "to get employees to want the company to succeed as badly as I did." On the other hand, Lincoln was convinced that appealing to the inherent self-interest of workers was critical to ensuring each person would work as diligently and smartly as possible.

A student of human psychology as well as a deeply religious man, Lincoln believed that "all acts of human beings are prompted by selfish motives." The key to creating a balance between trust and self-interest in any company was to appeal to what he termed "intelligent selfishness." It is "the incentive that causes a mother to sacrifice herself for the good of her child . . . the incentive that makes us loyal citizens who willingly sacrifice our lives in war that our country may survive . . . that causes a man to struggle toward perfection so that he becomes more prosperous."[20]

In 2009, guaranteed employment at Lincoln Electric survives because it continues to function as a powerful incentive that encourages employees to work hard for themselves and work together for the company as a whole. "People are nervous. We all watch CNN, and we see Paul Krugman warning how bad this will be," said Maffit. "It is nerve-racking, and I hope Krugman is wrong. I have a feeling things will get better. The old-timers have been through this before, and I don't hear much gloom and doom from them."

TAKING AN AMERICAN MANAGEMENT SYSTEM GLOBAL

Expanding beyond home borders always presents challenges, and Lincoln Electric has faced its share, especially surrounding the introduction of its unusual employee incentive system (including piecework, the Advisory Board, the merit-based bonus, and guaranteed employment) into foreign business environments.

Lincoln Electric has been an international company since 1916, two years after James F. Lincoln first took the helm, when a distribution office was set up in Canada. In the mid-1920s, Lincoln Electric Canada began manufacturing welding machinery and consumables in a new factory in Toronto. In 1938, a second overseas plant was opened in Australia. A third subsidiary was established in France in the 1950s, but apart from a short-lived venture in the United Kingdom, the company's global footprint remained unchanged until the mid-1980s. Then, in a burst of

energy from 1986 to 1992, Lincoln Electric expanded into fifteen
more countries, including Norway, Mexico, Brazil, Spain, and Germany. After 2004, when John Stropki became CEO and chairman,
the firm intensified its efforts to expand into China, Indonesia, and,
most recently, India. By 2009, the company had manufacturing
facilities in 20 countries, distribution and sales partnerships in more
than 160 nations, and a global workforce of more than 9,000 employees (roughly 3,300 of them in the United States).

Precise numbers are hard to come by, but the global welding
market represents roughly $20 billion in sales annually. Lincoln
Electric holds the largest market share—again, an estimate—of
roughly 14 percent. (Its nearest competitor is ESAB, originally a
Swedish company now headquartered in the United Kingdom,
which holds a market share of roughly 11 percent.) Like many
U.S. firms that operate around the world, Lincoln Electric's international sales are increasing faster than those at home. In 1998,
total sales to customers outside North America (the United States
and Canada) constituted 32 percent of overall revenue. By 2008,
that figure had soared to 58 percent.[21]

Canada and Australia, the firm's first two foreign ventures, operate largely as mirror images of the American company. Almost
from birth, the Canadian subsidiary adopted piecework, the Advisory Board (called a council), and the merit-based bonus with
virtually the same operating procedures as in Cleveland. However, guaranteed employment was never introduced (nor in Australia). There is no clear paper trail to explain exactly why, but
conversations with present and former employees on both sides
of the border suggest two major reasons. The first seems to be that
until James Lincoln died in 1965, the Canadian subsidiary operated quite independently from its parent company, although
American executives were dispatched to run the division. As long
as an acceptable level of profits steadily headed south each year
to Cleveland, Lincoln apparently felt disinclined to take a closer

hands-on approach to management in Toronto. And given that guaranteed employment became official policy only in 1958 in Cleveland, exporting it northward seems not to have been a priority for him in the last few years of his life. The second reason — which is more an explanation of why the no-layoff promise has yet to be introduced even fifty years later — centers on a complex issue that the company has dealt with, sometimes painfully, in all its international locations: Business cultures, social systems, and tax policies are different around the world.

Joseph Doria, a Canadian, has been the CEO of Lincoln Electric Canada since 1992, except during 1998–2001, when he headed operations in Europe. His estimate, supported by interviews with former and current employees, is that from the late 1940s until spring 2009, there have been fewer than three dozen permanent Canadian employees laid off for economic reasons (the current workforce is roughly 250 people across the country). As in the United States, workers in Canada have been terminated for consistently poor merit ratings over the years.

After the demand for welding products collapsed in late 2008, Doria made many of the same policy decisions to protect his skilled workforce that had been used in the United States: wage cuts for senior executives, the termination of contracts with outside suppliers and temporary staffing agencies, and shifting employees to new assignments ("the guy now on the main switchboard used to wind coils in the factory").[22] A few new employees who were still on probation were let go, with a promise that when business picked up, they would receive priority status to be rehired.

But it is in the area of reducing the hours of work where a clear difference between Canada and the United States emerges, a difference that gives Doria flexibility in different areas than his U.S. colleagues. By early 2009, the workweek for most of the company's Canadian workers had been slashed down to just twenty-four hours (compared to thirty-two in the United States). But under the terms of Canada's well-publicized *work-share* program, a federal government–funded plan, workers received an additional sixteen hours of "employment insurance" support, at roughly 60 percent of their hourly base wage: In essence, Lincoln Canada's workers took home almost the same wages of a normal forty-hour week. (According to the *New York Times*, seventeen U.S. states actually have work-sharing programs, but they are little known, and only a very few eligible employers apply for help.)[23] "We can go as low as sixteen hours out of a regular forty-hour week and still keep our people at work," explained Doria. "Canada is different with this kind of a different social safety net in place, and that is why we have never gone to the guaranteed employment program."

The greater annual cost to manage a workforce for Canadian employers (due to the taxes that every business pays into a government-run health insurance system and for a more generous and comprehensive system of unemployment insurance) has shaped the decision by successive leaders in Lincoln Electric Canada not to formally promise guaranteed employment, but the final outcome—steady long-term employment—is essentially the same as in the United States. Overall, said Doria, "it works for us." (A merit-based bonus has been paid to Canadian employees for sixty-nine of the past seventy years. Over the past decade, it has averaged roughly 25 percent of base wages. Again, the different tax regime and the higher cost for employers associated with a more comprehensive social safety net are identified as reasons why the Canadian bonus is smaller than in the United States.)

The rapid international expansion between 1986 and 1992 delivered a very costly lesson in the difficulties of exporting a unique corporate culture into different labor environments. Even the company's official history describes it as producing a "precipitous decline" in profitability.[24] In Germany, for example, guaranteed employment was already mandated under national labor laws, the normal workweek was shorter than in the United States, wages were proportionally much higher, and annual vacations were much longer. ("They have five weeks of vacation, and I can tell you that is more important than *any* merit bonus," remembered Doria.) According to labor laws in one Latin American country where Lincoln opened up, any profit-sharing bonus paid for two years in a row automatically became an entitlement that could not be rescinded. American managers quickly found out that it was impossible to operate with the same degree of flexibility they were used to, which was essential to maintain their system's profitability. Similar problems — including conflicts with powerful national labor unions — arose in the other countries, as did losses in the tens of millions of dollars. "The root cause of the crisis was that Lincoln's leaders, including myself, had grown overconfident in the company's abilities and systems," wrote Don Hastings a few years later in a blunt mea culpa. "None of us had any significant international experience. We had assumed that the incentive system and culture could be transferred abroad and that the workforce would be quickly replicated. We ignored the loud and widespread expressions of concern from employees. We did finally learn from our mistakes."[25] (The company quickly returned to profitability by the mid-1990s and has remained well in the black ever since.)

As expansion has continued since those difficult days, the company has continued to experiment with introducing elements of its U.S. operations' management style but at a more cautious pace, given what has been learned about differing cultural attitudes. In China, for example, one research study of the company noted that while "the traditional Lincoln system required the ability of the workforce to speak out and make suggestions for improvements in processes, [that openness] would not come easily in the hierarchical Chinese society, where superiors were expected to make initiatives and decide on most organizational matters."[26]

Jordan Siegel and a colleague at Harvard Business School have studied the relative profitability of Lincoln Electric's operations around the world.[27] They concluded that the best financial results have come in those countries where Lincoln Electric successfully found a middle ground in developing its local management style by, on the one hand, avoiding a wholesale (and ultimately futile) attempt to install the complete U.S. labor management system while, on the other hand, resisting a "total adaptation" to local work practices. More particularly, they found that the more any new host country's labor laws and institutions supported Lincoln's system of pay for performance, the better for everyone involved. "You can duplicate an asset, a process, a factory in six months," stressed Canadian president Joe Doria, "but a culture—that takes years. People look at things [like this system] very differently in other parts of the world."

Yet if the desired outcome is to keep talented workers on the job through thick and thin, consider the fact that Lincoln Electric Canada has adapted Lincoln Cleveland's management system to fit a different economic environment with great success, despite the fact it has not formally adopted the guaranteed employment promise. In 1996, when I first visited the Toronto factory, I interviewed seven employees. Ten years later, six were still on the job. The seventh had recently retired after more than forty years of continuous employment.

chapter four

"THE PROPER STEP FORWARD"

Irregularity of employment is to my mind the greatest of industrial
wastes and one of the greatest causes of social demoralization.
— JUSTICE LOUIS BRANDEIS, 1911

The idea and the reality of guaranteed employment are
well over a century old in the United States. Lincoln
Electric was far from the first company to guarantee that,
come what may, its employees would be able to keep earning a
salary and thus be able to provide for their families. Others both
big and small beat James Lincoln to the punch long before he offered a formal promise of guaranteed work in 1958. Yet only a
handful of these guarantees have survived and, arguably, none as
successfully as his.

The National Wall Paper Company of New York City seems to
have been the very first employer to guarantee work in the United
States, in the 1890s.[1] Born out of the merger of a few small firms,
the new company negotiated for several years with the union representing its employees, during a recession when customers and

sales fluctuated widely. Initially, the union asked for only a guarantee of eleven months' work and avoided demanding a wage
raise. But an improving economy apparently convinced the company to offer a twelve-month guarantee and even an increase in
pay: proof, one assumes, that the wallpaper business was improving, that the owners felt it was economically worthwhile to grant
the union's demands, and that the union was a strong negotiator.
The guarantee survived until 1930 when the Depression exerted its
deadly toll.

As the twentieth century unfolded, a few more companies
each year would make similar promises. A retail men's furnish-
ing store started guaranteeing fifty-two weeks' pay with full hours
in 1905, a coffee-roasting company in 1912 paying full wages even
during the off-season, a chicken processing plant in 1913 with
fifty-two weeks of full-time work for its permanent employees,
and so on.

Eastman Kodak, established in 1881, was widely regarded as
one of the most progressive of all the welfare-capitalist companies. Based in Rochester, New York, and thus far from hotbeds of
union-organizing activity such as New York, Cleveland, and Pittsburgh, Kodak by the 1920s presented itself as a textbook case of
workers who were given powerful financial and employment security incentives to work hard, develop new technologies, build
a sense of teamwork, and, yes, resist the siren call of unions.
George Eastman never hid his deep distrust of organized labor.

As described in wonderfully rich detail by UCLA economist
Sanford Jacoby, Kodak offered profit sharing as early as 1912, annual bonuses, a rudimentary form of health insurance, and an in-
sured employee pension plan by the mid-1920s.[2] Guaranteeing
the survival of these programs became important to everyone in
the company, although, as Jacoby reveals, no one in management
ever seems to have tried to accurately measure their cost-
effectiveness. With a commitment to hire from within, the idea

of *career employment* at Kodak was a virtual reality by the time the Depression began.

Sales of cameras and film did begin to fall after 1929, but far less dramatically than the losses incurred by most other manufacturing businesses in the country. In response, Kodak and its workers made use of virtually every tool in their welfare-capitalist arsenal to avoid layoffs. Hours were reduced dramatically, workers were shifted to assembly lines for products that remained in relatively strong demand, and pay cuts (never very deep) were imposed. It's not surprising that Kodak's employee turnover rate was a small fraction of that of other large American companies.

Kodak survived the Depression largely unscathed, and it continued to uphold many of its welfare policies well into the 1980s. By then, unfortunately, it became clear that the firm's overwhelming success in the world of photography over so many years had actually "reduced its incentive to innovate," and with the arrival of digital technology, that turned out to have been a dangerous miscalculation. Kodak was forced to terminate its no-layoff policy, ordering huge cuts in its workforce. Since 1988, when Kodak's workforce reached approximately 145,000 employees, it has been a downhill slide: By early 2009, it had dropped to below 25,000, roughly the same as during the Great Depression.

As noted earlier, many guaranteed employment promises at nonunion companies were made in hopes of fending off organizing campaigns from the labor movement. In the 1920s, Cleveland was a very highly developed union town and the second-largest center for the garment trade in the country after New York City. But in a rare departure from union practice, then or now, the Cleveland chapter of the International Ladies' Garment Workers' Union made guaranteed employment a priority in its negotiations with local employers, agreeing to accept cuts in pay in return for steady work. In the end, the union won a guarantee of forty-one weeks of paid employment, backed up by a

rudimentary unemployment insurance system in case that promise was broken.[3] (Surrendering ground on hard-fought pay scales
has always been strongly opposed by the vast majority of unions.
The painful deliberations within the United Automobile Workers
over the past several years regarding wage concessions are just
one example. Overtime provisions, health insurance, and pension plans have all been on the chopping block as the American
auto industry has foundered, but base pay has generally been the
last item up for negotiation.)

During the late 1930s, governments even stepped up to play
their part by passing legislative and regulatory incentives to encourage private companies to adopt guaranteed employment
plans.[4] The first state to do so was Wisconsin, with a provision in
1934 that exempted those employers who promised steady work
from paying unemployment insurance taxes; guaranteeing jobs in
the middle of the Depression seemed a fair trade-off for an already badly stretched state treasury as well as for the struggling
employers and workers involved. Forty states eventually passed
statutes allowing employers to pay lower taxes in return for concerted efforts to ensure steady work. A federal labor statute with
a similar goal became law in 1938: It exempted employers from
paying overtime (up to sixteen hours beyond the normal workweek of the time) in return for their guarantees of steady work
over a full year. None of these legislative attempts to nurture
steady work turned out to be very effective. Apparently, good intentions, even when backed by tax reductions, provided insufficient motivation for beleaguered employers to actually take
governments up on their incentives.[5]

In the 1920s and 1930s, three other large American companies—
Procter and Gamble, Hormel Meats, and the Nunn-Bush Shoe
Company—adopted versions of a guaranteed employment policy as part of their welfare-capitalist strategies and were often featured in newspapers articles as a result. But that seemed to be the

"high-water mark of guarantee voluntarism" among big business in America, and all three eventually abandoned their plans.[6]

When the war ended in 1945, exhausted Americans were yearning to rebuild their lives in a more secure environment than the previous decade and a half had allowed. The dream of guaranteed work held obvious appeal, and as a result, the idea began to be more openly and widely discussed in public. Chicago's charismatic Bishop Bernard Sheil, known and loved across the country for his commitment to social justice at a time when the Roman Catholic Church was often at odds with organized labor, even turned up at a national union convention to argue that a guarantee of steady work was "just, feasible and democratically necessary."[7]

During the 1920s and 1930s, union leaders had generally been nervous about accepting guaranteed employment offers from employers, regarding them with suspicion as a coercive strategy to buy employee loyalty instead of paying better wages. Union officials also worried that these plans could serve to erode their own influence over rank-and-file union members. Their fear was that once workers were wrapped in the warm embrace of an employment guarantee, they would never risk rocking the boat over other important issues that labor leaders might raise, for fear it could jeopardize their newfound financial security.

Slowly, however, organized labor began to mellow. The leaders of the CIO and the AFL, the two major labor organizations in the country, came out in favor of guaranteed employment as one way to cleanse the country of its gloomy wartime miasma and to ensure a speedy economic recovery. "A floor under the income of wage-earners," said the CIO's head, Philip Murray, "would mean a floor under the national income."[8]

The increasingly enthusiastic talk about the potential advantages of guaranteed employment was not matched by reality. A 1945 study by the Bureau of Labor Statistics revealed that only

42,500 workers out of a total American workforce of at least 8 million people were actually promised steady work by their employers; that's not even 1 of every 200 workers.[9] And though unions were tentatively becoming more favorably inclined toward guaranteed employment, employers—and especially big business—remained generally reluctant to engage workers on the subject. Many thought that any suggestion they should surrender the right to fire people was proof that the unions were really plotting how to grab a much bigger say in the day-to-day control of companies. The potential encroachment on management's authority, said one executive, was really about "a lust for power and a movement towards some form of socialism."[10]

A LATENT ABILITY TO WORK HARD

Why did James Lincoln ultimately offer his employees a guarantee of steady work? Why wasn't he threatened, like so many employers of the time, by the idea of giving up one of the most powerful tools available to any CEO, the right to cut his workforce whenever it seemed necessary?[11] It is clear that, in part, he was motivated by the religious values he was imbued with while growing up as the son of a deeply pious Congregationalist minister. He genuinely wanted to treat people well.

But as a student of human nature, Lincoln also sincerely believed in what he termed our infinite "latent abilities," abilities that could be developed only through a process of constantly testing ourselves against the world we live in. He felt it was the job of an honest business owner to find ways to test his employees in a fair environment where everyone would then share together in the results of their collective hard work. Lincoln knew that creating such a working environment—and the process of production involved—was impossible in the absence of trust shared deeply across an organization. Talk was too easy, he often wrote: "There is no claim more often repeated by management than that of 'cooperation.'" Unlike many at the time who were experimenting only with financial incentives, Lincoln was convinced that workers who feared for their jobs would never demonstrate much enthusiasm for their work, let alone any creativity. "There may even be no conscious effort to hold back progress," he cautioned, but a worker will never try to put his mind to creatively solving a problem if in doing so "he is threatened with the loss of his job by a better way of producing."[12]

To some observers, a guaranteed employment promise sounds like charity, not sound business management. Not to Lincoln: "It is no part of management responsibility to be merely kind to workers," he stressed in his writings. "Managers are responsible for efficiency in their industry . . . efficiency depends on human cooperation . . . cooperation [demands that] the fear of losing income will be eliminated. . . . This can only be done by guaranteeing continuous employment."[13]

Lincoln had no illusions that his management style would ever protect his company from the relentless cycle of economic boom and bust (although he did believe that it would be better for society as a whole if many more did!). In fact, he saw opportunity in the downturns, provided management didn't rush to lay off employees at the first sign of trouble. Over the years, he came to understand all too well how CEOs and their senior managers could become dangerously complacent during an economic boom. "Bad habits and consequent waste grow when business is at a peak," he wrote, adding a warning of the need to constantly plan for coming slumps.

For James Lincoln, being tested by hard times—whether personal or economic—demanded discipline to ensure survival. In the era when he ran the company, the role of outside investors and stockholders was much more limited than in our day. But even back then, he was well aware of the distorting financial pressures that could be exerted by those external actors on the company's management. He was adamant that good leadership meant resisting the temptation to give in, especially in times of uncertainty, when stockholders became nervous about their investments. More than forty years ago, Lincoln offered prudent advice about how to prepare for an economic crisis—save some money and don't sacrifice your employees: "Management should have the necessary assets on hand to take care of any circumstance. Lack of cash available has in some cases held up programs that should be followed. If that means fewer dividends, pay fewer dividends. . . . Do not threaten the future of the company by reckless spending, no matter how insistent on dividends the stockholder is. . . . Laying off the worker because of slackening of business is death to efficiency."[14]

"IT IS THE PROPER STEP FORWARD"

On Armistice Day, November 11, 1918, Lincoln wrote to one of his employees that the end of the fighting in Europe meant the end of Lincoln Electric's wartime role in the production of guns, tanks, and ships.[15] Tougher times lay ahead, yet he stressed that cutting wages was to be a last resort, and any cost reductions should be achieved through "an increase in efficiency." Still new to management, he worried that layoffs were unavoidable, but was equally emphatic that "in no case is any employee to be dropped who has done his work faithfully. Those who have taken advantage of the times and shirked their duties should be let out." This note foreshadowed not only guaranteed employment but also the use of rigorously enforced performance standards and the merit system.

In his 1945 letter to President Truman, Lincoln wrote that the last layoff at his company required "for economic reasons"—which has always been the wording used when workers were laid off for lack of sufficient demand from consumers—had been in 1925. That would seem to indicate that sometime in the mid-1920s, the company began a concerted effort to retain its employees at all costs. (In public comments these days about the no-layoff policy, Lincoln Electric states that the last layoff was in 1948, but there is apparently no documentation marking an exact event. A hesitation not to formally push that benchmark date even further back seems to derive from a vague sense among company elders that a few people may have been laid off just after World War II.)

By the late 1930s, James Lincoln had become a fixture on the management lecture circuit of the time, and he regularly wrote newspaper articles and letters to the editor, explaining how his company operated. In a 1939 series of articles for the *Christian Science Monitor*, he placed the responsibility for keeping working people on the job, even in hard times, squarely on managers: "Top management, including the sales manager, are not laid off when business decreases; their jobs are safe. The hourly worker is the one who suffers . . . because of the failure of those responsible."[16]

In a speech to the American Management Association in 1944, before an audience of the nation's business elite, Lincoln laid out the financial advantages of the various incentives the company was using. He emphasized that keeping employees on the job was not about paternalism but profits.[17] As he had done at a congressional hearing two years earlier, Lincoln stressed that paying blue-collar workers two and three times the national average wage was about good business, not good feelings. Look no further, he suggested, than the fact that his well-paid workforce has quadrupled in size over the previous ten years to more than

1,300 people. That could be achieved only through a steady growth in productivity.

Sometime around 1950, the idea of a formal guarantee of steady work was first raised at a meeting of the Advisory Board, and in January 1951, Lincoln began sharing his thoughts on the proposal with employees. Several memos speak of his conviction that a program that had already been in operation for roughly twenty-five years was probably worth taking to its logical conclusion, but he cautioned his employees that it could also bring hardships. Lincoln was trying to ensure that everyone would understand that while great shared gains were possible with guaranteed work, so too was shared pain in tough times.

> It is an experiment that poses many problems. Some of these must be answered, of course, by management, but some of them also must be answered by the producing worker. While continuous employment . . . would undoubtedly increase the total income to all people, yet there is little doubt that in extreme conditions it would reduce the bonus. . . . It is my belief that it is the proper step forward, but there are many problems which must be acknowledged if we are to succeed.
>
> —J. F. LINCOLN, JANUARY 16, 1951[18]

Lincoln's biggest challenge in implementing guaranteed employment—and it remains the biggest challenges for any employer—was to ensure that his employees trusted him to keep the promise. There would be many sacrifices required of employees in the short run to make the system work for everyone in the long term, and employees would never be willing to make those short-term sacrifices if they didn't believe Lincoln would deliver in the long term.

Trust is generally missing in a reading of the history of guaranteed employment over the past century, or indeed in the history of many other issues involving management in the America economy. Over and over, senior managers seem to have started down the road to a no-layoff policy (with a variety of motives, as described earlier), only to quickly resort to layoffs when they were faced with a serious financial crisis. Lincoln Electric approached a guaranteed employment promise extremely cautiously, however. The idea had been part and parcel of the day-to-day management system for several decades before Lincoln himself suggested that it could formally become company policy.

Once implemented, the promise could never be broken; there would be no second chances for guaranteed employment. Lincoln was convinced it was a risk worth taking.

FLEXIBILITY AND FEAR

If *trust* is the first overarching principle necessary in any workplace that hopes to thrive with a guaranteed employment promise such as Lincoln Electric's, the second is surely *flexibility*. Everyone—from the bottom to the top of the company—must be willing to be flexible about virtually everything involved with doing a job and being paid for it.

Unfortunately, as sociologist Richard Sennett has pointed out, in today's economy, flexibility has almost always come to mean that employees must learn to work and live with the near-constant fear and insecurity that their jobs might disappear at any moment. To do otherwise—by hoping for some degree of employment security and financial stability—means foolishly standing in front of the freight train that is the global economy, Sennett wrote in *The Corrosion of Character*. But the persistent uncertainty in the workplace required by what he called "flexible capitalism" exerts a terrible price on workers and their families: "It cannot give any guidance for the conduct of an ordinary life," and "the corroding of character is an inevitable consequence."[19]

Flexibility at Lincoln Electric does require employees to accept the possibility of change in their work, their hours, monthly
compensation, career development, merit rating, and, of course,
the size of their annual bonus—precisely the forms of institutionalized insecurity that Sennett decried. But in return for accepting this demanding degree of flexibility on the job, and
agreeing to meet the firm's rigorous performance standards, employees are guaranteed the certainty of steady work, which means,
in turn, the ability to support their families over the long term—
the very things that Sennett argued have disappeared from modern economic life, to such damaging effect on society as a whole.

Flexibility continues to be protected and nurtured as an important corporate value at Lincoln Electric because it has proved
to be extremely beneficial for the company, its customers, its employees, and its shareholders. Furthermore, employees understand
that being flexible is essential to the company's ability to remain
competitive, both in the United States and internationally.[20]

During the 1950s, while Lincoln Electric was moving toward
making guaranteed employment a formal company policy, there
were many voices raised in the business community and elsewhere that argued that the workplace flexibility essential to sustain a vibrant and growing American economy was starting to
disappear. These concerned commentators feared that there
would be a price to pay if too many rules came to limit the near-
absolute discretion of those in charge of the nation's private enterprises. The immediate impetus for their worries, of course, was
the growing power of organized labor in manufacturing and
many other sectors of the economy. (Almost 40 percent of U.S.
workers in the private sector were then in unions versus less than
8 percent today.)

It is of course crucial to recognize that the great expansion of
union power after World War II directly fueled a profound
change in the social and economic fabric of the United States.

The immense—and since unmatched—economic growth between the late 1940s and late 1970s created unprecedented nationwide prosperity. The relative wages of tens of millions of American workers steadily and significantly increased, which allowed them to join the middle class. Pensions, health care, and many other work-related benefits became commonplace to a degree unimaginable just two decades earlier.

But this transformation in the social and economic structure of the country didn't just happen because the economy was growing, argues MIT economist Frank Levy.[21] It took place precisely because many social institutions—the labor movement, of course, but also political and economic organizations—acted forcefully on behalf of an entire generation of Americans who were exhausted by depression and war and who adamantly wanted to create a more egalitarian society. (Later, after the Reagan revolution took hold, many of those same institutions changed their priorities.)

That said, the decade following the end of the war turned out to be a time of significant labor strife, with the proportion of employees involved in strikes up to forty times greater than in recent years. For many business leaders, unions became an unavoidable fact of life, and given their growing power, many corporations were forced to make concessions on a wide range of demands raised by workers, beginning with wages and job security, followed by other benefits. Those increasingly unavoidable concessions to labor worried CEOs from coast to coast, and gradually, the extremely rigid and ritualized culture of labor relations that developed after World War II came to be seen as a limit on innovation in the workplace.

The United Automobile Workers set the tone for collective bargaining in the postwar period for the union movement as a whole and, perhaps just as important, for nonunion workplaces, too. Whenever nonunion employers refused to match the (usually highly publicized) financial gains in new contracts for unionized workers in their communities, they inevitably faced stronger union-organizing campaigns among their own disgruntled nonunion employees, as well as increased difficulty in finding anyone to work for less than union scale in their businesses. In other words, the unions established a floor of comparative fairness. ("Unions raised the bar and the level of other people's wages, and we should never forget that," Joe Latessa Sr. told me, although he never wanted a union at Lincoln Electric. "Our company had to be competitive to get good people.")

The 1950 contract between General Motors and the UAW became a bellwether for labor relations across the whole American economy. Dubbed the Treaty of Detroit—at a time when Detroit was approaching the zenith of its national economic influence— it was a five-year agreement that spelled out in minute detail how power would be exercised and work performed in GM's factories.

Flexibility was not a word heard to describe the Treaty of Detroit, in fact or in spirit. The contract enshrined what were becoming case-hardened attitudes between employers and workers, and it defined a process of adversarial bargaining and work rules that lasted for decades. In this and other similar contracts, management retained near-complete control of the overall direction of production for the firms involved, while unions won the near-absolute right and power to negotiate the impact of those workplace decisions on their members.

A GM vice president of the time was unabashed about who did what: "Management establishes the rules and it disciplines for violations. The Union is free to challenge the application of any rule . . . and 'walk the last mile' with a disciplined employee." Union leaders were similarly blunt: "A union demand is a negotiable demand which if not satisfied can be met by a strike. How do you talk about job redesign questions in terms of a negotiated demand and a possible strike?"[22]

The financial costs of negotiating these contracts—let alone of violating them once they were in place—constituted a powerful incentive to try to spell out on paper every possible scenario for conflict that might develop in the workplace and then to specify appropriate remedies. Similarly, every effort was made to reach agreements that extended as far into the future as seemed reasonable. The end result was collective agreements of tremendous complexity and length, spinning a web of rules that detailed precise lines of control from the top of organizations down to the factory floor.

In this negotiating environment, the kinds of more consensually based management systems that had become essential to welfare capitalism simply didn't fit very well. Companies such as Kodak, Sears, and IBM were largely still extending workplace benefits to their employees, but there were few new acolytes—among workers or management. As labor scholar Sanford Jacoby has noted, many welfare-capitalist policies that emphasized cooperation and sharing (whether of profits or decision making) were dismissed as *touchy-feely* and potential tools of abuse by one side or another.[23]

Employers became more and more suspicious of profit sharing, as they sensed a general hardening of attitudes in their increasingly unionized workplaces: Senior managers feared that the joint decision making needed in an efficient profit-sharing system would be exploited by unions to win a much greater (and, for management, unwanted) say over company policies. In return, unions grew more nervous about profit sharing because as the normal business cycle ebbed and flowed, workers would necessarily be forced to sacrifice the certainty of being paid a fixed hourly wage for a fixed number of hours each week or month. A better option, both sides began to argue, was to sign off on convoluted yet ironclad rules that specified the exact pay premiums earned per quarter hour on double overtime on a

Sunday, or to spell out the byzantine actuarial issues of pension coverage.

Work-sharing and job-reassignment programs were also cause for union concern. The key goal of these policies may have originally been to keep more people employed in slow periods by reducing the overall hours worked by the average employee. But organized labor generally became suspicious that this approach was yet another back-door assault on the concept of income security and on the all-important principle of seniority.

It was this increasing rigidity in the postwar workplace, achieved through collective bargaining, that sparked growing worry. As early as 1948, Sumner Slichter, perhaps the most prominent labor economist in the country (and hence someone who might be seen to be "in labor's corner"), asked, "Are we becoming a 'laboristic' state?"[24] He feared that American workers, through the growing power of their unions, were exercising an undue influence on the direction of the economy. Slichter warned that collective bargaining was becoming a power struggle, not a discussion of principles. The inevitable strikes—which were significantly increasing in number at the time—could not bode well for society as a whole, he believed, especially if regular wage increases led to inflation.

A decade later, another prominent economist, Arthur M. Ross, asked a similar question: "Do we have a new industrial feudalism?"[25] Ross tackled the view, increasingly debated in public, that workers in America were becoming "chained to their jobs" precisely because the benefits they had fought so hard to earn were so rich that leaving a job was now considered far too risky. Working for big unionized companies, worried many economists, had become so financially profitable and secure that no worker could ever reasonably "afford" to quit in order to seek greener pastures elsewhere. This was dangerous, according to these experts, precisely because the vibrant American economy relied on people eager to move—perhaps across the country almost at the drop of a hat—to explore new economic horizons. Too much workplace stability was a threat to future prosperity. In the end, by analyzing the pattern of actual *quit rates* collected by the Department of Labor, Ross rejected the arguments about "workers-in-chains because their jobs were too good," but the idea retained a popular life of its own.

Prominent sociologist Clark Kerr worried about the effect of ever-increasing social stability on an even broader canvas, arguing that America in the 1950s was becoming such a comfortable place that it risked losing its "independent spirit."[26] Kerr believed that because jobs were becoming so effectively protected by unions—in essence, guaranteed through collective agreements— the restless energy and pioneering urge that had fueled the transformation of the American wilderness into an international industrial powerhouse were being dangerously dissipated.

Then in the summer of 1957, the United States came under attack—from the Toyota Toyopet Crown and the SONY TR-63. The arrival in the United States of the first Japanese automobile and first transistor radio heralded a traumatic period for everyone who played a part in the American economy. The Crown, the TR-63, and all their offspring were products of a manufacturing and management culture that differed dramatically from the "ritualized conflict" of union-management relations in most American workplaces.

Few Americans at the time noticed that Japan's dynamic system of manufacturing was remarkably similar to Lincoln Electric's way of doing business—and to that of other employers in the long-past era of welfare capitalism—with an emphasis on the importance of trust between management and workers and, for most employees, a promise of guaranteed employment.

JAPAN, LINCOLN ELECTRIC,
AND THE HIGH PERFORMANCE WORKPLACE

The revival of the Japanese economy after World War II is a well-known story, from smoking ruins in 1945 to international economic status as *Number One* in 1990, when one square yard of Tokyo real estate was said to be worth more than a quarter of a million dollars. Of course, Japan had been a significant presence in the world economy before the war, but its resurgence was phenomenal by any measure and especially in relation to the United States. By 1960, Japan's economy had recovered to be about 18 percent of the American economy; three decades later, it had more than doubled its relative size to 40 percent. In 1970, just thirteen years after the first Toyota arrived in California, Japanese car sales were still only 3 percent of total U.S. new auto purchases; by 1990, Japan's share had exploded to 30 percent—a tenfold increase.

In the United States, and indeed in other developed countries around the world, the arrival of Japan, Inc., gave birth to great angst about the future of American capitalism and its ability to compete on the world stage. In 1990, Charles Ferguson, an economist at MIT, cautioned, "US and European information technology companies face a stark choice: cooperate or become vassals of their Japanese competitors."[27] When huge Japanese conglomerates began to buy American cultural icons such as Rockefeller Center (Mitsubishi) and Hollywood's MCA Studios (Matsushita), there was a collective gnashing of teeth across America that the loser of the last war had somehow come out the winner, largely because of a too generous postwar reconstruction effort financed by American taxpayers.

After the Meiji Restoration of 1854, Japan had quickly set out to establish itself as a global power by building up its economy to rival those of Britain, Germany, and the United States. Japanese business, military, and academic experts were soon scouring the world for the best of Western technical know-how in a wide range of economic fields. By the first decade of the 1900s, F. W. Taylor's philosophy of scientific management had been translated and published in Japan, where it became widely influential in industry in the decades between the two world wars.

The basic principles of Japanese industrial management were divided into two broad areas: the management of employees and how their work was organized. At the heart of its "people-management" system were policies quite familiar to Lincoln Electric workers (or those at Kodak, Sears, and others) of the 1920s and 1930s: near-lifetime employment, an emphasis on equality among employees, a very flat management hierarchy, company associations and unions organized to encourage communications across the firm, and, finally, a focus on building a consensus among workers and managers regarding long-term goals. (The extent to which Japanese society, with its social norms of working in groups and joint decision making, renders this system unique has been debated for years.)

Lifetime employment in Japan generally applied only—and applies still—to a core of permanent male workers in large corporations as well as in government. Armies of temporary workers provided a necessary degree of flexibility. Women were largely excluded. Nonetheless, the system has functioned to provide a loyal workforce for the companies and security for workers who were confidently able to plan for their families' futures.

The status of specific jobs and career paths—so codified in union contracts in the United States—was minimized in Japanese industry in order to make it easier for managers to move employees within a firm as needed. Encouraging flexibility was also seen as important in nurturing a sense among employees that everyone was part of a team.

Much earlier than in the United States, Japanese industry embraced the belief that product quality must be part of the actual process of manufacturing, rather than something to be "fixed" at the end of an assembly line. It's been suggested that one reason Toyota became an early leader with its emphasis on quality as a production technique was precisely because it had *not* been involved in a joint venture with American car manufacturers between the wars, as had other Japanese auto companies.

By the 1950s, Japanese industry with the support of the national government adopted a growth strategy based on exporting to overseas consumers, particularly in the United States. Once again, an American played a key role in making that strategy work.

If F. W. Taylor may be called the influential wizard behind the curtain for Japanese industry in the first half of the twentieth century, W. Edwards Deming played a similar role in the second half, after he arrived to help in the postwar reconstruction effort. Deming believed that a manufacturing company needed to ensure that every last component of its organization was devoted to creating products of the highest quality; pursuing profits and market share came later. Low-key but charismatic, Deming advised many Japanese companies how to employ statistical techniques to achieve zero defects during production. With Deming's help, Japanese industry systematically fine-tuned the approaches to manufacturing that are now known so well in U.S. industry: *kaizen*, or continuous improvement; *kanban*, or just-in-time inventory deliveries; and the overall concept of *lean manufacturing*.

Retired Lincoln executive Dick Sabo remembered meeting Deming in the 1980s. Sabo said the two men "agreed about 90 percent of the time about everything to do with managing a manufacturing company," and particularly on the importance of guaranteed employment and other policies that raised levels of trust between workers throughout a company. Deming was not a great fan of Lincoln Electric's financial incentives and the merit system, according to Sabo, perhaps reflecting his then decades-long experience in Japan, where the culture would tend to downplay anything that might lead to overt displays of differences between people at work or, more broadly, in society.[28]

By the end of the 1970s, with Japanese products making huge inroads into North America, it was slowly becoming clear that responding to the challenge posed by the organization of work in Japanese manufacturing companies would be extremely difficult. Those who argued for a change in America's manufacturing methods faced a significant roadblock: The "fine-grained division of labor" that existed between management and workers in the United States meant that neither side seemed prepared to make concessions. The challenge ahead became all the more clear when an avalanche of books appeared detailing what American industry needed to learn from Japanese-style management policies. Two of these were especially influential during the 1980s.

The most popular was *Theory Z: How American Business Can Meet the Japanese Challenge*, by William Ouchi.[29] A best-seller for much of 1981, *Theory Z* argued that American industry's focus on achieving short-term success was a significant disadvantage when competing against Japanese companies that tended to take a much longer strategic view. Ouchi identified the rapid turnover of employees in many American firms—through layoffs and voluntary quitting—as a critical barrier to developing a broadly shared sense of loyalty among employees toward their employers. He also argued that this ever-changing makeup of a company's workforce limited the sharing of ideas on how to continuously enhance product quality.

The second book, published the same year, was *The Art of Japanese Management: Applications for American Executives*, which became more colloquially known as the *Seven S's*.[30] The book identified seven essential management priorities for any firm. The last three—shared values, staff, and style—were

described as the "soft" levers of good management that formed
the secret ingredient of Japan's success. The authors argued that
by taking a longer view of what constitutes success, Japanese
firms were more easily and effectively able to nurture a broad
company-wide consensus on goals and to build a loyal, flexible
workforce that would agree to make sacrifices for the overall
good of the company.[31]

James Lincoln would have had no disagreements whatsoever
with the overall thrust of these books or other similar appeals to im-
itate Japan. But if this latest message for American industry was
clear—*build a workplace where workers are trusted, decisions are
shared, and employers think long term*—bringing those ideals into
practice was exceedingly difficult, and has remained so in the
decades since. At the start, it wasn't for lack of trying. In the 1970s,
there were scores of programs undertaken by a wide variety of
American companies to increase the involvement of workers in
decision making. Quality circles were soon appearing on the shop
floor of many manufacturing companies. Jobs were redesigned to
emphasize a team approach to problem solving rather than individual classifications. A variety of profit-sharing schemes appeared.

One of the earliest and most influential efforts to rebuild a
whole American company to focus on the "soft" elements of
Japanese management took place in 1972 in Bolivar, Tennessee,
where Harman International Industries, a large American manufacturing conglomerate, owned an auto-parts company that supplied components to the Big Three automakers.[32] The president
of the company and a senior official of the UAW (representing the
workers) realized that, each for his own reasons, they both wanted
to demonstrate that a more collaborative workplace was, first of
all, possible and, second, more profitable than the adversarial
model they had become used to. With their support, the company was dramatically reshaped to involve production workers in

decision making and to give them increased flexibility at work as well as enhanced job security.

For a time, it all seemed to work. Product quality and job safety improved, employee turnover and absenteeism fell, relations between the UAW and management became less confrontational, and overall employment increased. But ensuring change over the longer term was harder. When the company's owner and the local union leader both left office, their replacements turned out to be much less committed to the experiment. "I didn't recognize soon enough how critical a role the managers have to play," the original owner told the *New York Times* when the Bolivar plant was eventually shut in 1998. "You don't go anywhere unless you get those guys to passionately sign on."[33]

It was only in the rarest of cases that well-established companies moved to embrace no-layoff policies similar to that of Lincoln Electric as part of developing new workplace relationships. The NUMMI car plant in California, a collaboration between Toyota and GM that opened in 1984, is probably the most famous. Toyota even agreed to the presence of a union, the first and only such arrangement with organized labor in any of its North American production facilities. In the collective agreement between the two companies and the UAW, there was no formal promise to avoid layoffs, but all sides accepted it as a shared goal. NUMMI's creation is often cited as proof that unions and management can find agreement on innovative changes in the American workplace. However, in the recession summer of 2009, first GM and then Toyota announced plans to end their collaboration. At the time of this writing, it is unclear what the demise of the NUMMI arrangement—and the likely closing of the plant— means for the UAW workers.

Southwest Airlines, which took to the air in 1971, was another firm that emphasized the importance of employee involvement at all levels of the company. It embraced a no-layoff policy along with a number of other strategies to involve workers at every level of the company and to build loyalty (by June 2009, Southwest had still been able to avoid layoffs).

For many years until the mid-1990s, Lincoln Electric hosted seminars on the inner workings of its incentive system for other interested companies. The workshops explained the complex interplay among piecework, the Advisory Board system, merit ratings, and guaranteed employment. Participants were warned that just cherry-picking one element or another (with high hopes for dramatic improvements) was unlikely to solve any of their HR or productivity problems. Dick Sabo recalled that in the early 1970s, as American industry was reeling from the invasion of high-quality Japanese imports of all kinds, between fifty to one hundred firms would attend every year: "They would range from small family-owned businesses to Caterpillar Tractor to Ohio-based steel manufacturer Worthington Industries to Air New Zealand." Most expressed great interest in guaranteed employment, remembered Sabo, but few seemed prepared to think critically about the changes in their hiring policies necessary to make the policy work. Former factory worker Terry Dattilio also remembered regularly seeing groups of visiting Japanese executives closely observing his assembly line during the late 1970s and early 1980s.

Toward the end of the 1980s in the United States, the so-called *Japanese management system* was rebranded by academics and industry experts as the *high performance workplace system*. To some extent, this reflected a concern that Japan's unique culture—with its great emphasis on social harmony, consensus building, and working together to solve problems—played such a significant role in its industrial management structure that trying to emulate that system in America was doomed to fail. And when the Japanese economy fell into a deep slump—the start of the so-called lost decade—it also seemed inappropriate to embrace the management philosophies of a severely weakened competitor. (There was also a great deal of schadenfreude at Japan's plight.)

A name change notwithstanding, one reality was clear: By the 1990s, only a few American companies were really serious about transforming themselves into organizations where employees were truly valued as decision makers as well as laborers, and where senior executives truly believed that a sharing of profits over the long term was a sign of good management.

In 1998, Thomas Kochan, now codirector of the Institute for Work and Employment Research at MIT's Sloan School, was frank about the grim future of labor relations in the United States. The traditional system of collective bargaining that had evolved since the end of World War II, warned Kochan, "cannot produce economic results for [U.S.] firms to be competitive in product markets that demand high levels of quality, customer service and productivity." More worrisome, he said, was the fact that despite the incessant talk about reform and Japanese management and high performance, all efforts to reshape the way large American businesses were being run had failed. A decade later, in early 2009, Kochan told me that little had changed and that "as long as there is a low-road alternative that is more comfortable for management" in the United States, they will take it.[34]

The employment and financial security provided by a no-layoff promise—long a key feature of Japan's management system as well as Lincoln Electric's—can still only be found on the margins of the American economy.

UNIONS AT LINCOLN ELECTRIC

There is no union now at Lincoln Electric, and there never has been. That's largely due to the fact that over the past 114 years, there have been only a very few moments when anyone inside the company has devoted much thought to unions and only a very few moments when unions have devoted much thought toward organizing inside Lincoln Electric. History shows that a union seldom has much appeal to workers in a company that pays well, shares a relatively huge proportion of annual profits with employees, provides a safe work environment, and offers a guarantee of steady work.[35]

It is true that James Lincoln did not want a union in his company and told his employees exactly how he felt. Labor leaders were generally the objects of bitter scorn in his writings and public speeches, and he dismissed the collective-bargaining process as "civil war." Yet at the same time, he never blamed workers who felt that they needed a union to protect their rights on the job. In Lincoln's view, good management set the tone for the workplace, and if managers "had intelligently and willingly given the workers what the labor unions had to fight for, no labor-management friction ever could have existed."[36]

From the 1930s through to the present day, there have been only a few short-lived attempts to organize workers at Lincoln Electric. As far as anyone inside or outside the company can remember, the UAW led the organizing drives, most recently in the mid-1990s; all faded fairly quickly. There are a few tales of tough talk and some intimidation surrounding those campaigns, but no collective memory of mass firings or workers threatened with violence. There is no evidence of what Cornell University labor scholar Kate Bronfenbrenner recently called the "standard practice for workers to be subjected to threats, interrogation, harassment, surveillance and retaliation" for union-organizing activity in American industry, especially during the past twenty years.[37]

The man whom most credit with initiating the last organizing drive in the mid-1990s is certainly no firebrand. Nor was his campaign. "A union wasn't necessary," said Bill Sass, waving his hand dismissively. "Our tenure is phenomenal, and our wages are phenomenal." Sass worked in the factory for thirty-eight years, retiring in 2002. His wife is still an office worker at the firm. "Did any of us really want a union?" asked Sass rhetorically, referring to the several hundred employees who signed membership cards, many of whom later met with union officials at Alexander's restaurant in Euclid. "No! We wanted to force management to get back to a better line of communication. Why would we want to hurt our livelihood?"

The campaign began, said Sass, after several new senior executives had been brought in from the outside, an unusual occurrence given the common practice at Lincoln Electric of hiring from within. What "really hurt" long-term employees, according to Sass, was that the newcomers (recruited from some very large U.S. manufacturing companies) were granted the same vacation privileges as if they had been with Lincoln Electric for twenty-five years. "They walk in off the street and get these benefits and then make statements that people on the factory floor are making too much money," said Sass. Some workers also had concerns about the financial health of the company pension plan.

Don Hastings, then company chairman, sent every employee a letter stating clearly that "the company does not want a union to take over our plants."[38] Other executives told me they spent time on the factory floor encouraging workers not to sign up with the union. They put the case to the employees that the future of the annual bonus would be threatened because any union would inevitably fight to end a system that allowed their pay to rise or fall depending on the overall profit situation.

Sass did use the word *intimidation* several times in our interview, saying that he felt that his own career had been hurt after the campaign "fizzled out," but he took pains to emphasize that "there is no dark underbelly" to labor relations at Lincoln Electric and little future for another union-organizing drive. Bill Burga, head of the AFL-CIO in Ohio from 1993 to 2007, affirmed Sass's claim. "We always looked at Lincoln Electric to see what

they were doing, and we never worried about them," Burga said.
"You have to give them credit. They have maintained a good history of decent pay and profit sharing." So why did they buck the
trend? According to Burga, "It's all based on corporate leadership;
that's the only explanation I have. They saw a way to run the company by treating people right, rather than paying people less with
less security."[39]

GUARANTEED EMPLOYMENT at Lincoln Electric, as one of the key components of its incentive system, has continuously evolved as the
American industrial landscape has changed over the years. The
constant element has remained the flexibility of the company's
workforce: The vast majority of employees have come to trust that
the sacrifices they make will be rewarded in the long run by those
charged with making decisions at the top of the company.

In the summer of 2009, the U.S. auto industry was struggling
to reform and rebuild itself after excruciatingly complex bailout
negotiations and remarkable union concessions, all unfolding
amid bruising market conditions. Similar struggles were under
way elsewhere across the economy. Everyone—CEOs, workers,
investors—seemed to be fighting off a sense of desperation, in no
small measure because they were unable to draw on a reservoir
of trust and flexibility similar to that of Lincoln Electric. For
those other firms and their workers, years of neglect were taking
a terrible toll.

"LAYOFFS AREN'T A BIG DEAL ANYMORE"

By pursuing his own interest [a man] frequently promotes that of the society more effectually than when he really intends to promote it. I have never known much good done by those who affected to trade for the public good.

—ADAM SMITH, *The Wealth of Nations* (1776)

How selfish soever man may be supposed, there are evidently some principles in his nature, which interest him in the fortune of others, and render their happiness necessary to him, though he derives nothing from it except the pleasure of seeing it.

—ADAM SMITH, *The Theory of Moral Sentiments* (1759)

More than two centuries after he published his great works, Adam Smith's words still resonate powerfully. Long before there were professional economists—let alone management consultants—Smith pointed out that every business enterprise had an impact on the society in which it was operating and that everyone running a company needed to deal with that responsibility. It wasn't—and isn't—a simple problem. A man had best focus on his own business rather than worry about how to make the world a better place, Smith argued. Yet how could any moral man blatantly ignore the condition of the people around him?

The resolution of this most human problem in economics is determined in our time, as in Smith's, by the values of the men and women in charge of running the nation's commercial enterprises, and it is hardly going out on a limb to say that many, if not most, Americans believe that there is something desperately wrong with the value system of modern business.

As the 2008 recession dragged into 2009, evidence of something amiss kept piling up: the collapse of Lehman Brothers, AIG's bailout, flagrant misuse of corporate jets, million-dollar retention bonuses, the Madoff fraud, and more. Of course, such a chronicle of deception, arrogance, and illegality might have only irritated rather than enraged Americans if it wasn't for the greater human costs that emerged at the same time. In December 2008, 681,000 U.S. jobs were lost; in January 2009, 741,000 were lost. February, 681,000; March, 652,000; April, 504,000; May, 345,000; June, 467,000; July, 247,000.[1] Mix all that together, shake, and then season with a dose of corporate-speak from CEOs such as Hewlett-Packard's Mark Hurd, and it's no wonder Americans are angry: "I am a big believer that having the most efficient cost structure directly relates to your ability to scale and grow. We've got to do tough stuff." Hurd then announced a layoff of 25,000 employees.[2]

There is an alarming disconnect at the core of our economy. Far too many business leaders seem to have decided that their solution to Adam Smith's dilemma is to simply ignore "the fortune of others" in favor of their own and to forgo the admittedly difficult challenge of balancing the complex needs of the firms that they control with the human needs of their employees, their families, and their communities. In particular, those in power have come to regard layoffs as simply *normal*, where that word embodies all its *Oxford Dictionary* meanings of "regular, usual, free from mental or emotional disorder."

Lincoln Electric, in contrast, has always operated under the assumption that an energetic pursuit of corporate profits is not inhibited by an equally determined commitment to raise the fortunes of its employees; in fact, the two are interdependent. As proof that Lincoln Electric's business model can survive the rough-and-tumble of Wall Street, consider the company's financial track record: an average growth rate of 19 percent per year from 2005 through 2009, an average annual return on investment of 16 percent during those years, a long-term debt-to-equity ratio of only 9 percent, a bank balance of $406 million in cash, and a larger global market share than any of its competitors.[3]

Of course, laying off employees has always been part of a growing economy. In 1942, German economist Joseph Schumpeter introduced "the perennial gale of creative destruction" to the language of economics, a phrase he used to describe the inevitable, necessary, and, in that sense, normal process by which old industries (and the jobs in them) died off to be replaced by newer ones. But as one of Canada's best-known musicians, Bruce Cockburn, warned many years ago, "The trouble with normal is that it always gets worse."[4]

The attitude that layoffs are just another everyday technique of modern management is now deeply embedded in corporate behavior in America. As an example, here's an executive's guide to good layoff procedures from *Personnel Economics in Practice*, a graduate-level textbook widely regarded as the standard reference work at many business schools across the country on how to manage your employees. Imagine that your company's sales are dropping, and your creditors are calling. Just flip to page 103:

> Downsizing can be highly emotional, and organizations that go through the process tend to find that workers are extremely unproductive while it is ongoing. One of the reasons for this is that workers focus, quite naturally, on who will be laid off, when, and under what terms. This can be quite a distraction from ordinary business. Thus, it often pays to get the pain over quickly, and unexpectedly.
>
> For similar reasons, a firm should consider laying off more workers than seems apparent at first glance. If it can do so, it minimizes the odds that it will have to do so again soon (many downsizing firms go through several waves of layoffs before they are finished). An additional advantage is that it makes it possible to clean house thoroughly in areas of the organization that need radical restructuring, because the costs of firing a worker tend to be lower when implemented in the context of a larger set of layoffs.[5]

The three immediately preceding paragraphs in the book suggest that managers can effectively use just the hint of layoffs to force some of their employees to voluntarily accept buyout offers and quit. If absolutely necessary, a few real layoffs may ultimately be required "to credibly threaten" people. There is even an upside to that somewhat unsavory decision, according to the authors: A small layoff generally turns out to be cost-effective, because letting just a few workers go "reduces the buyout that is required to motivate" a sufficient number of the remaining employees to see the light and leave of their own volition. The *drive system* of management so prevalent a century ago couldn't be described any better. It is as if many executives willfully minimize the significant human costs of layoffs on employees, their families, and the companies themselves.

Is this conclusion unfair to CEOs? At the end of the 1990s, a decade in which huge layoffs often seemed to be daily news events, an analysis by Bain and Company of the winning management strategies employed by Fortune 500 firms reported that 70 percent of senior executives who were surveyed disagreed with the statement that "layoffs show poor management."[6] Not much has changed, judging by the past couple of years.

Over the past two decades, however, a small number of labor economists and other social scientists have been examining what a layoff means for those who find themselves on the receiving end, that is, employees who, until the ax falls on them, have generally been performing exactly the work they were asked to do by the senior executives who are now delivering pink slips. These experts are asking questions such as: Are lifetime jobs really disappearing? What happens to the family finances of workers who lose their jobs in a layoff? How is their mental and physical health affected? Can layoffs kill workers? Researchers have also analyzed whether layoffs achieve the (not always loudly announced) goals of senior executives who call for them, such as: Will a layoff prevent a significant fall in the price of the company's stock? Do CEOs profit from making layoff decisions?

The answers to these questions—almost always published in academic journals with limited readership and seldom widely reported in the mainstream media, if at all—are drawn from extensive employee polling, census reports, tax returns, corporate survey results, annual filings to the SEC, and historical stock-market records, among other data collections, all analyzed with complex statistical techniques. While it might be comforting to learn that the final verdict on layoffs is uniformly negative—in other words, that layoffs consistently fail to achieve what executives who call for them expect and that, in fact, layoffs hurt everyone involved, from the workers who are let go to those who remain at the firms themselves—the picture that emerges is much more nuanced.

Layoffs are sometimes unavoidable in the real world. These researchers have no illusions about how our market economy operates. They understand that a corporation's future must be precisely plotted out with detailed strategies to ensure its survival, growth, the effective use of scarce resources (including employees, physical materials, and finances), higher share prices, and, ultimately, greater and greater profits. Lincoln Electric is no different in that regard: Every employee knows that if abandoning guaranteed employment is the only option left to avoid a bankruptcy brought on by cataclysmic economic conditions, senior management will make that decision, albeit very reluctantly.

Yet the following short road trip through the latest research on layoffs and their aftereffects seems to raise serious doubts about the corporate and social wisdom of regarding this strategy as anything but an absolute last-ditch survival option. The decision to order a layoff seems to be a choice that is, on the one hand, very risky for the firm and, on the other hand, almost always very costly in human terms for the workers let go and for society at large, which finds itself forced to deal with the aftereffects.

IS A LIFETIME JOB HISTORY?

Over the past couple of decades, there has been growing public concern that fewer and fewer Americans are able to find, let alone keep, jobs that will provide them with the financial and social stability needed to enjoy decent lives. In books such as *The Big Squeeze, Falling from Grace, The Disposable American,* and *The Two-Income Trap,* and in countless newspaper articles and television and radio documentaries, the plight of people who are unable to sustain long-term employment is chronicled in painful detail.[7]

Henry Farber, a labor economist in Princeton University's Industrial Relations Department, has been studying the changing world of work in the United States for decades; he is widely considered to be the leading expert on the past and future of job security in this country. Farber believes that a flexible labor market is an important strength of the U.S. economy, but he also considers long-term employment equally important for the economic health of the nation as a whole, and for the quality of life of individual working Americans. "The results are clear cut," according to Farber: The share of what most of us consider to be high-quality jobs (those with relatively high wages, long-term employment, benefits, and so on) has declined since the 1970s, especially for men, and, furthermore, jobs don't last as long as they used to. "By virtually every measure, males in the private sector have been with their current employers for less time . . . and have become much less likely to be in a long-term employment relationship," he wrote.[8] Farber's work confirms that men and women do better working in the public sector than in private industry, but since barely 20 percent of all jobs in the United States are in local, state, and federal governments, the impact of that relatively better news is small.[9] Calling the decline of steady work for men "dramatic," Farber said that overall, "the nature of the private-sector employment relationship in the United States has changed substantially in ways that make jobs less secure and workers more mobile."[10]

Farber sees something else at risk in an economy creating fewer and fewer long-term jobs: the ability of sons and daughters to follow their parents into work with a long-standing employer. This was a familiar pattern for more than a century and a half up until the past several decades, especially at manufacturing companies such as Lincoln Electric and others across the Midwest. It is destined to become extremely rare in the not too distant future, for two reasons. First of all, in the early stages of an individual's working life in the current economy, "the churn is definitely increasing in the under-30 age group . . . and nearly half of all new jobs end within the first year."[11] Second, even for those who are able to maintain a job into their thirties, the chances that they will be able to stay with that employer for another decade or more are falling.[12] The unavoidable outcome, said Farber, is that "young workers today should not look forward to the same type of career with one firm experienced by their parents."[13]

Some experts are less fearful about the future of long-term employment relationships. Ann Huff Stevens, an economist at the University of California–Davis, believes that the shift downward is too small to require writing an obituary for long-term jobs: "For the typical worker in this country, not differentiating by male or female, there is no decline [in the average tenure of jobs]. I do feel like a skeptic sometimes because there is more temporary employment in the U.S., but we just don't have evidence that those [temporary jobs] are replacing full-time employment."[14]

Nonetheless, Stevens sees real dangers for younger Americans arising from the spread of the conventional wisdom (erroneous in her view) that steady work is almost impossible to find. "Young people are constantly told, 'You're on your own, and you're going to be fired from any job you get, and so you should always be the first one to leave,'" said Stevens. As that perception increasingly shapes the views of many younger workers, she fears it will "discourage people from investing in the skills and relationships that would turn that job into a long-term relationship. It can become a self-fulfilling prophecy."

Despite their differing views on the decline of steady work in America, there is one area where Farber, Stevens, and most other experts on long-term employment agree: When a job ends involuntarily, "the consequences are astronomical."

WHAT DOES A LAYOFF COST A WORKER?

There is a newspaper clipping from the June 16, 2008, *Cleveland Plain-Dealer* taped to a shelf just above my laptop; it's a want ad from Lincoln Electric, looking to hire supply-chain and logistics experts. Among the benefits offered to new recruits are this one: "The company has not exercised its layoff options since 1948." While there hasn't been a layoff among those covered by the guaranteed employment policy in the United States in (at least) sixty-one years, virtually every employee knows exactly what losing a job means because a reminder stares them in the face every day when they leave work.

The area between the two railroad lines in Euclid where Lincoln's main complex is located was once home to five other large manufacturing companies: TRW, GM's Fisher Body plant, Euclid Road Machinery, Chase Brass, and Addressograph-MultiGraph. At their peak, they employed tens of thousands of people, many of whom were friends and neighbors of Lincoln Electric's workers.

By the end of the 1980s, all five were gone—closed down, bankrupt, or moved away—leaving employees and their families to cope with the following grim reality: "Job separations during the early 1980s led to large and persistent earnings losses that last over twenty years, initially 30%, still 20% [lower] after ten years and losses have not completely faded 20 years after."[15] This is the conclusion of a report by three economists from Columbia University, the Social Security Administration, and the Congressional Budget Office who looked at what happened to the lifetime earnings of hundreds of thousands of American workers who "left" their jobs during the 1982 recession. (The authors believe the vast proportion of workers surveyed lost their jobs involuntarily, that is, through layoffs, reasoning that very few people voluntarily quit a job when the economy is already in deep distress.) In short, the prognosis for the financial future of a laid-off worker is grim: When you are permanently laid off from your job, you will likely never again earn as much as you used to, even decades in the future, and there is little you can do about it.

Princeton's Henry Farber has looked at how the amount of schooling workers hold at the time they are laid off affects their earnings later in life (most people do eventually find some kind of work). From the early 1980s into the mid-1990s, he calculates that laid-off workers with less than a high school education suffered the worst decline in average annual earnings of all, somewhere between 15 and 20 percent. But Farber's research contains this shocker about the impact of layoffs from the 1990s onward: Americans with one and even two college or university degrees, the most educated people in this society, are suffering the greatest proportional decline in earnings after they lose a job. It's a point Yale University economist Jacob Hacker stressed in his recent book detailing the increasing risk faced by all Americans, regardless of how much schooling they may have: "High levels of education may be a prerequisite for success in today's economy, but they are by no means a guarantor of middle-class security."[16]

Finally, layoffs have one more punishing effect on future generations in a family. Ann Huff Stevens and two colleagues charted the financial and personal lives of 39,000 father-son relationships over three decades. They found that boys whose fathers lost their jobs when the children were between ten and fourteen grew up to earn roughly 9 percent less than boys whose fathers enjoyed steady work throughout their sons' childhood years. In adulthood, these men also were more likely to receive unemployment insurance and other forms of costly state-sponsored social assistance.[17]

Yet it turns out that the financial costs of layoffs to workers and their children may not be the most serious consequences.

DO LAYOFFS KILL?

In December 2007, economists Daniel Sullivan from the Federal Reserve Bank of Chicago and Till von Wachter of Columbia University published the astonishing result of their research into mass layoffs and mortality.[18] Their verdict: Layoffs are deadly.

After assembling a huge database from tax, employment, and health records, Sullivan and von Wachter investigated what happened to workers in Pennsylvania who were laid off during the recession of 1980–1982, when many manufacturing companies slashed huge portions of their workforces. Eventually, the authors were able to statistically follow 20,000 workers for nearly thirty years, from 1974 to 2002. Roughly a third had permanently lost their jobs in the early 1980s. The authors defined a "mass layoff" as a decision by a company to cut at least 30 percent of its workers. "We have checked since, and whether we use 20 percent or 50 percent, it really doesn't make much of a difference," said von Wachter.[19]

Their research revealed a disturbing fact: "Male workers who suffer a permanent layoff in the middle of their working lives suffer an increase of 15 to 20 percent in their probability of dying in the following twenty years. If you summarize what that means over a lifetime, it turns into a loss in life expectancy of one to two years." The impact of the financial damage was so great that "it changed their whole lives . . . and workers with the greatest losses have the greatest reduction in their life spans," said von Wachter. "Losing your livelihood speeds up your mortality."[20]

Employees in the middle of their working lives suffered the greatest decline in life expectancy, argued the authors, because the accumulated financial pain and emotional stress resulting from a layoff last for so many years. "If you're displaced just before retirement, your lifetime income is not affected that much," explained von Wachter, "but if you're laid off in your forties, your entire life has been downshifted, and you're exposed to the threats from lower income and higher chronic stress for thirty years. The bottom line is that we do establish a causal chain between mass layoffs and death."[21]

This is not the only evidence linking layoffs to an increased risk of dying. In the early 1990s, Finland experienced a severe recession that led to massive downsizing in both the public and the private sectors of the economy. Unemployment soared above 16 percent nationwide. A recent survey of more than 22,000 local government employees in communities across Finland that suffered layoffs revealed that those employees were up to five times more likely to die from cardiovascular problems than people working in offices that had not been downsized. But the amazing left hook in the study was that those 22,000 employees were not the people laid off: They were the ones who were spared and had continued to work.[22] In an interview with a British science magazine, lead author Jussi Vahtera of the Finnish Institute of Occupational Health blamed the higher risk of death for the survivors on the fact that they were forced to do much more work, with far less control and more job insecurity.[23]

Despite the causal link between layoffs and death that his research revealed, Till von Wachter still does not believe that layoffs are always unnecessary. "I think this is more a question for public policy, and maybe through better education [about layoffs' serious side effects] we can create better options. Layoffs remain a part of a dynamic capitalist economy, and it may not be right to get rid of them," he cautioned. "It is not necessarily clear that it is a CEO's responsibility to avoid layoffs; it may be his responsibility to keep the company growing to benefit the workers who stay on at the firm."[24]

DO FIRMS BENEFIT FROM LAYOFFS? DO CEOS?

While researchers such as Henry Farber and Till von Wachter have been exploring the impacts of layoffs on employees, others have been studying the effects of layoffs on the firms where they occur and the financial implications for the CEOs who order them. Which of the following propositions do you think is true? Which one do you want to believe is true?

- Companies that lay off more than 10 percent of their employees can expect to see their stock price fall 38 percent.
- The stock market has become more accepting of layoffs in recent years.
- The CEOs of firms announcing layoffs receive 22.8 percent more total pay the following year than corporate leaders who don't.
- Layoffs significantly increase CEO turnover in the following year.

The answers to the question "Can a layoff be good for a company?" are elusive and not always easy to measure; what is good for a firm in the short run may not play out as well in the long run, and the financial forensic work required to measure success and failure requires data that are not always easy to uncover or easy to compare. Most of the research in this area has looked at the impact of layoffs ordered by Fortune 500 and S&P 500 companies. The common measures of financial performance used to evaluate the effectiveness of layoffs include changes in the price of a company's stock and return on assets. (Unsurprisingly, none of the significant social costs to workers and their families is factored into these calculations.)

In all this research, there is also an important cautionary issue that economists call the *counterfactual problem*, or, in laymen's language, the what-if-we-didn't scenario. Even if it was possible to track with absolute precision what happens to a company after it decides to lay off some of its employees, there is no way to know whether things would have turned out better or worse if that decision had never been made in the first place. Nonetheless, given that caveat, are layoffs effective?

Broadly speaking, relatively small layoffs seem to be followed — sometimes — by small improvements in a company's financial position, while large layoffs generally don't help and may in fact cause long-term financial harm. The larger the layoff, the less the chance of any resulting financial benefit.[25]

Princeton's Henry Farber and Cornell University's Kevin Hallock looked at nearly thirty years of stock valuations and layoff announcements involving more than 1,000 large American corporations.[26] They found "clear evidence" that the stock market has become "less negatively inclined" to layoffs in recent decades. In other words, the decline in the price of a company's stock after a downsizing is announced has become smaller over the years. The authors believe that Wall Street may be responding favorably to a change in the professed rationale that has been normally offered to justify layoffs. Since the 1970s, American firms have increasingly defended their decisions to cut staff as being elements of well-thought-out strategic plans, rather than acts of desperation in the face of declining demand for their products or services. Perhaps, suggested the authors, Wall Street believes that a so-called strategic layoff decision is evidence of good corporate planning. Then again, Wall Street could just as easily simply be getting used to layoffs regardless of the excuse.

In the Bain study cited earlier, which focused on a layoff's effect on share prices, layoffs of between 3 and 10 percent of a company's workforce were reported to result in no change in share value, while companies that eliminated more than 10 percent of their employees saw the price of their stock drop as much as 38 percent. A large European research report summarizing studies from around the world argues, "Layoff announcements have an overall negative effect on stock prices, and this remains true whatever the country, the period of time and the type of firm considered."[27]

One study kindly offered some emotional comfort for CEOs contemplating layoffs, although it wasn't good news for their imminent victims: Because the impact of multiple layoffs on a firm's financial performance is usually only slightly worse than that of a single layoff, the authors believed that "executives troubled with the prospect of frequent layoff announcements should not be overly concerned."[28] In other words, take Nike's advice, Mr. CEO, and "just do it!"

The law of unintended consequences also plays a recurring role in the research on layoffs' implications. For example, as the management textbook cited earlier predicts, it turns out that once a layoff happens, a significant number of the employees who are left soon decide that it's a good time for them to leave the firm voluntarily. Survivors begin to ask themselves, "Will I be next?" and head for the exits, rather than waiting for the ax to fall again. This can create serious financial problems for a company suddenly forced to cope with unexpected departures: The costly race to recruit and hire suitable replacements often completely wipes out the expected savings used to justify the initial round of layoffs.

In a study titled "Keeping Your Headcount When All About You Are Losing Theirs," Charles Trevor and Anthony Nyberg found that in some situations, for every worker formally laid off, five more employees voluntarily decide to leave the firm within the following year. "The downsizing-turnover relationship suggests a sad irony," warn the authors, "in that employees are laid off by companies that may subsequently find themselves understaffed."[29]

✧   ✧   ✧

ASK WHAT LAYOFFS mean for the CEOs and senior managers who order them, and the evidence is equally troubling. Cornell's Kevin Hallock has interviewed dozens of Fortune 500 executives— CEOs, COOs, and senior VPs of human resources—in firms that ordered large layoffs in recent years, promising them absolute confidentiality.[30] Stripped of personal names and corporate affiliations, Hallock's interviews document a callous and growing acceptance of layoffs as normal: "Just about everyone that I interviewed seem to think layoffs aren't a big deal anymore." Very often during a first interview conducted soon after a layoff, "the CEO was crying, everyone was devastated, it was horrible, and they couldn't believe this had happened," remembers Hallock, "and then I'd go back in six months, and they were ready to do another layoff, saying, 'Hey, it's the way of the world, and it's just part of doing business.'"[31]

Hallock has also studied whether CEOs lose their jobs when a layoff decision goes bad for the company. His conclusion is that if the price of a company's stock falls after a layoff announcement, the odds are that the CEO will soon be on his way, just like the workers who were shown the door.[32] Given the now ubiquitous presence of very lucrative executive termination contracts in American industry, this is unlikely to be as painful for the boss as it is for those he let go.

Craig Rennie at the University of Arkansas' Sam M. Walton College of Business has no qualms at all in declaring that American CEOs who call for layoffs are paid extremely well for their decisions. After examining the compensation histories of executives in major U.S. corporations who instituted a total of 229 layoffs during the 1990s, Rennie and his colleagues concluded that in the year after a layoff, average total CEO pay increased by 22.8 percent.[33] He argues that because so many CEOs currently earn a much greater share of their total compensation package through stock options (i.e., the higher the stock price goes, the more compensation they earn) rather than from cash pay, there is a clear incentive for these leaders to institute layoffs (assuming, as Rennie does, that share prices do rise). "I have a built-in bias to believe the popular press, and in this case, the popular press is right when it says that executives are paid more after layoffs and it continues to be more in years after."[34]

DO MASS LAYOFFS DESTROY COMMUNITIES?

Though the answer to this question may seem obvious, it is worthwhile examining evidence of the harm that layoffs can inflict beyond a company's walls, if there is to be any hope that corporate executives might eventually begin to consider the social importance of a guaranteed employment program such as Lincoln Electric's. In recent years, writers such as Robert Putnam, Barbara Ehrenreich, Richard Sennett, and Katherine Newman have all explored how the increasing fragility of work in America profoundly damages the lives of individuals and their families and erodes the human connections within the communities where they reside. The powerful stories they tell speak loudly.[35]

Jennie Brand, a sociologist at UCLA, has documented how communities are directly weakened when people lose their jobs and suggested that the resulting downturn can threaten the very employers who made those decisions. Brand based her work on a truly amazing five-decades-old, and still ongoing, survey of 10,317 people who graduated from high school in Wisconsin in 1957. As she notes, these are the people whom Putnam, in his best-selling book *Bowling Alone*, called "the joiners," a reference to an era in American history when citizens were much more involved in the life of their communities than in our day. The postwar period up until the mid-1970s was also a time when growing economic prosperity was shared much more equally among all

Americans. The Wisconsin project has closely followed this group as they have grown up, subjecting them to repeated extensive interviews that uncover the minute details of their personal and financial histories. More than one in four of the group has been laid off at some point in their working lives, often several times. These are real portraits of the effects of layoffs.[36]

Drawing on these tens of thousands of interviews, Brand chronicles how people who are laid off from their jobs begin to retreat from life. Over and over, former employees told the interviewers that they started going to church less often than others who held on to steady jobs, they withdrew from participating in civic and neighborhood organizations, they quit volunteering for community and charity groups, and they stopped spending time helping young people in sports activities. More disturbing is that even when these people finally found work again, "they never get back on track with participating, ten years or thirty years later. It scars them." The financial threat to employers who lay people off is very real, argued Brand, because when citizens stop being part of their community, "it's a trickle that turns into widespread economic costs. People are depressed, they are less likely to consume, and so the effects are ultimately not just on the individuals, but on society at large, and, of course, eventually right back to the firms involved. Everybody loses."[37]

EVERYBODY WINS

Joe Latessa seemed to love gently embarrassing his wife, Melissa, by recounting how she had recently earned a Lincoln Electric "Man of the Year" award, even though it was actually a more politically correct Best Employee certificate.[38] The three of us, along with Melissa's twenty-year-old niece, Jessica Pitino, were sitting around the kitchen table of their spacious split-level house in Concord Township, just south of Painesville, Ohio. At the back of a two-acre wooded lot sits an old barn where Joe and his dad have been fixing up a 1970 Dodge Charger RT in their spare time. From here, the commute to Lincoln Electric through a few miles of quiet rural scenery to Interstate 90 and then west to Cleveland takes about half an hour. "I don't actually know anyone else who's ever got the award," Joe joked. "She never misses a day of work, she had a perfect quality rating, she trained about sixteen other people on the job, and was still the best in her department." At forty-six, Joe is incredibly proud of Melissa's achievements because as a Lincoln Electric employee himself, he knows exactly how hard his wife works. In fact, almost everyone in their extended family knows exactly how hard forty-year-old Melissa works because most of them also work at Lincoln Electric. I needed to draw a genealogical chart to understand the dense web of family connections to the company, spanning decades of work uninterrupted by layoffs.

On Joe's side of the family, his younger brother, Michael, is the technology specialist working in the welding-applications laboratory. Married with two children, Michael has actually been at Lincoln longer than Joe.

Their father, also named Joe, retired from Lincoln Electric in 2002 after nearly forty-one years on the job. ("In all that time, he never even sniffed a "Man of the Year" award," laughed his son.) Like his two sons, the elder Latessa is a big man, offering a handshake to match when I arrived at the beautiful ranch house he shares with his wife, Susan Lynne. Both sixty-seven, they live a few miles south of Michael and just added a separate wing for Susan's elderly mother, who lives with them. The huge lawn is immaculately groomed, professional putting-green quality; it would take a good drive to hit the nearest neighboring home with a golf ball.

Joe Sr. was not the first member of the Latessa family to work for Lincoln Electric. His uncle started on the factory floor in the mid-1950s. He convinced Joe, who at that point was "starving and just eking out an existence," as a newly married eighteen-year-old bank clerk in Cleveland, that he would do much better in the welding industry.

In 1961, Joe made $3,000 as a bank teller. In 1963, his first full year at Lincoln, he earned $9,300. "I had taken some courses from the American Institute of Banking," Joe recalled, "and so they made me a mail boy. They liked starting people at the bottom." Over the decades, he worked his way up from the mailroom to become a crane operator, a foreman, and, finally, finishing as a scheduler in the main factory. He also represented his fellow workers on the Advisory Board a number of times.

Jump over to Melissa's side of the family, and the web continues to spin out. Her stepfather worked at the company for more than thirty-two years. "My dad worked second shift [from roughly two in the afternoon until midnight] for a lot of those years," she remembered, which meant he wasn't around much while she was growing up. "He never talked about the work at Lincoln at all. Except at bonus time just before Christmas."

Melissa's older brother, Hobart McKinney, is a millwright in Lincoln Electric's maintenance department. Most of his work is in the electrode division. Divorced three times, Bart, as he's called, has two boys, aged seventeen and twenty-seven. He's helping Cody, the youngest, with tuition at a local technical training school. Jessie, his eldest, recently graduated from the Lincoln Electric Welding School (established in 1917), and with some financial help from his father, he's now studying advanced underwater welding in Florida. (Children of Lincoln Electric employees are eligible to take these courses almost for free, while outsiders must pay thousands of dollars.)

And finally there's Melissa's niece Jessica, sitting across the kitchen table. A third-year student at Cleveland State University studying American history, Jessica had just finished her first summer job at Lincoln Electric. She worked in administration for the clean-room division, where the printed circuit boards for the welding machines are designed and built. Her desk sits in the exact same room—albeit totally transformed—where her grandfather labored decades ago. "I have always had a job, but just never something this great," Jessica gushed, "and I got up at four in the morning all summer to go to work. It's awesome." (A few months after we met, as the effects of the recession began to hit home nationwide in 2009, Jessica decided to continue working for a few semesters before returning to college.)

If you're keeping track, that's eight people spanning four generations across six decades in one extended family who have worked at Lincoln Electric. Add in spouses, children, and siblings, and you have a small community that has grown stronger over the years because of the emotional security of steady work, the financial benefits of good pay, and the opportunities for career advancement. Guaranteed employment has allowed this family and many more to send children to college and to support relatives in hard times. Moreover, it is a group of people who have significantly contributed to the financial health of their communities, their state, and the country by regularly paying healthy income taxes over many years. Their histories as part of a strong community stand in complete contrast to the chaotic lives experienced by so many families of laid-off workers every day in America.

Most of the members of this clan have never worked anywhere else but Lincoln Electric, and so they almost take for granted their employer's unbroken promise never to lay off its employees when times get tough. Joe and Melissa Latessa do not. Like tens of millions of other Americans, they know firsthand the financial pain and emotional anguish of having had their lives turned upside down by a layoff announcement.

✦ ✦ ✦

"I'D KIND OF just resisted it, you know, what with my dad working there," recalled Joe when I asked why he didn't start at Lincoln Electric once he'd graduated from high school. "I had my mind thinking I'll only ever work there if I have to."

Instead, Joe took a job at TRW, the automobile-parts supplier that got its start manufacturing wooden wheels for Model T Fords in 1909. He worked his way through jobs in the foundry, the cutting department, and the testing labs. Along the way, he met Melissa McKinney. Soon after they became engaged, the division of TRW where they were both working was sold off to PCC Airfoils, which makes parts for both commercial and military jets.

In the fall of 1992, the couple had been working repeated seven-day rotations, a grueling schedule even for someone used to heavy shift work in a factory. "It was a Sunday night, just two weeks before Christmas. . . . We were both on third shift—the overnight shift—and they called us all into a room together . . . and we knew that was it." As Melissa and Joe described that evening, they tag-teamed in telling the story, not so much interrupting each other as ensuring that no grim detail was left out. "I'd actually forfeited four weeks of vacation that year because we got so busy," remembered Joe, "and I still got laid off. It was horrifying."

Several months later, despite extensive searching, neither of them had been able to find steady work. Then Joe's dad called to say that there were job openings coming up at Lincoln Electric. A decade and a half later, Joe still freely admitted that at first, he wasn't eager to apply, but in the end, he went in for a couple of interviews in the late winter of 1993. "Finally, in June, they called and said I was hired. That's when Melissa applied too, except that they called her back the same day. Four months for me, four hours for her," said the proud husband.

Joe and Melissa remain convinced that their employer will do absolutely everything it can to avoid condemning them again to the emotional uncertainty and financial nightmare of unemployment. They only need to consult the family historians over the Sunday dinner table for reassurance.

But the specter of a nightmare of another kind has also hung over them for many years, with potentially more devastating consequences. Soon after Joe was born, doctors discovered he had a congenital heart defect. At three, he had open-heart surgery, and in the years since then, he's endured a long litany of complicated, dangerous, and extremely costly medical procedures. A pacemaker in his near future now seems a possibility; returning to work anytime soon is unclear. But once again, the importance of steady employment—and a little luck—in building and protecting a good life in America is illustrated through Joe's health challenges. As a child and then a teenager living at home, Joe's staggeringly high medical expenses were fully covered by his father's medical insurance plan. Because Joe Sr. was steadily employed decade after decade, he was able to afford quality coverage, a luxury unavailable to many American families hurt by layoffs.

Lincoln Electric does not pay for medical insurance for its employees. Yet it requires every person in the company to show proof that he or she is covered by a comprehensive hospital and medical insurance plan from the moment they first begin to work. This seemingly harsh and almost contradictory policy is regularly cited by critics of the company's unusual business model as proof that Lincoln Electric can't—and moreover shouldn't—serve as an example for anyone else to emulate.

But think closely about those snap judgments. It is undeniably true that the United States urgently needs to reform the structure of medical insurance coverage if it is to, domestically, rebuild a humane and caring society and, internationally, restore its comparative advantage. The deplorable situation of more than 45 million people struggling to survive without the ability to pay for adequate health care seems proof enough that dramatic changes are needed quickly. Until that day arrives, however, Americans lucky enough to have decent jobs are generally able to pay for quality medical care.

This has been Lincoln Electric's operating goal for many decades: to ensure that the company continues to generate and distribute sufficient profits so that its employees can afford comprehensive health insurance policies to protect themselves, their spouses, and their children without crippling family finances. No system is perfect, and sometimes Lincoln Electric employees do face financial problems. Yet many have told me that when coworkers find themselves unable to foot the full cost of health insurance, the company has quietly stepped in to offer help.[39]

Out on his own in his twenties and then married in his early thirties, Joe's luck held: He had few serious medical challenges as he moved through his early employers. But in the mid-1990s, not long after he and Melissa joined Lincoln Electric, his health began to deteriorate once again, which ultimately led to a doctor's order that he take disability leave in 2007. Over their years of steady work, Joe and Melissa had been able to afford long-term disability insurance, and Joe's LTD benefits now replace 60 percent of his previous regular earnings.

In the spring of 2009, Joe received a call from Lincoln Electric's human resource department inquiring if he knew when he'd be able to return. As in many large companies, employees on extended disability leave can lose some priority claim on their old assignments when they eventually resume working. Joe was unable to provide a precise return date and requested additional time, arguing that he knew of others who had been granted extensions. When he was told that was impossible, Joe e-mailed Lincoln Electric's CEO, John Stropki, directly, confident that the company's open-door policy to the very top was his to use. A few days later, his extension was granted. "Joe's been off for more than a year, and I can't say that we've suffered," said Melissa. "Paying off our mortgage is still in sight, and it's comforting to know that I don't have to worry about being laid off. I just don't."

TAKING CARE OF FAMILY

The Mentor (Ohio) High School Cardinals had moved to an early lead against the St. Ignatius Wildcats with a touchdown scored by number 21, who was being pummeled by his happy teammates. Behind Mentor's bench, the school's cheerleaders in red were going wild.

Up in the stands of this brand-new stadium, James Maffit was not so happy, because he'd just realized the pause button was still engaged on his son's video camera at the precise moment number 21, his fourteen-year-old son, Jimmy, crossed the goal line. Now Maffit's Plan B was to pray that the high school's media department was also filming the game and might run off an extra copy, documenting Jimmy's triumph. "I was in at work at 2:30 this morning, so I'm a little tired," Maffit explained, although from the furrowed brow, he seemed to know that excuse was not going to appease number 21 at the dinner table later in the evening. "My normal shift runs from 7 a.m. to 3:30 in the afternoon, but today one of the guys took a vacation day, so on a three-shift cycle, someone from one of the other two shifts covers four hours, and another guy from the other shift covers the other four. So you're each working twelve hours that day."

Of the more than sixty Lincoln Electric employees interviewed for this book, Maffit was one of those who most easily helped me understand how such an unusual workplace feels so normal to the vast majority of people who experience it day to day. "Look, we come to a place to make a living. I mean, I enjoy my job, and it looks like you enjoy your job, but the bottom line is that you're here to make a living, and so you do things to improve that," he says. In other words, he's not much concerned about coming in at 2:30 in the morning on short notice.

"I DON'T KNOW if my kids would have ended up as good as they turned out if I hadn't had those rough years at the start working at Lincoln. I was a farm kid, used to throwing hundred-pound bales of hay, but I mean it was hard," said Bob Maffit, James's uncle. "He'd come home with his hands all cut up from the new tools, and he used to cry, 'I'm going to quit,'" chimed in Sandra Maffit, his wife, from across their wood-paneled kitchen. Bob, who is now sixty-three, started at Lincoln Electric in 1963.

Yet if a new employee could show that he knew how to work hard, the veterans would help teach him the ropes. Soon, Maffit was making good money winding electrical coils on the assembly lines. He moved on to building armatures for a line of electrical generators, finally ending up in the quality-assurance department until he retired in 2006. These days, Bob pursues his hobby of re-searching the military records of veterans of the Civil War buried in Mentor, where he and Sandra live. He's also dealing with an aggressive prostate cancer, but that merits little more than a shrug in conversation.

When Bob thinks back to what his years at Lincoln Electric meant, he talks a lot about how steady work allowed him and San-dra to build a good life not just for themselves and their children but also for relatives who never had his advantages of a stable ca-reer. "I come from a family of ten in Hopedale, down in the Ap-palachia part of Ohio, right near Wheeling, West Virginia. The best thing I ever did growing up in a little farming town of forty houses was watching cars go by after school," Maffit remembered. "I could have gone and worked on the railroad like my dad did and then my brother, or worked in a coal mine like I did when I was seventeen, but where would I be now?"

At the urging of Sandra's uncle, Bob moved to Cleveland and joined Lincoln Electric; his brother Jim, father of James, the failed video cameraman at the football game, moved north to work at Lincoln Electric as well. The rest of the family stayed behind in southern Ohio, working at jobs that stopped and started and sometimes just ended. "We helped my parents, and Sandra's mother and father really went through hard times. Her dad was often laid off, and because I was working, we were able to help them. My brother Jack was a truck driver, and I guarantee you he was on strike every six months or so."

The Maffits remember their early days at Lincoln Electric as "not living high on the hog, just getting by feeding our kids." But it did seem, said Bob, "that we were always way out front of others in the family and other people around us." And when things got bad for other family members, the Maffits would cash in some of the Lincoln stock that they were accumulating each year.[40] "We've been able to do what we needed to do to take care of our families," said Sandra with a smile. "We do feel lucky," added Bob. "There are so many people I knew that once had good lives. I mean, we could have ended up as greeters at Wal-Mart too, but we won't have to."

"I THINK THERE are things you can do here at Lincoln Electric to control your future." James Maffit and I were watching the end of the football game at Mentor High School, and his wife, Teffin, had joined us up in the stands. "I worked swing shifts for three years to get a day job in order to have more time with my family, and I knew that was going to happen," he said. Working a normal eight-hour day job rather than piecework on shifts with a lot of overtime meant less money coming in for the family. But because Maffit is convinced his position at Lincoln Electric is secure for the long haul—as long as he continues to perform on the job—it was a decision, and not a gamble, that made sense. "I'm a father these days; that's my role in life. I coach my eleven-year-old girl's softball team, my seventeen-year-old boy's baseball team, and help with football too. We don't live a real flashy lifestyle; we live in a three-bedroom split level, and I've got some debt, but not a lot."

"We're comfortable," agreed Teffin, "and we wouldn't be without his job. I never had to work, and I stayed home until Aubrey [their youngest, now eleven] was in kindergarten. And our kids really don't want for anything." I mentioned my conversation with James's uncle Bob, regarding his ability to financially help so many relatives as a result of steady employment at Lincoln Electric for so many years. "I don't know that we could really help quite as many family members now," said Teffin, "because things aren't quite like they used to be. But I feel secure, and no, I don't worry."

WHY DO LAYOFFS remain such a common choice for CEOs despite the lack of convincing evidence that they can improve a faltering company's financial health? Peter Cappelli, who teaches management at the University of Pennsylvania's Wharton School, blames the addiction to layoffs on the tragic lack of imagination of America's corporate elite. Most senior executives have absolutely no clear idea if slashing large numbers of employees is a good strategy, according to Cappelli. "They don't have a systematic way to assess what is the net present value of the decision whether or not to lay people off," he warned, using the precise language of managerial economics. As a result, Cappelli argued that a decision to lay off employees without a clear idea of the potential costs and benefits makes a mockery of a cherished assumption embraced by the U.S. business community that most corporate leaders "think carefully about what they ought to do to make profit-maximizing decisions." Furthermore, bemoaned Cappelli, the addiction to layoffs is very deeply ingrained: "In the Reagan era, people used to say that the ability to fire people was the great advantage of the U.S. system, and that was why we were doing so well in the 1980s. You'd ask them why the Japanese were doing even better in the 1980s, and they would wave their hands a lot. Ask them now why Indian companies are paying so much attention to their employees, and you get a lot of that same hand waving that there is only one way to run a business. It is a belief perpetuated by the business community that 'we don't have a choice, that we have no options.'"[41]

So why does that belief persist?

chapter six

"A TERRIBLY NONOPTIMAL AND INEFFICIENT POLICY"

The assumption that laying off employees can be an efficient management strategy remains largely unchallenged inside corporate America for five reasons: the widespread ignorance of any equally effective and profitable alternatives, the value system of business education, Wall Street's current fixation on short-term gains, the self-interest of senior executives, and, finally, a paralyzing, although admittedly well-earned, lack of trust inside the average American workplace. Mutually reinforcing, these five currents support the default position adopted by most executives in tough times that "we have no options," and thus they serve to keep the idea of guaranteed employment off corporate America's radar screen. All this despite the fact that profitable companies such as Lincoln Electric and a few others have thrived in our very midst for so long.

Analyzing these roadblocks is vital if those in decision-making positions in the national economy are ever to come to an understanding that there *are* alternatives to laying people off.

IGNORANCE AND THE HERD

When I entered the word *layoffs* into Amazon.com's search engine a few moments ago to see what popped up, only two of the first hundred results—in both book and electronic download formats—had anything to do with exploring alternatives to layoffs, and one of those was a costly reprint of an article first published in 1930. The other ninety-eight hits comprised how-to-prepare guidebooks for when layoffs loom and how-to-survive guidebooks once the ax has fallen on you. Try it for yourself at your local bookstore.

There is virtually no easily accessible information about how an American company in the twenty-first century could remain profitable over the long term after making some sort of a detailed promise to its employees that layoffs would be the absolute last thing to happen before the business shut down. More important, there is virtually no awareness in America that such a thing is even possible, let alone that history can provide proof. In other words, when corporate executives say, "I have no option but to order this layoff," what they are really saying is, "I have never heard of an option that might help me to avoid laying off my employees."

During the process of researching this book, I cold-called executives across the country in companies of all sizes, labor lawyers in universities and private practice, financial analysts in Wall Street investment banks, union leaders, community organizers, and many others to discuss the challenge and importance of ensuring steady work in our society. Almost uniformly, none had ever heard of Lincoln Electric and its guaranteed employment program. A small handful of people knew something about Southwest Airlines's admirable record (it has avoided layoffs since taking to the air in 1971). There were a few nostalgic references to IBM, in the halcyon days when Big Blue prided itself on offering lifetime employment (that ended nearly two decades ago), as well as vague recollections of the near-ironclad union contracts between the Big Three automakers and the UAW in the immediate postwar era. But there was almost no awareness of any contemporary models of a successful no-layoff policy.

What's worse, argued Wharton's Peter Cappelli, is that the majority of executives who order layoffs (with no defensible economic justification for their decisions) operate by "rules of thumb, and the most important one is 'What is everyone else doing?'" The resulting herd behavior creates a perfect feedback loop of reinforcing causality, where everyone comes to believe that there is only one way to reach the destination of sustaining profitability and growth: Keep the layoff lever close at hand.

Economists actually have a name for this phenomenon—path dependency—which is often described as the problem where "you can't get there from here because the road has been dug up." Their favorite example to cite is the persistence of the QWERTY keyboard that was patented in 1878 and is now used on virtually every computer in the English-speaking world. Over the past century, several other alphabetic keyboard arrangements have been invented whose supporters have argued—and some modern experts on ergonomics have agreed—are easier to use. But because the original format established such an early beachhead, those other formats have never been able to crack the QWERTY monopoly. Only one road to fast, accurate typing has survived and thrived, although that destination is clearly reachable by taking different highways. Similarly, the goal of sustained profitability is reachable via several approaches to managing a workforce, but only one seems to live on as a viable strategy.[1]

Guaranteed employment has had several seasons in the sun during the economic history of this country (granting its over-whelmingly marginal status these days), and for that reason alone, it deserves to be better understood. But "reconstructing lost alternatives," as David Noble, the noted historian of technology, once put it, serves an additional crucial purpose.[2] In filling out the historical record, Noble wrote, the revelation that there are other effective ways of doing business shines a critical spotlight on the currently accepted mainstream assumptions, asking why they persist and who benefits from keeping equally viable options in the shadows.

"I DON'T BELIEVE WE SHOULD BE GIVING ANY GUARANTEES IN LIFE"

Every year, roughly 150,000 students graduate with advanced degrees from business schools in the United States, the vast majority earning the much coveted MBA. From Harvard, MIT, Chicago, NYU, Stanford, and hundreds of other less well known but equally good universities (reaffirmed as such by the many annual ranking surveys), they pour forth to take up positions of power and influence throughout the American economy.

The MBA has been taking a high-profile beating since the turn of the century, starting with the pivotal role Jeffrey Skilling played in the Enron debacle and, more recently, with the performances of John Thain at Merrill Lynch and Dick Fuld at Lehman Brothers, just to name a few. But millions more MBA graduates labor in relative obscurity, in American companies large and small, working as CEOs and senior managers, making decisions day by day that affect the lives of their employees, their families, and their communities. They are guided by the values and skills absorbed during two intense years at business school, when much of their time was devoted to reading the ubiquitous case studies that constitute the core of most MBA programs. Countless more senior corporate employees attend executive seminar programs every year where they too are immersed in the same case-study method of teaching. The education of American MBAs powerfully shapes how our economy operates, and it effectively sets the ground rules for what is considered the normal way to treat employees. It would be completely unrealistic to assume anything else.

It will probably surprise you, then, to learn that the best-selling case study in the history of Harvard Business School—a case that is also taught in countless other business schools in the United States and around in the world in different languages— is a detailed examination of Lincoln Electric.

NORMAN BERG never planned to write a worldwide best-seller about a little-known welding company. He just wanted to write something for his students that would help them understand how a successful firm encourages its employees to work hard.

In 1975, Berg was head of the general management program at Harvard Business School, where he had been teaching for more than decade. He'd already written and supervised a number of case studies, because that's what professors at the world's most famous business school are hired to do. But Berg, who had earned an MBA and a Ph.D. at Harvard, had no way of knowing that his next case about Lincoln Electric would ultimately become the most popular in the B school's history and destined to be taught around the world for years to come.

The "case study" forms the basis of learning at Harvard Business
School. Pioneered by HBS faculty in the 1920s, the case method
brings business reality into the classroom, placing students at the
center of the learning experience. It is designed to challenge students by bringing them as close as possible to business situations
of the real world. Judgment and experience lie at the very core of
managerial success.[3]

An HBS case study is a detailed analysis of a specific business
crisis that is facing a firm in the real world. Over the years, Harvard has been able to convince an astonishing array of companies, mostly American, to let researchers from the school
document from the inside how and why a crisis has developed,
what the implications are for the company if the situation remains unresolved, and what options seem to be available to the
firm's senior executives. The case is then written up as a twenty-
to thirty-page document, complete with financial figures from
the company's books, and, generally, ends with a series of questions designed to force the reader to explain what he or she would
do in this situation—and why.

Over the course of a two-year MBA program at Harvard, most
students will read more than five hundred case studies. Many say
they feel lucky if they are able to spend even a full hour studying
a case the night before it's scheduled to be covered in class. Then,
in an eighty-minute session, the students, not the professors, are
expected to analyze what led to the crisis, what is the best way
forward, and what is the "takeaway"—that is, the lesson learned.
Then it's on to the next case.

In 1975, Norman Berg (now professor emeritus) was concerned that too many cases had become unnecessarily complicated and that given the frantic pace at which students had to
race through them, important lessons were being missed. "We

had lots of cases featuring new approaches to management and innovation," he remembered, "and we were going to fly to the moon with new strategies. I thought it would be very useful to have a case on a rather simple, old-fashioned manufacturing company that had done very well over many years and in an understandable industry, so you could focus on what they do, rather than get lost in the complexities of the product. I also wanted something that emphasized workers and productivity, and was successful on a continuing basis, and Lincoln Electric fit that very well."[4]

Berg didn't pick Lincoln Electric out of the blue. When he was an undergraduate in mechanical engineering at Case Institute of Technology in Cleveland (now Case Western Reserve University), Lincoln Electric had been a significant recruiter on campus every year. "I knew of the company from the time I was in college, and I even interviewed for a job there, although in the end I went to U.S. Steel," he recalled.

In addition, Harvard had already commissioned a case on Lincoln Electric in 1947, when two professors (who later taught Berg) visited Cleveland and interviewed James F. Lincoln.[5] But by the 1970s, that case was no longer in wide circulation. Berg's research assistant, Norman Fast (who went on to earn a doctorate at HBS), interviewed employees at every level of the company, from assembly-line workers to then president George Willis, who provided the first words of the completed case: "We're not a marketing company, we're not an R&D company, and we're not a service company. We're a manufacturing company, and I believe that we are the best manufacturing company in the world." Millions of MBA students around the world have read those two opening sentences since HBS Case 376-028 was published in 1975.[6]

✧　　✧　　✧

"THE FUNDAMENTAL QUESTION about the Lincoln Electric case study is
to understand what induces or encourages people to work hard,
both in their own interests and in the interests of the company,
and to do this on a continuing basis," explained Berg when I
asked what he had initially hoped his students would get out of
the now famous case. "It creates the opportunity to ask questions
such as 'Is Lincoln ahead of, or behind, good management practice?' Some students will always say, 'It's perfect capitalism where
workers have control over exactly what they do and get rewards
based on their own efforts,' while others will say, 'This is practi-
cally a form of communism, not putting the stockholders first.'"

Over twenty-five pages, the case explores Lincoln Electric's
history, compensation system (including piecework, the bonus,
and guaranteed employment), manufacturing challenges, and
financial performance, all interspersed with employee interviews. The second paragraph of the case takes pains to emphasize the firm's track record of profits: "More significant than a
single year's results was Lincoln's record of steady growth over
the previous four decades." At the end, students are asked to predict whether the company circa 1975 can continue to exist in its
then current form.

There are only two paragraphs explaining the promise not to
lay off workers during tough economic times. Berg says that he always made it clear to his students that the promise would be broken if the survival of the firm was ever in doubt.

The accompanying teaching notes, which have guided business school instructors at Harvard and other universities around
the world for decades, emphasize that Lincoln Electric's management system contains "significant obstacles" that most companies probably could not overcome. But instructors are also
reminded that the case is not about whether Lincoln's unusual
management approach "*might* work—it *has* worked, and very
well."[7]

Two miles east of Harvard, and more than three decades later, Thomas Kochan, of MIT's Sloan School of Management, issues a similar reminder to his MBA students when they're about to read the case: "They are amused, in a positive sense, that this case was written in 1975, before they were born. So I bring them up-to-date, show them the company still seems to be doing well, that they've expanded internationally, and yet still have this unique system." Kochan thinks the case is so widely used because "it illustrates the whole system that has to go with guaranteed employment. It shows how you need piecework, some form of employee voice, and a business strategy that is integrated with the workforce strategy. As well, very few organizations are willing to have as egalitarian a compensation system in terms of the income levels from top to bottom. . . . You need all those supporting elements, and that's what the case is all about."[8]

Across the country, at Stanford University's Graduate School of Business, Jesper Sorensen said he waits for the *aha!* moment whenever he teaches the Lincoln case. "It has a kind of bait-and-switch element to it, so when students walk into the room, they're thinking that the whole key to success at Lincoln is the piece-rate system. But by the end, it's clear that piece rates are important but more so because they are part of a system, including guaranteed employment and a very strong culture, and the leaders of the firm are committed to all that."[9]

"The case doesn't present answers, and that's why it endures," said Berg, who estimated he'd taught it hundreds of times to Harvard MBA students. "It tells students that here's what somebody else does that has been successful for them and that you have to be careful with guaranteed employment, but does this have applications elsewhere? The burden is on the students to figure that out."[10]

What students figure out about guaranteed employment, at HBS and other business schools, depends to a great extent on what their various teachers feel about this unusual management policy. And in academe, there is a great variety of opinion about the virtues of a no-layoff policy. As German philosopher Freidrich Nietzsche once remarked, "There are no facts, only interpretations."

"I WILL TELL YOU a story. John Akers, the CEO of IBM, came to speak at the department as a guest of our organizational behavior people, the sort of touchy-feely types." George P. Baker and I were sitting in his spacious office on the fourth floor of the Baker Library at Harvard Business School. Baker holds a Ph.D. from Harvard in business economics and cochairs the school's doctoral program. It was the morning after Barack Obama won the election, and everyone at Harvard, indeed everyone in Boston, including Baker, seemed to be extremely happy.[11]

"Akers was a hero of the organizational department for maintaining IBM's lifetime employment program in the face of really hard times.[12] The firm was struggling, and he was trying to hold on to lifetime employment because it was right and good and all this crap. A colleague of mine was invited to this dinner, and to the department's tremendous chagrin, he stands up and says, 'Do your patriotic duty and free up those underutilized resources to flow to their highest value,'" remembered Baker with a laugh. "Everyone was in shock, falling back in their chairs. But he was right."

"That's the real problem with a lifetime employment policy," said Baker, leaning forward to help make his point. "Why do we think that the optimal use of society's resources is to keep people locked in their firms? It's actually not, and for most of the time, it's better to allow those resources to flow freely."[13] James F. Lincoln would be rolling in his grave if he could hear that.

George Baker is respected worldwide as an expert in *principal agent theory*, often called "the economic theory of incentives." It is an arcane division of economics utilizing game theory and other complex mathematical techniques to model a workplace in which an employee (called an "agent") performs tasks on behalf of a supervisor (called a "principal") in order to achieve the principal's goals. In other words, agency theory tries to figure out how incentives such as stock options, piecework, profit sharing, and guaranteed employment can motivate employees to work hard (and for whose benefit, as in the case of Wall Street's extravagant bonuses).

Business schools like HBS (and most others around the world are modeled on Harvard, whether they admit it or not) can seem like rather balkanized environments. In one of the many academic corners sit distinguished economists such as Baker, who tend to see business in terms of equations; in another corner sit management and strategy experts such as Norman Berg; and in a third sit industrial relations specialists like MIT's Thomas Kochan.

Over the course of a normal two-year MBA, students are exposed to many conflicting points of view emanating from the various B-school fiefdoms on how best to manage a firm in a modern global economy. In recent years, agency theory has offered a new perspective on the lessons of Lincoln Electric.

John Roberts has been teaching economics at Stanford University's Graduate School of Business for nearly thirty years. In the late 1980s, Roberts and fellow Stanford economist Paul Milgrom began writing about how the various strategies that a company can employ to motivate its workers interact with each other in the workplace. They called the effect "complementarities," that is, doing more of one thing in the structure of the company makes it more profitable to do more of another.[14] And Lincoln Electric has become almost a poster child for their elegant mathematical analysis, which is now widely taught in many MBA programs.

In his book *The Modern Firm*, which the *Economist* called the best business book of 2004, Roberts explains how Lincoln Electric's merit-based bonus system, which penalizes workers for shoddy production, corrects for the standard shortcoming of a piecework system, that is, the lapse in quality resulting from the rush to earn more for each completed task.[15]

In discussing guaranteed employment, Roberts explores another complementary relationship: how eliminating the threat of layoffs encourages workers to be more productive because it eliminates any fear they may innovate themselves out of a job. "It has stuck by this promise even in severe recessions, when it put production workers to painting the factory rather than lay them off. This policy [of no layoffs] also *probably* contributes to the trust that supports the credibility of the piece rates. So another policy that might be of *questionable* attractiveness in isolation becomes very valuable in the context of what Lincoln seeks to do and how it seeks to do it."[16]

Many experts share this reluctance to consider steady work (through some version of a no-layoff promise) as a basic priority around which a modern firm should build its management agenda. Robert Gibbons, the Sloan Distinguished Professor of Management at MIT and another widely acknowledged expert on principal agent theory, seemed unconvinced that Lincoln Electric's guaranteed employment policy significantly increased the levels of trust inside the company and, as a result, could help the company's operations: "I'm not at all sure it is safe to regard guaranteed employment as a major aspect of Lincoln's success."[17]

"I'm not unsympathetic to guaranteed employment and the long-term social strength it builds," James Rebitzer told me, "but I'm not as sympathetic as I used to be." Rebitzer chairs the Economics Department of the Weatherhead School of Business at Case Western Reserve University in Cleveland and was the first to introduce me to John Roberts's work on complementarities.

"I think there are only a few very special circumstances where a commitment to no layoffs actually improves operating efficiency, and in a lot of cases, there may be other ways to deal with the disruptions caused by layoffs that are less economically costly."[18] Rebitzer was particularly concerned about the potentially fatal costs of honoring a no-layoff policy when a company finds itself having to turn on a dime, perhaps by changing its whole product line in order to survive some dramatic shift in market conditions. If your existing workers simply don't have the new skills needed for the transformation, survival would be severely in doubt, he argued.

Guaranteed employment can be an anchor around the neck of an executive, according to Rebitzer, and an unnecessary one at that: "Why should I artificially constrain myself when I don't have to? If I want someone to stay with me twenty years, I know how to structure the employment relationship [i.e., by paying more money] so that they'll stay those twenty years, but I will still have the option of letting them go if I need to." Rebitzer believes that is why so few companies follow Lincoln's example of employment security: "You have to tell me as a manager about what do I get for giving up that freedom of action. If you're trying to make the case that guaranteed employment is something we don't have enough of, you're going to have to make the case why the natural resourcefulness of most managers in pursuit of profit isn't enough to do it."

At the University of Texas at Dallas, John McCracken uses the HBS Lincoln Electric case "to get students to think about the *economic* model of human behavior as opposed to the *good citizen* model, which is when you ask someone to do something that is in effect a benefit to you, but a cost to them."[19] A former investment banker on Wall Street with a Ph.D. from the Wharton School at the University of Pennsylvania, McCracken now teaches in the executive MBA program. He said he loves introducing students

to the Lincoln Electric case because it is such a good example of
a company with clearly defined "organizational architecture": that
is, every employee understands who makes what decisions, how
the results are evaluated, and how people are rewarded.

But McCracken also encourages his students to share his view
that in many, if not most, business environments, any form of
guaranteed employment is a nonstarter, especially if the social
benefits of steady work enter into the discussion. "I teach it for
one key purpose only, and I go through this over and over and
over again: No rational economic actor is going to bear the cost
for a social benefit. I worked on Wall Street, and I tell you that I
would have grabbed that company in a second and broken it up,
but I couldn't get it. [Lincoln Electric] is a situation where management makes long-term decisions for the benefit of the employees which are always a cost to the shareholders. It's a
zero-sum game."

I asked George Baker why so many of his intellectual colleagues share his skepticism about a guaranteed employment policy such as Lincoln Electric's, even as they teach the case study
that profiles what is arguably its most famous exemplar. "Lincoln
Electric is a special case, and by the way, it is not a panacea for
them," he responded. "When they go into tough times, it's really
expensive for the company, and unless there is some other good
reason for having it, as part of an incentive system like Lincoln's,
in my view, you would be wrong to recommend it. The reason
that people are so in-their-guts opposed is that most of the time,
it is really a terribly nonoptimal and inefficient policy."

HARVARD BUSINESS SCHOOL had just celebrated its one hundredth anniversary when I sat down in November 2008 with three second-
year MBA students who had read the Lincoln Electric case study
just a few days before.[20] Distinguished alumni such as GE's Jef-

frey Immelt, former eBay head Meg Whitman, James Wolfen-
sohn (who ran the World Bank for ten years), and many other
luminaries had all been on campus in recent days to reminisce
about their student experiences, to praise HBS's role in their subsequent success, and to look ahead to the school's new challenges
and responsibilities.

The average age of MBA candidates has crept up in recent
years — it's now twenty-eight — a reflection of the administration's
belief that students need to have three or four years of real-world
work experience under their belts to get the most out of their Harvard education. The three sitting with me in Cotting Hall (a classic redbrick, gray-roofed, white-windowed Harvard building)
certainly fit the bill.[21]

Corey Crowell, MBA 2009, was born in Ogden, Utah. He
served in a church mission in Spain for the Church of Jesus
Christ of Latter-day Saints before getting an undergraduate degree in international business at Brigham Young University.
Crowell then worked for International Armoring Corporation,
a Utah company that produces bulletproof passenger cars
("We've done pope mobiles," he said with a smile). The dream
of a leadership role in a larger international business led him to
Harvard.

A native of South Dakota, Jennifer Timmerman, MBA 2009,
went to Wharton at the University of Pennsylvania for an undergraduate degree in business and then joined a consulting firm in
Hong Kong for a few years. Cochair of the school's Asia Club,
she plans to return to Asia to work in the technology sector.

And finally, Giovanni Carraro, MBA 2009, is from Milan,
Italy, where he graduated with a master's in electrical engineering. Fluent in English, Carraro came to the United States to work
for International Rectifier and several other high-technology
companies. His hope is to stay in America in a senior management position.

Halfway through their third semester at HBS, these three had each read roughly 350 case studies, including Lincoln Electric, and so I began by asking what struck them, if anything, about this particular one. (A disclaimer for those concerned about bias: The students knew in advance that I was writing a book about the company and its guaranteed employment policy, although none had been aware of the case's best-seller status.) "To read that there is a company still today that works with real piecework, a principle that was labeled as evil in the late 1800s and early 1900s, was fascinating," jumped in Carraro, "because in Europe, it was considered a social achievement to protect workers from this kind of thing. I was really surprised at the other practices they use, like a no-layoff policy, which are something out of the distant past. I was even more surprised when I watched the 60 *Minutes* TV show, and the workers say they love it. It is clearly odd," Carraro offered, shaking his head in disbelief.[22]

Timmerman said what caught her eye was that Lincoln so successfully used a different management strategy from so many of the other companies she read about in her case studies: "It's great to see the cases where they use tried-and-true methods, but it's always more interesting when we read about companies which try something new, not a traditional compensation system." Of course, Lincoln's "new" incentive system is actually decades older than the "tried-and-true" alternatives such as Six Sigma and Total Quality Control that are featured in so many case studies.

"A lot of positives in the way they guarantee employment" was the instant reaction from Crowell, "and I think it's a great way to design a human resources program. I definitely think it's a step forward for employees because it gives them a sense of being in a family. It's value-added for everyone."

They were clearly intrigued by Lincoln Electric, especially because the company was continuing to prosper. (The recession was well under way as we spoke in late 2008.) But when my questions turned to whether another company could—or should—adopt some form of a no-layoff promise, intrigue quickly transformed into doubt.

"I just worry that the sense of a guaranteed job and just coming in, checking in every day, would create a bit of complacency," said Crowell, "and to some extent we are seeing that already in the world, a lot of complacency. Look at the auto industry!" He also worried about the alleged efficiency of keeping people "working" in a downturn due to a no-layoff policy: "Can you really keep painting a wall over and over? And with piecework, what's the difference between being laid off and employed with almost zero salary?" He sounded a lot like George Baker.

Carraro was more explicit. "I actually do not believe that you can take this system [of incentives] and put it somewhere else, although I do recognize the great advantages of a no-layoff policy and the social ethics of taking care of employees. Guaranteed employment works at Lincoln because of the synergies surrounding it [he meant piecework and the bonus system, among other elements], but there is something of an intrinsic culture in every industry, and I honestly don't see how guaranteed employment could be put into another environment without significant disruption or even destroying the system."

For Timmerman, there was a huge difference between trying to "retrofit" an existing company to embrace some form of a no-layoff policy and creating a start-up: "If you were starting a new company, that would be one thing, because you could say that these are our values, and we really will focus on, for example, lifetime employment, as we build the company. Then the people you hire start to feed on those values, and it will work well. But if you are trying to suggest to another firm to do this, you will have some employees who will like these values and will stay and other people will leave, and you would have to be really prepared for that." Then she mentioned another issue: What would Wall

Street think? "If a public company did [embrace some form of a no-layoff promise], it would take time to work. But Wall Street would look at the quarterly earnings and say, 'Uh-oh! This company is taking a new initiative, and we are not seeing the results,' and it would definitely hurt, at least in the short term."

We finished up with Timmerman reflecting on her roots: "In the places where I grew up, in the Midwest, which has more traditional and religious values, I think a no-layoff promise would be appreciated. You see plants shutting down, and in those companies, people all know each other, they've been there three generations, and those communities are really having a tough time. Do I think that you could force a sense of family on everyone? No, that's not realistic."

DHRUV MEHROTRA was a first-year MBA candidate at MIT's Sloan School of Management at the other end of Cambridge. Mehrotra earned two degrees in electrical engineering from the University of Texas at Austin and worked as a consultant for five years before deciding in his late twenties that he needed to learn a lot more about how to run a company before starting one of his own.[23]

Mehrotra's first exposure to Lincoln Electric had come just a few days earlier through reading a recent offspring of the original Lincoln Electric case, written in 2006 by another HBS professor, Jordan Siegel.[24] This case details the decision facing current CEO John Stropki as the company considers expansion into India: Will it purchase an existing Indian welding manufacturer, form a joint venture, or build its own production facility from scratch? "Our class really became heavily divided on the cultural issues [such as piecework and guaranteed employment]," Mehrotra recalled. "The polarization was very interesting, and we had a heated discussion about this. A lot of the international folks—or at least people with an international education or experience—tended to view piecework, in particular, as a very evil thing. The people who had not traveled much outside of North America saw it as a capitalist economy where they are not forcing anyone to work and you are rewarded for what you do."

Like the three Harvard MBA students, Mehrotra was deeply skeptical that Lincoln Electric's management structure had much relevance for other businesses. It was certainly not what he would introduce into any company he ended up building. "We talked a lot about guaranteed employment, and I don't believe it means much. It's something of a management tool, something that is good to say to attract people, but it doesn't mean a whole lot. No one can guarantee you anything, and while the intentions are noble, what happens is that motivation and productivity would decrease. I don't believe we should be giving any guarantees in life."

Younger students at MIT who had been exposed to the Lincoln Electric case were slightly more optimistic about the applicability of guaranteed employment and the other management policies to other companies. Tanya Goldhaber, an undergraduate mechanical engineering student with double minors in cognitive science and music, offered an interesting perspective on Lincoln Electric's future, echoing concerns expressed to me by some older employees on the factory floor in Cleveland: "I think the system takes patience and work ethic, but I don't really see [those values] in my generation. It will be interesting to see what my generation does to Lincoln Electric."

"I ONCE ASKED a guy in the business school world, 'How come you're still using Lincoln Electric? Don't you have another case?' And he said, 'No, it's the only really good case we have.'"

Richard Freeman is widely considered to be one of the pre-eminent labor economists in the world. He teaches in Harvard's Economics Department and also heads the Labor Studies Program of the National Bureau of Economic Research in Cambridge, where we discussed the enduring popularity of the Lincoln case.[25]

The MBA students and the university administration officials whom I interviewed at Harvard and other business schools all seem in agreement on one point: During their two years of study, the Lincoln Electric case is likely the only exposure students are given to the concept of a guaranteed employment policy, apart from a few brief references elsewhere to lifetime employment in the Japanese economy. As a result, it's hardly a surprise that the impact of one case study out of five hundred, read over for an hour at most and then discussed for another eighty minutes in class, is insufficient to convince future leaders of industry that a no-layoff policy can be a powerful strategy.

But Freeman argues that it's not just the rarity of the Lincoln Electric case in the average business school curriculum that limits its influence on how students think about employees and employers. Freeman is convinced the value system it espouses is profoundly at odds with the norms of those institutions. "I am sure that no business school encourages students to think about a scenario where one of their job responsibilities is to make sure that the one hundred employees who are given to them by the hiring process are fruitfully engaged, because they don't have the option of getting rid of them. The kinds of guys who do take on that kind of responsibility are working for unemployment offices and social service agencies," not for private businesses, said Freeman, "and it requires a different set of skills, which I don't think our B schools are very good at."

Norman Berg acknowledges the intense pressure on MBA students to absorb a huge amount of study material. But like Freeman, he is convinced that perhaps the most important message in his original analysis of what makes Lincoln Electric tick simply doesn't register with most students or faculty, at Harvard or other business schools.

Lincoln Electric's success challenges its readers to examine the basic tenets of our economy, argued Berg, but too few who make it to such rarefied educational heights as Harvard and other influential business schools are able to recognize this, let alone question it. "You are looking at two views of what is the purpose of a company and what is the purpose of a society and why does a country permit corporations to exist. Lincoln Electric has felt all along that job security is important to people and that the company will provide it to employees to the best extent it can. But most [students and professors at business schools] have no personal experience with layoffs, probably no family experience either, or are even familiar with people for whom this might have been a problem. It does not fit their view of the world. It's unfortunate, but not surprising."

LINCOLN ELECTRIC AND THE MBA

Three of the past four chairmen/CEOs have MBA degrees: George Willis (1986–1992) and Don Hastings (1992–1997) from Harvard and current head John Stropki from Indiana University. Anthony Massaro (1997–2004) took advanced executive seminar courses at Harvard Business School. Clearly, there is a different culture (perhaps an antidote?) at work inside the company.

WALL STREET JUST SCOFFS AND ASKS "WHY?"

"Here's the thing. Stock going up or stock going down, that's all I care about. Lincoln Electric has one of the top-three management teams that I cover, and it is that simple."

He was an equity analyst with a well-known Manhattan investment house, and he had been following Lincoln Electric's financial situation closely for years. Whenever his predictions for a company's financial performance over the next quarter are published in his firm's e-mail newsletters, the price of that company's stock can be driven up—or down—in minutes. For that reason, he shall remain nameless, as will two other analysts in similarly influential positions whose comments from separate interviews are included here. They all shared a professional enthusiasm for Lincoln Electric's "excellent management structure" that ensured its leading position in a competitive industry.

Does anyone on Wall Street believe that the company's guaranteed employment policy plays a role in ensuring its long-term success? I asked, mentioning the basic principles. There was a three-second pause: "I had no idea they had one. I couldn't even repeat what you just said! Besides, while it doesn't surprise me that they have an excellent track record with their employees, it is just not something that *anybody* [his emphasis] here would follow closely."

"For my shareholders," said one of the others who had heard of the no-layoff policy, "it's cut-and-dry. It's how much money are they making and how much more will they make in the future, and whether the company has a guaranteed employment plan or not makes little difference." He added that it had always seemed like an idea "out of left field."

Fair enough that people on Wall Street might not know much about Lincoln Electric's human resource management system. For most of its history, the company has been decidedly low-key about everything other than its acknowledged expertise in welding. Glossy sales catalogs make no mention of the no-layoff policy. The promise slips by in one paragraph in an equally fancy recruiting pamphlet. Even the company's annual 10-K report to the Securities and Exchange Commission—which financial analysts might be expected to at least glance through—has only a brief reference to guaranteed employment (at the end of note 1 in the 2008 submission).[26] Solid financial performance understandably keeps investors focused on profits, not internal policies.

What would be the reaction on the Street if another publicly traded firm, equally well managed and profitable, announced it was going to adopt a no-layoff policy similar to Lincoln Electric's? I then asked. Any indifference immediately evaporated. "It would be looked at extraordinarily poorly," said the first. "There would be a very negative reaction," replied the second. "I just don't know why they would," said the third, adding, "There would be a lot of unhappy investors if they tried this."

These conversations took place during the fall of 2008, when the world of Wall Street investment banking and securities investing seemed to be imploding. Two of these analysts mentioned, with some anger, that they had seen colleagues lose their jobs in recent days. The idea of guaranteeing employment to anyone did not go down well with them. "Let's keep the math simple," said one. "You did one hundred dollars in sales last year, and this year you're only going to do fifty because the economy is in the dumps. My administration costs are the same, and the price of my goods sold is the same. So because I have guaranteed these people employment, shareholders are supposed to take a hit on the bottom line?" He sounded incredulous. "Every investor would look on this poorly."

One of the analysts said he just couldn't fathom why any company would want to strike such a deal with its workers: "This just does not make sense from a capitalist viewpoint."

✧   ✧   ✧

THE CAPITALIST VIEWPOINT à la Wall Street has lost a lot of its luster
these days, given convincing evidence that it was Wall Street's
financial skullduggery that led to the recent financial meltdown.
Milton Friedman's defense of Wall Street, immortalized in a famous 1970 essay where he wrote that the only point of the stock
market and the only job of a good CEO is to make money, now
reads like an invitation to the bad behavior of the past several years.
"In a free-enterprise, private-property system, a corporate executive
is an employee of the owners of the business [the stockholders].
He has direct responsibility to his employers. That responsibility
is to conduct the business in accordance with their desires, which
generally will be to make as much money as possible."[27]

Understandably these days, a young MBA equity analyst rendering judgment on what "makes sense" for the economy doesn't
garner much respect from working or retired people who have
seen their life savings shrink by half and more, or from those who
have lost their jobs in the recession. The unseemly disbursement
of multimillion-dollar retention bonuses at Merrill Lynch and
other banks and investment firms that had received taxpayer
moneys just a few months earlier seemed to confirm for many
Americans that excessive greed was actually all that makes sense
to those in positions of power in the higher echelons of finance.

That suspicion of Wall Street was largely shared by James F.
Lincoln. In fact, it was only in 1995, when the company was cel-
ebrating its one hundredth anniversary, that shares of Lincoln
Electric stock were finally made available for sale to the public
(the company's symbol on the NASDAQ is LECO). Until that
time, shares issued by the company had been privately traded,
and largely owned by members of the Lincoln family and the employees. Lincoln himself had always believed that when it came
time to divide up any annual profits that had been earned by the
company, customers must be taken care of first (through keep-

ing product prices low), followed by the employees (through the merit-based bonus system), and only then the stockholders. Lincoln was a stickler for proportioning profits according to effort, and "there is usually no evidence that the stockholder did much to increase the profit. His proper share therefore is small."[28] Limiting the number of external stockholders also limited their ability to influence senior management, which meant that as a private company, an internal policy such as guaranteed employment was spared the scrutiny of Wall Street skeptics.

The decision to go public was eventually made after the series of ill-fated, costly expansions into Europe in the late 1980s and early 1990s discussed in Chapter 3. In 1992, for the first time in its history, Lincoln Electric borrowed money in order to pay the annual profit-sharing bonus to the employees. Three years later, with losses still mounting, public shares were finally issued to help defer the growing debt.

Don Hastings, the CEO at the time of the share offering, said that when Lincoln Electric pitched the stock to Wall Street, they told potential carriers they were "not interested in attracting short-sellers." But once the shares were on the market, he said that the pressure from the incessant quarterly reporting schedule began to grow. "We'd be down 2 percent on estimated income, and the stock would drop 15 to 20 percent. It was very difficult, but fortunately we had a good bottom line so we could say our system works long term." Jon Glick, a mechanical engineer with Lincoln Electric in the early 1990s who is now a high-tech executive in Silicon Valley, remembered guiding Wall Street analysts through the factory when the initial stock offering was being evaluated. "Their mission was not to get any sense of how the company operated," he said. "Their mission was to get an inventory value" in case the company had to be liquidated.[29] He also remembered the analysts' amazement at the high wages being paid to the factory workers.

Current chairman John Stropki told me that the pressures on short-term performance are just part of life, but like Hastings, he said the company tries to be clear that it is focused on long-term growth. "We generally don't have those kinds of [short-term] investors because we are so clear about our strategies, our employment practices, and our profit-sharing plans." Investors sometimes ask about the guaranteed employment program, said Stropki, and some questioned paying out $80 million in bonuses to workers in December 2008. But overall, given that the guaranteed employment program has been in place at Lincoln Electric for more than a half century, the policy is not under regular attack.

YOU WANT TO DO WHAT WITH THE PROFITS?

If there is any small upside to the financial chaos of the past few years, surely it is an increased questioning by the American public of the basic values of this country's economic system, given the ease with which it has inflicted such pain on so many.

As has been stressed already, Lincoln Electric's embrace of a guaranteed employment policy grew out of the desire of its founders to build a successful commercial enterprise. The ultimate goal was to ensure long-term growth and a steady stream of profits. In order to do that, the founders believed it was necessary to run a financially solid company that avoided taking undue risks or going into debt, to provide their employees with steady work, and to share a significant portion of the profits with them. It was a question of balance for James Lincoln, as it was for other employers and employees during the era of welfare capitalism, and as it is in our day for the relatively few other companies who try to maintain no-layoff policies. A sense of balance in the American economy, however, is widely accepted to be out of whack, and any discussion of the reluctance of most American businesses to consider a guaranteed employment policy must deal with this reality.

Lincoln Electric—the company and its employees—benefits significantly from a much more egalitarian work environment, in terms of pay and working conditions, than is found in the vast proportion of other American corporations. While the current economic crisis has certainly reenergized a debate about the growing financial inequality of American society, the value system that has produced the bloated executive salaries in so many sectors of the economy will not be transformed quickly. In the meantime, it's understandable that the vast majority of working Americans generally do not feel as if they are part of the same team as their company's CEO.

The Institute for Policy Studies reports every year on the exorbitant annual compensation paid to corporate leaders in America. Its latest estimate, for 2008, is that the average CEO in the S&P 500 makes 344 times more than the average American worker ($10.5 million versus $30,617).[30] According to Lincoln Electric's annual report to the Security and Exchange Commission, CEO John Stropki made $4.6 million in 2008; that's just 150 times more than the average U.S. worker (still a lot of money, without question). But consider this as well: At Lincoln Electric, the average worker made approximately $70,000 in 2008, more than twice the national average.[31] Using that as a basis of comparison, Stropki makes just 65 times more than the average worker in his company. In addition, Lincoln Electric's executive ranks are relatively small for a company of its size, and in 2008 only four other senior executives earned more than $1 million (and none more than $2 million) in total compensation.

The father of modern management, Peter Drucker, once argued that no chief executive should receive more than 25 times the salary of the lowest-paid employee in the company, in order

to avoid problems of productivity and morale. It is certainly hard
to compare pay ratios over decades, but Bill Burga, the former
head of the AFL-CIO in Ohio, believes that Lincoln Electric's
relatively low CEO and executive pay has been an asset over the
long term: "It takes out the greed factor which has ruined so many
of these multinational corporations. That's what makes Lincoln
Electric a success."

"I've asked lots of senior American executives if their son or
daughter was interested in manufacturing, do they think Lincoln
Electric would be a good place to start," said Harvard's Norman
Berg, "and they say yes. Then I ask, 'Would *you* work at Lincoln?'
and most say, 'I don't want to work that hard for that kind of
money.'"

It's not just the relatively low salaries of Lincoln's senior executives that serve to dissuade others who might otherwise be interested in emulating the company's management system in their
own companies. "People do make different amounts of money at
Lincoln, but the company tries hard to make you feel like you
are part of a team," said Berg. "The differential in symbols is enormous in most corporations, but Lincoln has always tried to minimize that—no preferred parking lots, no measurement of
someone's status by windows—and those things appeal to most
people."

Status symbols are almost nonexistent at Lincoln Electric.
The roughly 3,000 employees at its Cleveland headquarters, from
the CEO to the cleaners, enter the factory through one main
door. There are no personalized executive parking spots. Only
the CEO and a few vice presidents have offices with windows,
while other senior executives work in windowless rooms that can
best be described as bland, olive-green cells filled with a hodge-
podge of mismatched office furniture that could never have been
coordinated by an interior designer. There is no executive dining
room: Everyone eats in the basement-level cafeteria, where vice

presidents line up with welders and engineers to receive trays of the hearty daily lunch specials. "I felt like I was in a state correctional facility," Jon Glick told me, laughing as he recalled descending to the underground tunnels his first day on the job as a mechanical engineer. Glick grew up in Cleveland, studied mechanical engineering at Cornell University, and joined Lincoln's electric motor division in 1990. He later earned an MBA at Harvard (where he studied the famous case), went on to oversee Yahoo!'s search-engine development program, and is now vice president for product search at Become.com, a California-based Internet shopping search engine. "Forget 'no expense spared'; this was 'no expense spent'!" according to Glick. "I have nothing but good memories of Lincoln Electric. This was a company that made sure you got everything you deserved and nothing you didn't, and for me, that gelled. I saw what people are truly capable of when limitless opportunity is available."

IS A LESS DISTORTED executive compensation structure necessary to the smooth operation of a no-layoff policy? Does the CEO of a company contemplating the adoption of a guaranteed employment promise need to accept that he or she will likely have to forgo earning the stratospherically high salary enjoyed by most other American chief executives?

Perhaps the better question to ask is why year after year, a company such as Lincoln Electric shares 32 percent of its profits with its employees through the annual bonus. It's an amount that industrial relations experts such as MIT's Thom Kochan called "extraordinary." Rutgers University labor economist Douglas Kruse, one of the nation's leading analysts of profit-sharing companies, termed 32 percent "extremely generous." And David Wray, president of the Profit Sharing/401k Council of America, which represents more than 1,200 companies across the country, said, "Lincoln is clearly putting money into its [profit-sharing] program, and this one is about as generous as it gets."[32] Remember as well that the base wages that are paid to employees in Cleveland *before* the bonus is distributed each year have always had to remain competitive in the Northeast Ohio labor market. Otherwise, the company would never be able to attract talented new employees whenever it puts out the "help wanted" sign.

Ultimately, the answers to the questions above define the values of a corporation. Recall James F. Lincoln's initial motive for starting the Advisory Board in 1914: He needed his employees to want success as much as he did. When a CEO first makes a proclamation like that, he is, by definition, mouthing a platitude. When he and his successors act on it over decades, and as a result the company grows while the employees consistently and significantly share in the accumulated profits, that commitment comes to define the culture of the organization.

TRUST

Transforming a platitude into a culture is a process built on trust, and, sadly, there is a pervasive lack of trust corroding the American workplace. Over the past several decades, businesses of many shapes and sizes in the United States have steadily moved further and further away from the goal of building a collaborative relationship between employees and senior management. The justifications offered for management decisions that often seem explicitly designed to make employees unhappy include, among others, the pressures of a global economy replete with low-wage competitors, the relentless demands of a just-in-time business environment (which requires that everyone involved must embrace change and flexibility at all times), and the cruel financial calculus of international investment, mercurial in its loyalties at best.[33]

For tens of millions of American workers, the collective impact of these economic currents is that employers have downloaded onto the shoulders of their employees many risks that had formerly been undertaken by the firms themselves. This process is usually accompanied by a gentle admonishment from those on top that while the changes may seem unsettling at first, the new structure of personal risk (couched as *personal responsibility*) actually constitutes an exciting and fulfilling opportunity for employees to finally make intelligent decisions about their future. President George W. Bush made what he called the *ownership society* an important cornerstone of his domestic policy, putting the full weight of the administration behind a process that systematically increased the everyday risks faced by workers across the country.[34]

Because most working Americans and their families quickly found this experience to be extremely unsettling and often very painful, it has understandably led to the widespread and severe erosion of trust that employees hold for their employers and, particularly, trust in those at the very top levels of management. Survey after survey of how people feel about their work and their bosses confirms this, and virtually every analysis of the future of work suggests the situation will continue to worsen. One recent report on employee engagement suggests that one out of every two American workers now distrusts those at the top of their company, "the people who set the tone for organizational culture and need to inspire high-performance and commitment." Another extensive poll of employees by the consulting firm Towers Perrin gave CEOs a failing grade on five different measures of leadership behavior, reporting that 75 percent of employees do not believe senior management is helping them to contribute to their companies' success.[35]

One would think that every employer now understands why a lack of trust in the workplace has a tremendous negative effect on productivity, quality, and the financial health of the company. Certainly, a mountain of academic research in recent years on the advantages of *high performance workplaces* — gleaned from the profitable experience of the few companies that have embraced and stayed with these management approaches — offers proof of that.[36]

Being able to trust your boss is exceedingly important to employees. Researchers in the burgeoning new discipline of behavioral economics — fertile ground for several recent winners of the Nobel Prize — have determined that a wide range of employees in the North American economy would be willing to forgo significant increases in salary if instead they could enjoy even a small increase in their ability to trust the people who run their companies.[37]

At this writing in the summer of 2009, the survival of the Big Three American automobile manufacturers is still up in the air, even with the government bailouts and some evidence that consumers are heading back into car dealerships. But regardless of the final outcome for the companies and the unions that have been at such loggerheads during the restructuring, whatever trust ever existed within the largest industry in the country seems unlikely to be rebuilt in the foreseeable future. Looking back on his thirty years as a truck chassis assembler in Warren, outside Detroit, former Chrysler worker and local union leader Larry Christensen told me that "we didn't really trust more back then. We didn't know to be suspicious back then, as we now know to be suspicious. It was all a lie, and that never changes."[38]

What has made the erosion of trust particularly acute and generated such bitterness has been the relentless repetition of the same mantra emanating from the highest levels of businesses everywhere, a chant that "workers are vital to this corporation." There is little evidence that the vast proportion of American corporate leaders really believe what they say on this issue. "People don't really matter at all," said John Phillips Jr., a former vice president of Coca-Cola Enterprises and now a labor lawyer in Chattanooga. "Every company, no matter how large or small, whether publicly traded or not, lists as one of its core values that 'our people are our most important asset,' and it has become just meaningless." Phillips said he regularly urges his clients, mostly large American corporations, that unless they are serious about these statements, it would be infinitely better to leave them out. They seldom take his advice, according to Phillips, adding that the constant dishonesty "really annoys me."[39]

In February 2009, just weeks after the drug manufacturer Pfizer announced thousands of layoffs in the United States, CEO Jeffrey Kindler assured a disgruntled shareholder, who had written him to complain, that "loyal and committed employees are critical to any organization's success, and we are committed to treating all our colleagues fairly and with respect." GE's head Jeff Immelt, who laid off more than 15,000 employees in 2008 and 2009, told the same unhappy owner of his company's stock that "we value our dedicated employees and will be compassionate and respectful when difficult decisions have to be faced."[40]

A guaranteed employment policy like Lincoln Electric's is not realistic for every business: Schumpeter's "creative destruction" remains a fact of life in our economy. But consider this question: "Would you even think for one minute about trusting a CEO who promised that if you worked hard and agreed to share the ups and downs of economic cycles with all your fellow employees, he or she would never lay you off?" Sadly, the vast majority of Americans would say no.

chapter seven

"THIS IS NOT ABOUT ALTRUISM"

Winter 2008–2009 was in its last week when Ben Bernanke, chairman of the Federal Reserve, first spoke of seeing the "green shoots" of a recovery, although he was quick to warn that it would probably take at least a year before a revival finally took root in the American economic landscape.

By mid-summer 2009, farmers and home gardeners may have been happy with nature's bounty sprouting in their fields and backyards, but the majority of Americans were still mired in the financial chaos of a wounded economy. Hundreds of thousands of jobs were still disappearing each month as businesses across the country struggled to stay open or shut their doors forever.

In Cleveland, Lincoln Electric's production lines were still churning out welding machines, including some new energy-efficient models, and electrodes. But with sales off 40 percent (almost equally around the world), the company was definitely not operating as normal. "What is so clearly different in this recession, more than anything I have ever seen, is the amazingly broad

nature of it," said John Stropki, a few days after returning from
opening a new electrode plant in India, "and so we are really
pushing the envelope of all the techniques that we are able to use
to preserve guaranteed employment."[1]

For most pieceworkers and hourly paid employees, the workweek remained where it had been for the previous eight
months—at thirty-two hours, well below the more normal forty-
five to fifty hours. Salaried employees had seen their wages cut by
5 percent, and most were also working longer hours, including
Saturdays. Management salaries had been reduced by 10 percent,
and the senior executive team, including Stropki, faced cuts in
total compensation for 2009 of between 20 and 45 percent. More
ominously, there were fewer people working at Lincoln Electric
in Cleveland in summer 2009 than a year earlier. Had the famed
no-layoff promise been broken? No, said Stropki, and that answer
was echoed by the workers I spoke with soon afterward. But was
this just evasive semantics?

In February the company had announced a voluntary retirement incentive program. It's a tool that "we've never really used
before," said Stropki, but "some employees said to themselves,
'I've had a great run, earned a good living, I'm well set financially,
hours are much lower, and obviously the bonus will be much
lower this year.'" Two hundred people accepted the offer, and
most had left by late March.

As emphasized throughout this book, Lincoln Electric has always had well-defined and well-publicized performance standards, and has always been up front regarding the serious
implications for employees who consistently fail to meet those
standards, regardless of whether they have reached the three-year
mark (when they become covered by the no-layoff promise).
Everyone seems to understand that in boom times, the system is
more relaxed about enforcement. They also know that in tough
times, Lincoln Electric has never avoided making hard decisions:

Somewhere between one and two hundred people were terminated for performance reasons in the first six months of 2009.
(The company declined to disclose exact numbers.) In total, the
departures reduced the Cleveland workforce by more than 10 percent. "The parking lot is definitely looking a little thinner," tool-
and-die expert Mark Wells told me, but he believed, as did many
other employees, that the decisions to let those workers go for failing to meet the company's rigorous performance standard had
been made fairly.[2] Not everyone agreed, of course. An anonymous
blogger, the online author of "Welding a New Career," who
claimed he was a technician in Lincoln Electric's research labs,
argued that hours were being slashed arbitrarily and work rules
harshly imposed in order to crudely force up to a third of the staff
to quit voluntarily.[3] Interestingly, the author admitted he'd been
with the company for less than a year.

Like almost every publicly traded company in America, Lincoln Electric had seen its stock pummeled in recent months. At
one point, shares had lost 70 percent of the historical peak value
reached in the summer of 2008, but by August 2009, the share
price was hovering around the 50 percent mark.

During the spring quarterly report conference call, Stropki
had been pushed by industry analysts to predict when and where
a recovery in the welding industry would first show up. Like most
CEOs whose companies operate on a global scale, he pointed to
India and China in his "green shoots" answer, but understandably
ducked the question of when.

Lincoln Electric's success over the past century has been due
to much more than its smart HR policies, which include guaranteed employment. One other equally deep-rooted operating
principle—a tradition of fiscal prudence championed decades
ago by James Lincoln—has proved to be extraordinarily important during the recession, said Stropki. After all, it's Lincoln's
strong balance sheet boasting very large cash reserves—and not

the company's employment policy—that keeps Wall Street analysts so consistently enthusiastic about the company's future.

From 1895 until 1991, Lincoln Electric had no external debt whatsoever.[4] Then came the first outside borrowing when a rapid global expansion program had proved to be unexpectedly costly. These days, the firm's long-term debt load is a small fraction of the average for large American companies.[5]

A huge bank balance, $406 million in cash, is another payoff from that cautious management style.[6] "It is a very big advantage," said Stropki. "We are not sitting here worried about where our next infusion of cash is going to come from to pay our bills [including wages] or how to capitalize on any short-term opportunities which come along" (such as opening a new $20 million factory in India or spending $38 million to take full control of an electrode plant in China, both in the first five months of 2009).

Will Lincoln Electric's arsenal of good management policies—from the commitment to honor guaranteed employment to the other HR elements such as the merit system and the Advisory Board, the premium placed on innovation and quality manufacturing, and its discipline in following conservative financial operating procedures—help the company endure the worst of this recession until the economic horizon brightens? According to John Stropki, "As we have shown in the past, when the recovery does come, Lincoln Electric will be able to take advantage of it quicker than our local and global competitors who have chosen other ways to achieve their short-term cost needs such as layoffs." In Mark Wells's opinion, "It's got to turn around eventually. It can't stay like this forever, and until it does, I will still have a job."

BUT WHAT OF OTHER companies in our time who have tried to be equally committed to their employees, their customers, and their investors as Lincoln Electric has been? What has this recession meant for their fortunes and their workers? And are there lessons for other corporate leaders who would like to have a viable option to culling their workforce long before they find themselves backed into a corner, with their hands poised to pull the layoff lever? Some of the answers lie with two very different companies, far from the beleaguered industrial heartland of Cleveland, on America's East and West Coasts.

HYPERTHERM

"The Hypertherm sign at the entrance is small and may be hard to see," warned my travel directions, and on cue, I missed the turnoff, driving along Great Hollow Road in Hanover, New Hampshire, in a light rain. The headquarters of the world's leading producer of plasma arc metal-cutting technology resembles a university campus: ten low-level buildings spread across 120 acres of evergreen forest, connected by walkways lined with pine-chip gardens.

It's a far cry from the garage where, in classic high-tech tradition, Dick Couch and his partner started their business in 1968. Hypertherm is an international success story, with its products distributed in more than sixty countries, generating annual sales of between $250 and $500 million. The company is privately held, with a majority of shares owned by employees. Over four decades, the workforce has expanded to more than 1,000 permanent workers—and no one has ever been laid off for economic reasons. "I'm not sure that I call it a goal," said Dick Couch, who at sixty-six is still CEO. "I call it an operating principle which is defensible in a cost sense."[7]

The technology at the heart of Hypertherm's business—cutting metal apart rather than welding it together—was developed in the Second World War and involves the creation of a jet of highly energized, or ionized, gas at temperatures many times hotter than the surface of the sun. In the mid-1960s, Dick Couch, a recent engineering graduate from nearby Dartmouth College, invented a technique to more precisely and easily control the powerful stream of superheated gas by surrounding it with water. The firm has remained the leader in plasma cutting technology ever since.

When he started the business in 1968, Couch said a no-layoff policy was not uppermost in his mind. What was crucial was "a concept of fairness about human beings being important and how could I get people excited about improving productivity and reducing costs." The echoes of James Lincoln circa 1914 were everywhere as we talked, and there are many other similarities in how the two companies have nurtured a culture of technical innovation and employee stability.

Couch wanted to structure his company to avoid "the artificial division between plant workers and office employees—you know, where the front part of the building is carpeted with air-conditioning . . . and then you'd walk back into the plant and it's cold in the winter and hot in the summer." As at Lincoln Electric, there are few visually discernible status symbols at Hypertherm. On the main building's second floor, Couch has one of the few separate offices, but it exhibits none of the trappings of a very successful entrepreneur: Neighboring executives and administration staff all have great views of the surrounding forest. Hypertherm is a manufacturing company, but it can hardly be described as "heavy industry" in the same breath as Lincoln Electric. Its research labs, production facilities, and distribution warehouses are much sleeker and more modern, and it's visibly obvious that a professional industrial designer was paid to oversee the architectural integrity of the buildings, inside and out.

Like Lincoln Electric, there is no union at Hypertherm. Just as in Cleveland, until the recession hit full-force in late 2008, most production workers were putting in ten hours or more of overtime every week. By early 2009, that overtime had evaporated. By May, there were contingency plans—but only plans—to further reduce the workweek to thirty-two hours. "Our worst-case scenario is a drop in business of at least 40 percent, so given we're now down about 35 percent, we still have a way to go," Couch told me.[8]

When production started in 1969, Couch created an annual profit-sharing plan that has paid out every year since the early 1980s: Over the past ten years, the average bonus payment has been 25 percent of an employee's base salary. Unlike Lincoln Electric, there is no individualized merit-rating system. Hypertherm does monitor employee performance, but not to Lincoln Electric's extremes of subjective and objective measurement.

The first real test of Couch's commitment—and that of his employees—came in the recession of the early 1980s. Hypertherm's sales dropped off so dramatically that, as Skip Gould, a thirty-one-year veteran told me, "We'd come in the morning, work for twenty minutes, and spend the rest of the day just cleaning the machines. We worked four days a week at one point, but were paid for five!"[9] There was no profit to distribute that year, yet Couch dipped into his own savings to send every employee a crisp new one hundred–dollar bill with a personal note that he appreciated their efforts. "By then, I kind of understood that Dick was serious about the no-layoff policy," laughed Gould. (Like many older employees, he has two children working in the company; both are in management. His wife is also an employee.)

"This is not about altruism; it's good business," replied Couch when I asked him about the potential cost of his commitment to avoid layoffs at all costs. "But it is not a straight line, and that's the expectation that is the most damaging in public ownership, the belief that every quarter must yield good news." The major problem with America's business culture, Couch believes, is the "deeply entrenched" philosophy that stock dividends must always go up. Public companies that refuse to play that game face terrible penalties, said Couch, regardless of their own unique financial situation or unique strengths such as a commitment to avoid layoffs (which Couch believes is—by definition—a strategy for long-term growth). "Having profitability go up and down is a natural phenomenon," argued Couch, and forcing a firm to pay a dividend when its profits don't rise is "unreal." That's why he's avoided Wall Street and the industry analysts discussed in the last chapter. Instead, whenever Hypertherm has needed capital, he has sought out private investors. Given the company's impressive financial history, they have never been hard to find.

Couch believes that starting a company that values innovation and sharing and then growing the firm (while protecting those values) is much easier for a private, rather than a public, corporation: It simply takes a long time for a culture of trust to take root, and Wall Street has no patience. However, the current recession provided an opportunity to see trust develop quickly in one employee.

In October 2008, just before the bottom really dropped out of Hypertherm's sales, Melissa Carlson, the head of human resources, led me through the intricacies of managing with a no-layoff goal. Carlson joined the company in 2004 after working in Silicon Valley where layoffs were a daily fact of life. Her time in New Hampshire had been a period of "unprecedented growth": In the previous two years, Hypertherm had hired three hundred full-time employees, roughly a 25 percent increase in the workforce. She'd heard how Hypertherm survived tough times without layoffs, but had yet to experience a down cycle herself with the firm.

I asked Carlson for her thoughts on a commonly raised fear about guaranteed employment—whether embraced as a goal (Hypertherm's choice) or as a formal promise (as at Lincoln Electric)—that it can nurture a dangerous sense of complacency.

Her answer took me aback: "My personal fear is that the dark side of a no-layoff policy is that you're not able to weed out the dead-weight and bring in fresh perspectives."[10] She was quite prepared to concede that the extreme loyalty that Hypertherm's employees felt for the company grew out of its four-decade-old history of avoiding layoffs. But she returned several times during our conversation to the idea that there is "a finite opportunity cost" to retaining people for long periods of time, saying she had "huge skepticism" about the coming downturn.

"I stand corrected," said Carlson forcefully and quickly, six months later in April 2009, when I asked her again about the no-layoff goal.[11] By then, the flexibility offered by Hypertherm's HR policies had kicked in. Some production workers were even doing the landscaping maintenance (the equivalent to painting walls at Lincoln Electric). But no permanent employee had been laid off. "I really have to say that, looking at human nature, I am so proud to see people rallying together to say we *are* in this together and let's make sure we do it so that no one loses their job," Carlson told me. "I never thought I would have seen that."

Although Couch still radiates an enthusiasm for leadership, at some point, he will step aside. He is uncertain how he'll ensure that his replacement will share his commitment to avoid layoffs. "How can you figure out if the next generation of leaders agrees with your values?" He paused. "I'm not quite sure how you do that."

Ultimately, said Couch, the sad reality is that "our economic system is terribly resistant to change about what is the basic purpose of a business." It cannot be just about the primacy of those who own stock, as it is now, he argued. "We need a balanced approach to a workforce, the shareholders, and the community. It would be just as harmful to skew it all the way to workplace primacy [such as mandated guaranteed employment]. But the pendulum has swung too far in the direction of Wall Street and shareholders, and it has to somehow work its way back to a sense of balance."

Despite the current clamor for dramatic changes on Wall Street—especially the calls for more accurate methods to gauge sustainable economic strength—any transformation won't happen quickly. In the meantime, avoiding Wall Street is hardly a realistic prescription for the economy as a whole. In Lincoln Electric's case, I'm convinced that by the time the company began issuing stock—one hundred years after it was founded—its commitment to guaranteed employment was essentially immutable. Hopefully, Hypertherm's upcoming leadership transition process—its first in forty years—will produce a new CEO who shares Couch's values. But what about an established public company? Could it break away from the pack to assure its employees that layoffs will never be considered *normal*, yet still be able to remain profitable?

XILINX

"The reason why stability is so important in a workforce is that if you are an innovator, you have to stick your neck out," said Wim Roelandts, the chairman of Xilinx. "True innovation means you don't know if it's going to work—but if you're worried about your CEO planning layoffs, you won't stick your neck out, and you'll never get a breakthrough."[12]

The value of stability in the workplace is not a concept most people expect to hear espoused by a Silicon Valley pioneer like Roelandts, 3,100 miles west of the bucolic woods of New Hampshire. The geographic heart of the global high-tech industry just south of San Francisco Bay has long prided itself on a high-flying embrace of profits and impermanence. Talk of a no-layoff philosophy was definitely not what the board of directors of Xilinx wanted to hear when Roelandts was brought in as president in

1996 after a twenty-nine-year career with Hewlett-Packard. For a while, he won them over. But in the end, the board—and the rest of senior management—had it their way.

Xilinx was started by three entrepreneurs in 1984 to manufacture integrated circuit chips that could be individually programmed to perform whatever computer logic tasks a customer might need. Currently a Fortune 1000 company with sales in 2008 of almost $2 billion, Xilinx is the leading maker of programmable logic chips in the world; they're key components in everything from wireless telephones to computer servers to military communications devices.

In the mid-1990s, when the founders were looking for a new CEO, they reached out to Roelandts, then vice president of HP's massive computer systems division. A native of Belgium, trained as an engineer, Roelandts credits his belief that good managers can—and must—avoid layoffs to his three decades of working under Bill Hewlett and Dave Packard.

From the moment he arrived at Xilinx, Roelandts found that several members of the board and others at senior levels of the company were adamantly against his plan to establish a no-layoff work environment. They urged him just to stick with more familiar Silicon Valley practices—let employees go when management felt under pressure. Yet he persevered. "We never had a [formal] policy against layoffs," Roelandts told me, "but layoffs were always going to be the absolute last resort. If the company were going to go bankrupt, you'd have no choice. But because I had an alternate plan to reduce costs, that satisfied most people." That plan was based on his conviction that "companies with a no-layoff policy or goal are more innovative, more open, have more discussions, and the return on human capital is hugely improved."

From 1996 until 2000, Xilinx rode the tech boom on the way up. Its share price rose from $7 to $95. Sales quadrupled, and

Xilinx grabbed more than a third of the global market for its products. Layoffs were the furthest thing from anyone's mind. In fact, recruiting and retaining talented people on staff was the real challenge. If a Silicon Valley firm did encounter serious financial problems, the subsequent layoff of employees seldom meant that the people who were let go had their lives destroyed; stories of being able to walk across the street and get a new job by the end of the day were not apocryphal.

Then the bubble burst. In the blink of an eye, the challenge became finding customers and investors. From summer 2000 to summer 2001, shares of Xilinx dropped 75 percent. In 2001, revenue dropped more than 50 percent. With the market crashing, Roelandts and Peg Wynn, then vice president of HR, faced a real-life test of his no-layoff philosophy.[13]

The annual bonus—roughly 10 to 20 percent of base salary—was killed first. Then came graduated pay cuts, from 0 percent for the lowest-paid employees up to 20 percent for Roelandts. Six months later, in mid-June 2002, came an additional company-wide 7.5 percent salary reduction. Employees could choose between that additional cut and taking every second Friday off without pay: three-quarters chose the latter. Roelandts's total compensation was slashed by 50 percent, Wynn's by 45 percent.[14] "People were dancing in the street," said Wynn. "They were very excited by the fact that we were doing this instead of a layoff."[15]

As the tech economy tanked, the company shut down for two weeks. A voluntary severance program was introduced, regardless of tenure. People were encouraged to take a sabbatical year and promised that they'd suffer no financial or status-related penalties on their return. If an employee on sabbatical worked for a nonprofit organization, Xilinx offered to pay $10,000 to support that choice. And if an employee wanted to go back to school, the company would contribute $10,000 to help cover the costs.

By mid-2002, more than a year into the crash, Xilinx estimated it was saving more than $13 million each quarter with its innovative HR policies. By year's end, the tech market began to stabilize. Pay cuts were soon rescinded. Through it all, no Xilinx employees were laid off for economic reasons, and, in fact, turnover (through normal attrition and terminations for cause) was less than a quarter of the norm for Silicon Valley.

In the years following the tech bubble's burst, Xilinx regularly appeared on *Fortune* magazine's annual list of "100 Best Companies to Work For," placing in the top ten for four years in a row.

Then, on June 4, 2008, Xilinx laid off 250 employees, 7 percent of its workforce.[16]

On April 15, 2009, a further 200 employees were laid off.[17]

What happened?

Roelandts had retired as president in January 2008 to become chairman of the board. "The new CEO didn't believe in this philosophy, and the first thing he did was order a layoff," he says. That new CEO, Moshe Gavrielov, was an outsider whom Roelandts had helped select. "Our new CEO decided to go from a very fractionalized business structure with a duplication of resources which was limiting to a more functionalized model," explained Kathy Borneman, Xilinx's vice president for human resources.[18] She was brought into the firm in early 2008 by Gavrielov, soon after he took over from Roelandts, and just a few months before the first layoffs.

"No one brings up [the no-layoff days] directly anymore," said Borneman when I asked her if there was any corporate memory of the policy. "Some people look back to the kinder, gentler times when they lived on the entitlement of being taken care of, but they also say, 'We get it—the business reality and the need for competitive actions.'"[19]

In late spring 2009, after the second rounds of layoffs, Xilinx was relatively healthy, financially speaking, given the general carnage of the recession: "Better than most everyone else in this sector" was a common assessment by industry observers.

"Xilinx is doing reasonably well because we have some very good products," admitted Roelandts, who had just stepped down as chairman to become a director. (He resigned completely from Xilinx's board in August 2009.) But he worried about the impact of the layoffs and the resulting shock on the company's culture: "It will be negative because talent and experience and know-how will leave. The new management believes head count is head count, and everything comes down to being tough."[20]

Borneman doesn't disagree. "There are no absolutes," she told me. "We're looking at a very healthy company with strong fundamentals. We try to retain best performers . . . but coming out and saying we are a no-layoff company . . . is like saying, 'Reality can't happen here.'"

THERE ARE A NUMBER of lessons to be learned from Wim Roelandts's experience introducing a no-layoff goal into an established public company like Xilinx. They highlight the significant difficulty of changing the current cultural values of business in America. "He came in with this [no-layoff idea], and people said, 'Okay, this is kind of worthy, and we can get behind it,'" remembered Bruce Schlegel, who was in charge of compensation and benefit policies until he retired in 2007. But he also recalled that there was no "hard-core discussion" of how a crisis would be met, and no vote was ever held on the idea among senior managers. As the high-tech bubble inflated, Roelandts's enthusiasm for the no-layoff goal remained untested because no one had to do anything new, said Schlegel. But when the bottom suddenly dropped out, many people at the top levels of Xilinx felt unsure about what to do next. They also felt threatened. "It was unfortunate because it wasn't anything the key stakeholders decided on," according to

Schlegel. "It was pretty much all Wim, and he didn't have the support of the board, and at the end he didn't have the support of many of the thought leaders in the company."[21]

As a result, even when the worst was finally over and no employees had been let go, when revenue had recovered and Xilinx's global market share had grown to more than 50 percent, and when the company was winning those workplace awards, there still seemed to be a perception within much of the company's senior management team that the no-layoff initiatives were simply too radical and that, ultimately, "just doing what everyone else does" was easier. Avoiding layoffs "really requires great managers," said Peg Wynn. "You need to have tactical people in strategic roles who need to think two to three steps ahead of everyone else, and, generally, we all don't do a good-enough job at that."

Schlegel agreed with one commonly raised criticism of no-layoff policies—the potential danger of encouraging employee complacency, especially in the fast-moving high-tech economy. "We did get stagnant in the ability to renew ideas," he said, "especially the research and development people who were insulated from the real world. We weren't able to slow expenses there, and maybe a layoff would have given them a jolt to see the real perspective of the organization."

During the early 2000s, the pressure on Roelandts from Wall Street analysts and investors was intense. "It was absolutely a perennial struggle in those quarterly report calls. Wim and the CFO were questioned on and on as to why we weren't doing layoffs," remembered Wynn, even after markets recovered in 2002. Skepticism about the financial risks of pursuing a no-layoff goal was often just as intense inside the company, said Wynn, where it "was *not* part of the genetic code" (her emphasis). One vice president called it "bullshit."

Is a guaranteed employment policy simply not sustainable in a high-tech company like Xilinx versus in manufacturing firms such as Lincoln Electric and Hypertherm? No easy answers to that, said Jon Glick, the former Lincoln Electric engineer and now a high-tech executive in Silicon Valley. "It is certainly outside the ethos of these companies where there *is* an incredible amount of experimentation," admitted Glick, "because you do want the flexibility to move in and out of different areas quickly." Yet Glick also argued that in a business based on creative thinking, "if someone is always worrying about their job, they're thinking about updating their résumé and putting their creative energy somewhere else."

Roelandts admits he made a serious mistake in not adequately training someone inside Xilinx to fill his shoes. "Once you go outside, there is a high risk that you are not going to bring in the right person," said Roelandts. "They don't understand the power of the culture. If they have never seen something like this, they see 'softheartedness.'" Moshe Gavrielov was an extremely experienced and respected high-tech veteran when he took over from Roelandts as president in January 2008, but he was completely new to the firm. The first layoff came just five months after he arrived, the second less than a year later. In the end, it came down to the inability of a visionary leader to forge a permanent consensus within the senior management levels of the organization—and on its board—to create a new company culture.

Bucking the conventional wisdom that layoffs are normal was personally very difficult, Roelandts told me as he recounted conversations with his fellow CEOs in other Fortune 500 high-tech firms: "Most of them think I'm a lunatic. It's a sad story, and to be honest with you, it is one of the big disappointments in my life that people don't see the value of this."

WHOSE RESPONSIBILITY IS THAT?

Through the story of Lincoln Electric, these brief snapshots of Hypertherm and Xilinx, and a look back over the last century, one pattern emerges: The decision to consider and then adopt some form of a guaranteed employment goal in American business enterprises has almost always been made by individual CEOs determined to buck conventional management practice. Furthermore, the most common scenario has been for the founder of a new business to introduce some form of no-layoff practice from the company's birth. Since the Second World War, it has been rare for an established company, especially a larger public corporation like Xilinx, to dramatically revamp its conventional employment practices to end the use of layoffs. But apart from the road through the CEO's office, are there other potential routes by which guaranteed employment might become more common in the American economic landscape?

One possibility is to imagine workers in an existing firm approaching senior management to discuss how, together, they might reorganize their workplace in order to provide real job security while ensuring the company would remain healthy. After all, that happened at Lincoln Electric, when the employees reached out to James Lincoln in the depths of the Depression and suggested that both sides could hammer out their own private New Deal.

For some, the dream of a resurgent American labor movement holds out such promise. By reenergizing and then exploiting the power of collective action, advocates argue, unions might be able to force employers to fully appreciate that workers are best seen as valuable assets to be retained for as long as possible rather than cost elements to be slashed whenever needed. At a minimum, the groundbreaking work of labor economists such as Richard Freeman — especially in books such as his *What Workers Want* — has conclusively shown that a significant majority of American workers want to cooperate much more closely with their employers to ensure the long-term health of their companies, to avoid confrontation, and to improve their own job security.[22]

(What they adamantly do not want, said Freeman when we met in his office at the National Bureau of Economic Research in Cambridge, is a return to the near-ritualized combat of so many union-versus-management relationships.)

A second possible trajectory is that a campaign for the introduction of guaranteed employment policies might arise out of economic institutions and community structures much larger than individual companies or organized groups of workers, whether in unions or not. One example of this is the Mondragon cooperative in the Basque region of Spain—that nation's twelfth-largest commercial enterprise consisting of banks, manufacturing companies, and retail corporations—which has a form of guaranteed employment operating across its diverse and sophisticated network of employers. In the United States, there are initiatives (albeit on a much smaller scale than the Mondragon) that share similar goals through the establishment of broad-based coalitions of private and public organizations, such as the Chicago Manufacturing Renaissance Council.

Richard Trumka, the incoming president of the AFL-CIO at the time we spoke in the summer of 2009, believed that only a systemic change in national labor policy at the highest levels could encourage the spread of no-layoff initiatives. "This needs to be institutionalized and sustained on a much larger scale [than trying to support individual companies with enlightened CEOs]," he told me, "because many times, when these leaders go, their program goes as well." Trumka argued that building support for a wider embrace of no-layoff policies would help enhance the United States' ability to compete internationally: "Look at Denmark. They have essentially a national no-layoff policy. If an individual company has to cut back, the government offers a bridge salary and retrains people because they see that as necessary for the country to succeed."[23]

But given where history and the state of the American economy find us right now, it seems fair to suggest that these possible approaches might require a very long time to generate the significant improvements in job security that are so urgently needed by many Americans. Ultimately, the spotlight keeps returning to the responsibility of corporate leaders and the choices they make.

James F. Lincoln, in his day, was well aware of the immense difficulties of creating or transforming a business in ways that challenged conventional management thinking. He too emphasized the paramount need for a business leader to forge a binding consensus among his senior managers long before any new policy was formally adopted. Leadership was about more than simply advocating new ideas such as guaranteed employment or an advisory board or a merit-based bonus system, Lincoln argued, regardless of their alleged virtues. Effective leadership demanded having a strategy to build trust among employees that they would be protected during any transition process; it's called "buy-in" these days. Over and over, Lincoln came back to the belief that if the American workplace was going to be made a more productive place—for the benefit of companies, their employees, and society at large—it was CEOs who were "on the spot."[24]

CAN CEOS BE ENCOURAGED TO CONSIDER ALTERNATIVES TO LAYOFFS?

Pose this question to many experts in management and labor economics, and their answers will depress you. The people who have spent years studying why America's business leaders have so forcefully resisted embracing the *high performance workplace* (with its fundamental respect for the economic value of employees) seem to end up banging their heads against walls. Take Jeffrey Pfeffer of Stanford University's School of Business, one of the country's most respected experts on management: "We are getting nowhere. I think frankly that many U.S. managers don't think. Their brains are not engaged."[25]

There is also a goodly dose of testosterone involved here. Making a tough decision like ordering a layoff has long been regarded in the male-dominated upper echelons of American management as proof that a CEO "has what it takes" to be successful. This is a huge problem for every person in the country—in good times, let alone now, in the midst of a deep recession—and it bodes ill for the future. Waiting for the leaders of corporate America to voluntarily adopt the kinds of management structures that a few companies such as Lincoln Electric, Hypertherm, and Xilinx have proved can protect people as well as profits is not an effective strategy. They need a nudge in the right direction. Let me suggest some possibilities to get them started down the right road.

Education and Awareness. As discussed in Chapter 6, very few business executives are aware that there are viable options to the practice of "layoffs as normal" in the modern American economy. Where do they *not* learn that? At the nation's business schools, where the reading of one famous case study on a little-known welding company understandably has, at best, scant impact. Like it or not, the MBA degree has become a required admission ticket for corporate leadership and power in the United States. So given that a business education is an important force in shaping the attitudes of future business leaders, the challenge becomes one of introducing many more students to the idea that greater employment stability does not necessarily stand in the way of greater corporate profits. In fact, it might even enhance the bottom line in some situations. Given the terrifying tsunami of layoffs since this latest recession began, now more than ever, it is the responsibility of business educators to train their students to embrace a wider view of what are the responsibilities of a corporation in this society.

An education initiative need not be confined to business schools, however. The United States is a country of huge charitable foundations that spend hundreds of millions of dollars each year to fund research and public education programs on important economic and social issues. Harnessing the intellectual resources and outreach skills of these organizations could do much to build a wider public appreciation for the competitive economic advantage of truly valuing a company's workforce by making sure employees stay on the job even when the going gets tough. Jack Litzenberg, the senior staff member of the Charles Stewart Mott Foundation's program on economic opportunity, had never heard of Lincoln Electric's fascinating history, but its lessons were instantly clear to him: "Our whole purpose is to support job retention and wage advancement, and if this isn't job retention, then I wouldn't know what that is."[26] The challenge, he says, is finding effective ways to encourage CEOs to explore guaranteed employment's potential advantages.

Many foundations fund their research programs through universities and, including some like Mott, through graduate business schools. Why shouldn't foundations and other organizations that are interested in exploring the admittedly difficult challenges of guaranteed employment policies create financial support for business school professors and their students to research these concepts? Litzenberg raised the idea of foundations like his collaborating with individual businesses in different regions of the country to determine how a no-layoff program might benefit their work practices.

There is nothing like the glare of good publicity to push an issue onto the front burner of the national agenda, and nothing generates good publicity like awards. In recent years, "best of" lists have become increasingly popular in the media, including the Great Place to Work Institute's annual rankings and *Working Mother* magazine's publication of "100 Best Companies for Working

Moms." To date, neither has included specific measurements of steady work. Is it too much to dream, for example, that Forbes's "400 Best Big Companies in America" list—where rankings are now based on sales and earnings growth, debt to total capital, earnings outlook, and stock-market returns—might someday include a measure of employment stability as an important criterion to determine its annual winners?

Since any list of potential candidates with real no-layoff policies would be embarrassingly short, more inclusive criteria for comparing companies on such a ranking might include "average tenure of employees" or "lowest layoff rate." Admittedly, *longer employment* is not as impressive sounding as *guaranteed employment*, but (to paraphrase Voltaire in the extreme vernacular) there is little purpose in making the *ideal* into the enemy of the merely *better*, given the current unacceptably high unemployment rates.

Change on Wall Street? As anyone who has made it this far through this book will know, there is a tremendous resistance on Wall Street (used as shorthand for the broad world of private investment in America) toward any firm-level initiatives to reorganize the workplace that could pose a short-term risk to a rise in the price of that company's stock. Every CEO of every public company in America understands this, even as some bemoan the fact in private.

The quarterly report fixation—aided and abetted in recent years by a banking and investment system that relies on mathematical models constructed out of sand—is now coming under attack, in the wake of the recession and its painful effects. Yet despite the public pillorying of CEOs from major financial corporations such as Lehman Brothers and AIG, the attack is largely still at the rhetorical stage. Substantially altering the value system of those working on Wall Street—if a broad consensus develops that it is a desirable goal—will take time.

Joe Keefe is the CEO of Pax World Investments, a leading socially responsible mutual fund company. Widely acknowledged as an expert on corporate ethics, Keefe said that the only way to convince the current generation of analysts and traders of the potential strengths of a guaranteed employment policy is to continue to make the strongest possible business case for the idea. Unfortunately, given that so many investment professionals "have been badly burned with an economy down the tank," Keefe warned that in the short term, the best that can be hoped for is that "this might be a teaching moment on issues like these."[27]

Socially responsible investing (through the pooling of money in mutual funds) holds out one possible strategy to put some new pressures on companies and their CEOs to think more carefully about how employees are treated before layoffs loom. These funds currently use criteria such as environmental footprint and treatment of minorities to guide their investment decisions. Using indicators to compare workplace stability or job tenure seems a logical extension. The ravages inflicted by this recession may also result in many more Americans who are worried about their shrunken 401(k)s and IRAs bluntly ordering their financial advisers to get serious about adopting a sensible and cautious long-term planning perspective with the hard-earned life savings placed in their care. Just don't hold your breath, however, waiting for a burst of enlightenment among those on Wall Street that might render stockbrokers and investment analysts more receptive to a (rogue) CEO's musing about putting his employees on an equal par with shareholders.

Can Government Play a Role? You can almost feel pulse rates soaring on cue in corporate boardrooms, conservative political think tanks, and coffee shops across the country when this question is asked. So let me make two points quickly before anyone calls the paramedics.

First, the issue here is not whether any level of government in the United States should force American business executives to adopt some form of a no-layoff policy. The question is whether governments might feel that encouraging a CEO voluntarily to explore strategies to keep American citizens at their jobs longer, while ensuring that her company remains profitable, is a legitimate use of public policy. Washington already plays a large role in shaping the American workplace through OSHA, the EEOC, and the Wage and Hour Administration. Every state has its own labor regulations. For example, there are strict legal limits on what larger American employers can and cannot do when they decide to lay off workers, through the 1988 WARN act.[28] Suggesting that government might want to proactively encourage companies to avoid layoffs—while at the same time keeping the bottom line healthy—hardly seems like an invitation to the abuse of legislative power.

Second, since the recession began in 2008, two administrations— one Republican, one Democratic—have created, through the use of almost incomprehensively large amounts of taxpayers' money, the largest job-creation program since the Great Depression. Surely, if the full force of government is being marshaled to dramatically increase employment across the country, it is not a radical proposal to suggest that some additional effort be devoted to encouraging (and then checking) that employers who receive "stimulus money" are doing their best to ensure that those jobs last.

There are many ways in which federal and state governments might play a role in this process. Start by increasing both corporate and public awareness of management concepts such as guaranteed employment, said MIT's Thom Kochan, one of the leading academic experts on work in America. Kochan and a number of colleagues have suggested the creation of a National Workplace Advisory Council in which public funds are invested to bring together representatives from government, business, labor, and academe to explore innovative workplace practices.[29] The organization could then also serve as both a clearinghouse and a sponsor of further research.

One of the first initiatives taken by Vice President Joe Biden when the Obama administration took over in January 2009 was to set up the White House Task Force on Middle-Class Working Families, which brings together under his leadership the secretaries of labor, health and human services, education, treasury, commerce, housing and urban development, transportation, and agriculture.[30] The task force's mandate is to raise the living standards of middle-class working families in America. The vice president said his goal is to "get the middle class—the backbone of this country—up and running again." One effective and entirely appropriate approach to help reach that goal would be for Biden's task force to support and then publicize research on management systems that avoid layoffs by creating longer-lasting jobs inside financially healthy companies.

Throughout federal and state governments, there are currently a myriad of programs to support workplace training for both managers and employees, especially in the tens of thousands of small businesses across the United States. The history of guaranteed employment so briefly covered here suggests that the best chance for the successful adoption of no-layoff programs, whether as a simple goal or a formal promise, seems to be in smaller start-up companies. Using government training resources to ensure that more small business owners and managers—who are already the targeted customers for these training programs—are introduced to the potential advantages of these innovative policies would seem a wise investment.

The question of whether and how governments might provide direct financial incentives to encourage the adoption of a no-layoff goal or policy is complex and admittedly fraught with the potential for controversy and abuse.[31] Linda Barrington, managing director of human capital at the Conference Board, a forecasting and research organization supported by the biggest corporations in the country, suggested two problems with the creation of government financial incentives to nurture a concept such as a no-layoff philosophy.[32] First is a concern about the unintended consequences of encouraging a policy initiative for American business for which business itself is not clamoring. Second, she suggested that it is nowhere near certain that financial incentives would work, given the immense challenges of changing contemporary business cultures.

Yet the idea of government employing financial incentives to encourage innovative workplace practices in American industry is not new (see Chapter 4). Consider two further possible ways in which government might encourage CEOs to avoid layoffs. Both are inspired by recent proposals made by others.

In 2000, the Russell Sage Foundation published a report on the future of work in America authored by William Niskanen (chairman of President Reagan's Council of Economic Advisors), Rebecca Blank (currently undersecretary for economics affairs in the Department of Commerce), David Ellwood (currently the dean of Harvard University's Kennedy School of Government), and other distinguished experts.[33] One of the key concerns in the report—back then, as now—was the failure of the business community to adopt *high performance workplace* strategies. As an incentive to change this, the authors proposed business-tax reductions (through lower rates or increased credits) based on the adoption of multiple elements of the high performance methods: for example, high annual expenditures on training, a majority of employees organized into self-managed work teams, and so forth. Why not, then, expand their list of desired workplace practices to include some measure of "significantly better-than-average" employee tenure or "lower-than-average" involuntary departure rate (that is, fewer firings and layoffs)?

In 2007, Representative Jan Shakowsky (D-IL) and six fellow Democrats introduced what they called the Patriot Corporation Act into the House, while three Democratic senators, including Barack Obama, introduced a similar bill, titled the Patriot Employer Act, in the Senate. Both of these pieces of legislation proposed that American companies that met a set of "patriotic" criteria would receive preferential treatment in the awarding of contracts with the federal government—all other things being equal—as well as a corporate-tax reduction of up to 5 percent. The bills (Shakowsky reintroduced hers again in 2009) understandably sparked intense debate about the dangers of protectionism, given one key stipulation that a so-called patriot corporation must conduct 90 percent of its business in America. (Another criterion limited the pay of a patriotic corporation's CEO to just one hundred times that of its average worker—that's surely a less contentious litmus test!)

But using this kind of inducement as a model, why not try the following: Dump the controversial limitations on trade, introduce procedures to compare companies bidding for government contracts on the basis of how often they purge their employees through layoffs (or some other quantifiable measure of workforce stability), extend preferential treatment on that basis alone—and only then call the winner "patriotic"? Such a bill's chances of being passed by Congress—especially after this brutal recession—will almost assuredly be much greater. Companies would profit. And employees would benefit. In other words, government can encourage, and need not force, the adoption of improvements in the workplace that voters regard as important.

The notion that our economic system exists in a state of nature is absurd. As Joe Keefe, the CEO of Pax World, reminded me: "Markets were constituted by English common law. They

required antitrust acts, SEC acts in the 1930s and 1940s, and because markets are created by governments, governments end up
regulating markets. Markets have always run based on public
policy incentives to try to affect behavior. We are going to have
to accept the role of public policy in getting us to where we need
to go."

Trying to minimize the number of working Americans who
are laid off unnecessarily each year because too many CEOs believe they simply have no option *is* where the country needs to go.
The alternative—an economy that continues to tolerate the waste
of productive energy when large numbers of people are laid off
and the human pain suffered when those lives are destroyed—
is simply unacceptable.

A FINAL LOOK BACK—AND FORWARD, TO THE FUTURE

Let me be clear about what Lincoln Electric's century-long experience does—and does not—tell us about the possible future of
work in the United States.

The business model that Lincoln Electric has built over the
past 114 years has proven phenomenally successful, by any measure used to gauge success in the American economy. Since the
1930s, the company has retained its position as the largest manufacturer of welding equipment in the world. The company now
has production facilities in twenty countries and has been expanding its global footprint even during this punishing recession.
Since becoming a publicly traded corporation in 1995, the company has earned an excellent reputation on Wall Street for consistently solid performance due to the skill of its senior
management team. It has kept open, and even expanded, its main
production base in Cleveland while dozens of other large local
employers have closed up shop and moved away, with devastat-

ing consequences. Finally, for at least six decades, the company has honored a promise to its American employees never to lay them off for economic reasons.

Yet Lincoln Electric's way of organizing its employees is not being held up here as *the* right model for any other company in the United States to emulate. The peculiarities of its own history in Cleveland; the particular demands of technological exploration and manufacturing excellence in the welding industry; the unusual mix of complementary workplace policies, including guaranteed employment, piecework, the Advisory Board, and the merit-based bonus; its financial discipline—it is possible that all these elements create a unique business culture that cannot be replicated.

But is there any rational upside to surrendering to that possibility, given the human pain suffered by so many people who have lost their jobs in the latest downturn? Dismissing Lincoln Electric as an anomaly is nothing but an easy rationalization for continuing business—and layoffs—as usual. If Lincoln Electric can make guaranteed employment work, while achieving steady profits for the company and its shareholders and sustaining the otherwise decimated local community tax base, don't other employers have a social responsibility at least to try to understand how the policy operates and then to try in their own fashion to travel the same road?

The history of Lincoln Electric and the few others over the past century who have experimented with no-layoff policies does suggest that guaranteed employment may be easier to develop as part of the business plan of a start-up company than by attempting to introduce the idea into an existing business, especially a large publicly owned corporation. Consider the auto industry, which once prided itself on offering such steady employment to American workers that for more than three decades, it led the way in creating a strong middle class in America. It's hard to imagine this now beaten-down industry having the vision, let alone taking the initiative, to recapture its past leadership role in this area.

That said, if a "religious conversion" to guaranteed employment—as suggested by James F. Lincoln—seems a somewhat remote possibility for most established Fortune 500 companies, there are still many midsize businesses in the United States in which a visionary CEO could step up to the plate to commit her organization to a new and better relationship with its employees.

But the good news is that the United States is a land of start-ups; nearly a million new companies with employees (i.e., not one-person businesses) open their doors every year.[34] That's nearly a million new workplaces, filled with entrepreneurial enthusiasm, where a discussion of a no-layoff policy might begin early on *if* more employers knew what a few companies such as Lincoln Electric had achieved before them.

What is fascinating about Lincoln Electric—and what might, I hope, serve as an inspiration for some small company just starting out—is that after one hundred years as a private business, Lincoln Electric was able to make the transition to become a public corporation, issuing shares and coping with all the complexities of external scrutiny while, to this point in time, still largely living up to the principles of its founders and its employees. The current CEO, John Stropki, like most employees at Lincoln Electric, seems to take this legacy almost for granted, but it remains an impressive achievement for the people who have built the firm over the past century.

> We believe that guaranteed employment is good for *all* of our stakeholders—shareholders, customers, and employees. I think that is very important in understanding why we work so hard in trying to do the things we do. There are a lot of policies

which you could implement, such as layoffs, terminations, all the things you hear about, which are good for one or another of those constituencies, but generally not good for all three at the same time.

   If we are proven to be right and can go through these very troubling times while keeping our core people energized and committed to the company, as we have done many times before, it is pretty easy to see how our shareholders and customers will benefit from that.[35]

Lincoln Electric's history also serves as a reminder of the substantial impact every business has on the community beyond its doors. Most of us instinctively know what steady work means to ourselves and our families. We sometimes forget what it means to the places where we live, perhaps because one out of eight Americans moves every year.[36] Paul Oyaski was raised in Euclid, the industrial suburb of Cleveland where Lincoln Electric has been located since 1951. A lawyer, he later served as mayor of Euclid and is now director of development for Cuyahoga County, which holds Greater Cleveland within its boundaries. Oyaski has watched the region—his home—shrink from 1.7 million people in 1970 to less than 1.3 million in 2008.[37]

   When I graduated from high school in 1970, there were six large plants, and the city was booming. They generated disposable income that fueled retail and the taxes to build infrastructure. It was by degrees a much stronger community for families and the tax base. The only one still here now is the Lincoln plant because of their system. TRW abandoned us. Addressograph-MultiGraph went bankrupt. Chase Brass had horrible strikes. Euclid Road moved their plant to Canada. GM's Fisher Body moved to Mexico. So God save Lincoln Electric, because now, there is nothing even close.[38]

Finally, I believe Lincoln Electric's success can serve as a symbol of hope at a time when the American economy doesn't seem to be working well for many citizens and their communities. It is easy to be depressed by the events of the past couple of years, even though this recession, like every recession, was a long time in the making and there is a lot of blame to be widely shared. One of the worst outcomes has been the growth of widespread cynicism about the business world as a whole and its leaders in particular. In the course of writing this book, I have found it continually amazing—and sad—that so many people find the very idea of a modern successful company that tries so hard to protect its workers to be a novelty. Their experiences in the world of work— whether in manufacturing, the service industries, or high-tech—simply do not allow them to conceive of a no-layoff goal, let alone a promise, as a realistic option for the modern age. Ray Hogler, a respected scholar of labor history at Colorado State University, isn't surprised:

> What happened to the idea of a guaranteed employment promise like Lincoln's, which was so popular in the 1930s, is what happened to democracy in America. We have stopped thinking about a democracy as a country of mutual obligations and reciprocal relations with each other, and we started thinking about it in terms of individuals amassing wealth. There are a lot of people using the Milton Friedman model that says this is all good for corporations, and just let employees look out for themselves. The important point is that the corporate titans of the "Gilded Age" were in fact the ones who linked their economic activities with ideals of democracy and a measure of equality. We have drifted so far away from that concept—even though the corporate marketing mavens pay lip service to social responsibility—that a policy of guaranteed employment like Lincoln Electric's never pops up on the radar.[39]

A Greek chorus of CEOs chanting "I have no option" as they announce layoff after layoff is really an admission of failure. With millions of Americans forced out of their jobs over the past several years, there is simply no excuse for continuing to accept failure as normal. It doesn't have to be that way.

Lincoln Electric offers proof that if a company truly values its employees, works to instill trust in the workplace, and commits itself to ensuring the long-term financial stability of those workers, then that company can still thrive, innovate, and survive the perpetual boom and bust cycles of a capitalist economy. It may even do so better than its competitors.

The story of manufacturing in America need not go the way of the dinosaur. Embracing flexibility and trust in the workplace is difficult work, not only for management but also for employees, and the way toward a brighter, more secure economic future is not easy. The long and particular road that Lincoln Electric has traveled is not for everyone. But it is one that must be considered. This country desperately needs more businesses to decisively set foot on a similar journey if it is ever to aspire to rebuild the social stability and widespread prosperity that have made America great.

ACKNOWLEDGMENTS

SPARK WAS BORN in the summer of 1996 while my wife and I were on holiday in Maine. One noon hour, tuning in to the local NPR station as a fog horn boomed in the distance, we stumbled on Don Hastings, the CEO and chairman of Lincoln Electric, speaking about his company's commitment to retain its workers in hard times. We were inspired to hear him excoriate the culture of layoffs that seemed to have settled over corporate North America, and when I headed back to work with the Canadian Broadcasting Corporation, I called him.

In the thirteen years since — Don retired in 1997 — we have spent many hours talking about the company that was his life for forty-five years. When I raised the idea of writing a book about Lincoln Electric, Don contacted Cleveland on my behalf and later walked me into his old boardroom, where I presented my proposal to John Stropki and his executive team. I am very grateful for Don's support, and I hope I have done his ideas justice.

John Stropki said no the first time. But the rejection was delivered with grace and politeness, and so I waited, periodically bombarding him with what I was learning about the history of guaranteed employment policies. A year later, John said yes. From then on, he provided me with virtually unlimited access to

employees at every level and to every corner of the Cleveland facilities. During the trying times of the past two years, John kept
the doors open. I trust he's not second-guessing that decision. I'm
completely in his debt for the green light.

Carol Skoglund, director of communications, and Roy Mor-
row, director of corporate relations, coordinated my endless in-
trusions, personal and electronic, with great patience and humor.

Thank you to the men and women of Lincoln Electric—current and former employees—who spent hours talking about their
work and how guaranteed employment makes a difference to
their families and their communities. They invited me into their
homes and family picnics across Cleveland. I hope I've captured
their respect for this unusual employer. If I have missed anyone,
I apologize: Chris Bailey, George Blankenship, Gabriel Bruno,
Bruce Cable, Terry Dattilio, Roger DuBose, Gretchen Farrell,
Jon Glick, Jeff Iannini, Erin Justice, John Konich, Damian
Kotecki, Doug Lance, Joe and Susan Lynne Latessa, Joe and
Melissa Latessa, Michael and Heidi Latessa, Emma Lincoln, Bob
and Sandra Maffit, Carl Scott Maffit, James and Teffin Maffit,
James Peter Maffit, Tom Matthews, Bart McKinney, Yonatan
Necoechea, Ron Nelson, Ed and Peggy Pipik, Jessica Pitino,
Dwight Rorabaugh, Richard Sabo, Bill Sass, Lee Seufer, Richard
Siktberg, Robert Siktberg, Steve Simcak, Jeff Traynor, Fred and
Helen Wells, Mark and Rebecca Wells, Ted Willis, Chester
Woodman, and Tony Zalar.

Joseph Doria, president of Lincoln Canada, and Michael
Vuchnich, who's held a number of senior positions in Toronto,
kept me plugged in to the firm's operations in my homeland.
Thanks to Bob Stevens, who let me bother him on the assembly
line in Toronto in 1996 and was so patient again in 2006.

In Cleveland, Dr. Virginia Dawson shared the files she built
while writing a corporate history of the company in the mid-
1990s. John Grabowski, director of research at the Western Re-

serve Historical Society, introduced me to the collection's incredible archival resources.

While this book was a labor of love for me, it probably wasn't as much fun for my personal Advisory Board, who were endlessly peppered with questions and rough drafts, regardless of the demands of their own busy lives. I first met Gordon Betcherman (formerly with the World Bank in Washington, now teaching international economics at the University of Ottawa) when I produced a radio documentary on the company in 1996. Gordon speaks economics-in-English, a rarity, and we became close friends as a result. Also in Ottawa, Bill Breen challenged me to stop talking about the company and write a book. A former CEO of several Canadian-based high-tech firms, Bill helped me understand what it's like to sit in the executive office and make tough decisions. Till von Wachter (Columbia University) and Anil Verma (Rotman School of Management at the University of Toronto), both prominent labor economists, were always eager to share their expertise. Linda Tarr-Whelan (Beaufort, South Carolina) is one of the most insightful people I know about American politics and social change; she founded the Center for Policy Alternatives in Washington and helped me think about the big picture with this story. Finally, Ted Jackson (associate dean in the Faculty of Public Affairs at Carleton University in Ottawa) and Sean Moore (widely regarded as one of Canada's leading experts on public policy) provided support and intellectual stimulation with their smarts, their challenging questions, Ted's puns, and their enduring friendship.

At Harvard Business School, Norman Berg, professor emeritus and the author of the classic 1975 case study, shared his fascination with Lincoln Electric. Associate Professor Jordan Siegel, who wrote follow-up studies in 2006 and 2007, convinced Jim Aisner, director of HBS Media Relations, that the case's great popularity deserved a closer look. Their cooperation was vital.

Many experts in labor economics and industrial relations shared their insights with me. Particular thanks to Thom Kochan (codirector, Institute for Work and Employment Research at MIT's Sloan School of Management), James Rebitzer (chair of the Economics Department, Weatherhead School of Management/Case Western Reserve University), and Ray Holger (professor of management and law, Colorado State University). Thanks also to George Baker (Harvard Business School), Jennie Brand (University of California–Davis), Peter Cappelli (the Wharton School, University of Pennsylvania), Thomas DeLong (Harvard Business School), Thomas Eagar (Materials Science and Engineering, MIT), Henry Farber (Economics and Industrial Relations, Princeton University), Richard Freeman (Harvard University), Robert Gibbons (MIT Sloan School of Management), Kevin Hallock (Cornell University), Bruce Kaufman (George State University), Peter Kuhn (University of California–Santa Barbara), John McCracken (University of Texas–Dallas), Jeffrey Pfeffer (Graduate School of Business, Stanford University), Craig Rennie (Sam Walton College of Business, University of Arkansas), John Roberts (Graduate School of Business, Stanford University), Jesper Sorensen (Graduate School of Business, Stanford University), and Ann Huff Stevens (University of California–Davis).

Wim Roelandts (former CEO and chairman of Xilinx) and Dick Couch (founder and president of Hypertherm) spent many hours explaining their challenges in trying to avoid layoffs.

I have been a journalist with the Canadian Broadcasting Corporation (CBC Radio) since 1982, an incredible experience that provided me the opportunity to work and live around the world. My thanks to Jamie Purdon, director of news gathering, for letting me pursue my interests with this book.

At PublicAffairs in New York, Clive Priddle and Niki Papadopoulos, my editors, and Annette Wenda, my copy editor, deserve more credit than you can imagine for rendering the book into what I hope readers find to be a very good story about a very smart idea. My sincere thanks to Clive for giving me the opportunity to tell it.

My agent, Denise Bukowski of the Bukowski Agency in Toronto, saw the potential in this story from the very start. Thank you for your dogged enthusiasm and determination and for your sage advice about the publishing world.

My mother, Marjorie, who is now ninety-three, will enjoy reading the book, although woe to me if she finds a dangling participle. Her unflagging encouragement over so many decades of my life has been amazing. My father, Phillip, was a labor economist who studied under Joseph Schumpeter (the author of the phrase "creative destruction") and Max Weber at Heidelberg University just after World War I. Somewhere, I hope he enjoys this small attempt to follow in his shoes.

Finally, there never would—or could—have been a book without the incredible support of my wife, Elizabeth McAllister, who was with me when we first heard that radio broadcast. She, more than anyone else, endured the insecurities (another word, dear?) of a first-time author. A widely respected expert in the world of international development, she has helped me to understand how difficult it can be to buck the conventional wisdom of large bureaucracies with unusual ideas such as guaranteed employment, but also how important it is to try. We have traveled the world together for nearly thirty years—I usually follow—and it still is a wonderful trip. Thank you.

NOTES

CHAPTER ONE

1. Raymond Moley, *The American Century of John C. Lincoln* (New York: Duell, Sloan, and Pearce, 1962), 41. For biographical information on both John and James Lincoln, I've drawn extensively on this reference and from the comprehensive official company history, *Lincoln Electric: A History* by Virginia Dawson (Cleveland: Lincoln Electric, 1999). *Spark* is not a book about Lincoln Electric's groundbreaking track record as the developer of leading-edge arc-welding technology over the past century. Suffice it to say that without that legacy, good management of its employees wouldn't have meant very much. Much of that story is told in Dawson's fascinating book.

2. Dawson, *Lincoln Electric: A History*, 16.

3. Moley, *American Century of John C. Lincoln*, 35.

4. Ibid., 60.

5. See J. Norberto Pires et al., *Welding Robots: Technology, Systems Issues, and Applications* (London: Springer-Verlag, 2006), 7–8.

6. F. E. Denton, "The City of Cleveland," in *Prospectus of the National Convention, League of Republican Clubs, Cleveland, June 19, 20, 21, 1895* (Cleveland: Cleveland Printing and Publishing, 1895), 52, available at http://www.archive.org/stream/prospectusofnatioonatirich/prospectusof natioonatirich_djvu.txt (accessed June 9, 2009).

7. Naomi Lamoureux and Margaret Levenstein, "The Decline of an Innovative Region: Cleveland, Ohio, in the Twentieth Century" (paper prepared for the annual meeting of the American History Association), September 12, 2008.

8. Rick Fantasia and Kim Voss, *Hard Work: Remaking the American Labor Movement* (Berkeley and Los Angeles: University of California Press, 2004), 34–77.

9. Frederick Winslow Taylor, *The Principles of Scientific Management* (Mineola, NY: Dover Publications, 1998), 1.

10. Andrea Tone, *The Business of Benevolence* (Ithaca: Cornell University Press, 1997), 91.

11. Theodore Roosevelt, State of the Union address (December 3, 1901), available at http://www.theodore-roosevelt.com/sotu1.html (accessed June 9, 2009).

12. John Lincoln remained head of the company for many years, as president and, later, as chairman. He continued to play a significant role in developing technology that helped the company grow and maintain its leadership position. But increasingly, John left the running of the firm and the planning for its future in the hands of his younger brother, James. The elder Lincoln died in 1959.

13. Donald Hastings, interview with author, Cleveland, June 16, 2008.

14. Bob Maffit, interview with author, Cleveland, June 16, 2008.

15. Moley, *American Century of John C. Lincoln*, 19.

16. John C. Lincoln, *Christ's Object in Life* (New York: Henry George School of Social Science, 1948), v (with thanks to the Robert Schalkenbach Foundation, New York, http://www.schalkenbach.org/); James F. Lincoln, *A New Approach to Industrial Economics* (New York: Devin-Adair, 1961), 22, 88.

17. I have relied heavily on Sanford M. Jacoby's exhaustively researched *Modern Manors: Welfare Capitalism Since the New Deal* (Princeton: Princeton University Press, 1997) for background information on this historical period as well as Tone, *The Business of Benevolence*.

18. David Brody, "The Rise and Decline of Welfare Capitalism," in *Workers in Industrial America: Essays on the Twentieth Century Struggle*, 2nd ed. (New York: Oxford University Press, 1993).

19. Lizabeth Cohen, *Making a New Deal: Industrial Workers in Chicago, 1919–1939* (New York: Cambridge University Press, 1990), 163.

20. Tone, *The Business of Benevolence*, 82.

21. For a discussion of employee representation plans, see, among others, Raymond L. Hogler, "Exclusive Representation and the Wagner Act: The Structure of Federal Collective Bargaining Law," *Labor Law Journal* (Fall 2007): 157–182; and Raymond Hogler, Bruce Kaufmann, and Daphne Taras, *Nonunion Employee Representation: History, Contemporary Practice, and Policy* (New York: M. E. Sharpe, 2000).

22. Tone, *The Business of Benevolence*, 99–139.

23. John Commons, *Industrial Government* (New York: Macmillan, 1921), 263, available at http://ia311306.us.archive.org/2/items/industrialgovern00comm/industrialgovern00comm.pdf (accessed June 9, 2009).

24. Julius Rosenwald, quoted in Jacoby, *Modern Manors*, 26.

25. Chiaki Moriguchi, "Did American Welfare Capitalists Breach Their Implicit Contracts? Preliminary Findings from Company-Level Data, 1920–1940," NBER Working Paper Series, Working Paper 9868, July 2003, 16–28.

26. J. F. Lincoln, *New Approach to Industrial Economics*, 8.

27. James F. Lincoln, *Lincoln's Incentive System* (New York: McGraw-Hill, 1946), 29; James F. Lincoln, *What Makes Workers Work*, speech delivered to the Canadian Club of Toronto, published in pamphlet form (Fair Lawn, NJ: Liberty Library, 1947), 28.

CHAPTER TWO

1. Jacoby, *Modern Manors*, 74, 101 (see chap. 1, n. 17).

2. Tone, "Benefits for Breadwinners," chap. 7 of *The Business of Benevolence*, 226–244 (see chap. 1, n. 10).

3. The sale of "consumables" normally constitutes 55–60 percent of average annual sales revenue for Lincoln Electric. In the first half of 2009, as customers cut back on capital expenses, it had increased to more than 66 percent.

4. Dawson, *Lincoln Electric: A History*, 63 (see chap. 1, n. 1).

5. See, for example, "Address Before the Federal Council of Churches of Christ in America," December 6, 1933.

6. The idea of sharing company profits with employees, a common policy of many welfare-capitalist firms at that time, had actually been tried once before at Lincoln Electric. Soon after James took over from his brother in 1914, he had introduced an annual profit-sharing bonus that paid employees roughly 3 to 4 percent of their annual earnings. But he canceled the plan after only a few years when he realized it did nothing to increase productivity. The reason, Lincoln believed, was that the bonus was too small to really matter to the workers, and as a result, it was regarded as little more than a paternalistic gesture, like the proverbial frozen turkey given away just before Christmas. "It is not given as a result of good work," he wrote. "It is only a tip to all, no matter what their efficiency. In general, few worthwhile people respond enthusiastically to a tip" (*Lincoln's Incentive System*, 65 [see chap. 1, n. 27]).

7. House of Representatives, Committee on Naval Affairs, "Investigation of the Naval Defense Program: Hearing Testimony of James F. Lincoln," 77th Cong., 2nd sess., May 27, 1942, 4:906–930.

8. "The Congress: Again, NLRB," *Time*, March 18, 1940; House of Representatives, Committee on Naval Affairs, "Investigation of the Naval Defense Program," 919.

9. House of Representatives, Committee on Naval Affairs, "Investigation of the Naval Defense Program," 918.

10. Dawson, *Lincoln Electric: A History*, 63.

11. House of Representatives, Committee on Naval Affairs, "Investigation of the Naval Defense Program," 918.

12. J. F. Lincoln, *Lincoln's Incentive System*, 117–118.

13. Quoted in Dawson, *Lincoln Electric: A History*, 34. Because senior executives now travel frequently to visit the company's international operations, Advisory Board meetings are sometimes held up to a month apart.

14. Ibid., 38.

15. See also Thomas W. Gerdel, "Lincoln Electric Experiences Season of Worker Discontent," *Cleveland Plain Dealer*, December 10, 1995.

16. Dwight Rorabaugh, interview with author, Lincoln Electric, September 10, 2008.

17. J. F. Lincoln, *Lincoln's Incentive System*, 146.

18. James F. Lincoln, "The Lincoln Electric Company Incentive Plan," in *Industrial Engineering for Better Production*, Production Series 153 (New York: American Management Association, 1944), 36 (courtesy of the Western Reserve Historical Society in Cleveland, hereafter cited as WRHS).

19. J. F. Lincoln, *A New Approach to Industrial Economics*, 92 (see chap. 1, n. 16). According to information supplied by the company, the highest-paid pieceworker at Lincoln Electric in 2007 earned $151,000 (including the annual profit-sharing bonus).

20. Edward P. Lazear, "Performance Pay and Productivity," *American Economic Review* 90, no. 5 (December 2000): 1358.

21. Ibid.

22. Lincoln Electric, *Employee's Handbook*, 17.

23. Melissa Latessa, interview with author, Lincoln Electric, September 11, 2008.

24. Once when I was interviewing workers in Lincoln Electric's factory in Toronto, Bob Stevens, a final inspector on the line, terminated my questioning after about fifteen minutes with a quick glance at his watch and a grunt that I now owed him roughly $10. Do the math: $40 an hour, with a fifty-hour week, translates into roughly $100,000 a year. He then joked, I think, that I didn't have to pay him the $10.

25. Doug Lance, interview with author, Lincoln Electric, September 11, 2008.

26. A "multiplier factor" that applies to the piece-rate system as a whole is regularly adjusted to account for changes in the local cost of living. See Joseph Maciariello, *Lasting Value: Lessons from a Century of Agility at Lincoln Electric* (New York: John Wiley and Sons, 2000), 50.

27. Jeff Iannini, interview with author, Lincoln Electric, September 5, 2008.

28. Steve Simcak, telephone interview with author, January 18, 2008.

29. Joe Latessa Sr., interview with author, Cleveland, June 15, 2008.

30. Robert Clapp, interview with author, Cleveland, August 23, 2008.

31. Raymond Hogler, telephone interview with author, August 15, 2008.

32. J. F. Lincoln, "Lincoln Electric Company Incentive Plan," 37; James F. Lincoln, *Incentive Management* (Cleveland: Lincoln Electric, 1951), 111.

33. Fred Wells, interview with author, Painesville, OH, September 4, 2008.

34. Joe Latessa Jr., telephone interview with author, August 14, 2008.

35. Yonatan Necoechea, interview with author, Lincoln Electric, September 9, 2008.

36. Michael Jensen, *Foundations of Organizational Strategy* (New York: Wiley, 1998), 208, quoted in Maciariello, *Lasting Value*, 57.

37. Michael Latessa, interview with author, Lincoln Electric, September 5, 2008.

38. Richard Siktberg, telephone interview with author, January 19, 2008.

39. John Konich, telephone interview with author, February 9, 2008.

40. Bill Sass, interview with author, Madison, OH, September 12, 2008.

41. Tony Zalar, interview with author, Lincoln Electric, September 13, 2008.

42. James F. Lincoln, "An Open Letter to President Truman," *Industrial Engineering Digest* (Chicago), January 1946, WRHS.

CHAPTER THREE

1. Lee Seufer, interview with author, Lincoln Electric, September 8, 2008.

2. For example, since 1990, Lincoln Electric has collaborated with FANUC, the Japanese firm widely regarded as the world's leading manufacturer of industrial robots, to produce a line of sophisticated automated welding systems.

3. It's a different story in the eastern half of the factory, where welding rods and wires are made. The noise and heat are intense, there is a pervasive smell of chemicals in the air, and some of the machinery dates back more than fifty years. While I was allowed access to the consumables division, many employees are not: The proprietary technical and scientific information surrounding the makeup of the company's variety of welding fluxes is closely guarded.

4. George Willis, telephone interviews with author, March 18 and June 9, 2009.

5. Roughly two hundred sales staff around the United States are not formally covered by the guarantee, but, in practice, they have long been treated as if they were. When the plan was first adopted by the board in 1958, the probation period was set at two years; it was increased to three years in 1991.

6. Mark Wells, interview with author, Mentor, OH, December 10, 2008.

7. George Blankenship, interview with author, Lincoln Electric, December 12, 2008. Blankenship was promoted to senior vice president of North American operations in August 2009.

8. John Stropki, interview with author, Lincoln Electric, December 13, 2008.

9. Rebecca Wells, interview with author, Painesville, OH, September 9, 2008. There are no "sick days" at Lincoln Electric, except as mandated by state and federal laws regarding job-related illnesses and injuries. As with many larger American employers, annual vacations begin with two weeks per year, and rise, with accumulated service, to five weeks a year after twenty-five years of steady employment.

10. Terry Dattilio, telephone interview with author, March 21, 2009.

11. James Maffit, telephone interview with author, August 28, 2008.

12. Damian Kotecki, telephone interview with author, August 19, 2008.

13. Tom Matthews, interview with author, Lincoln Electric, September 11, 2008.

14. Thomas Eagar, telephone interview with author, November 3, 2008.

15. Dick Sabo, telephone interview with author, March 18, 2009.

16. Gretchen Farrell, interview with author, Lincoln Electric, September 17 and December 11, 2008. Farrell was promoted to senior vice president for human resources and compliance in August 2009.

17. Bruce Cable, interview with author, Lincoln Electric, September 8, 2008.

18. Lee Seufer, telephone interview with author, March 26, 2009.

19. James Maffit, interview with author, Mentor, OH, December 10, 2008.

20. J. F. Lincoln, *Incentive Management*, 90–91 (see chap. 2, n. 32).

21. Sourced from documents supplied by Lincoln Electric, ESAB, and conversations with other industry experts.

22. Joseph Doria, telephone interview with author, May 19, 2009.

23. See the "Work-Sharing 2009" Web site of Service Canada, part of the government of Canada, http://www.servicecanada.gc.ca/eng/work_sharing/index.shtml (accessed June 12, 2009); and Steven Greenhouse, "Out of Work, Part Time," *New York Times*, Business sec., June 16, 2009.

24. Dawson, *Lincoln Electric: A History*, 140 (see chap. 1, n. 1).

25. Donald F. Hastings, "Lincoln Electric's Harsh Lessons Form International Expansion," *Harvard Business Review* (May–June 1999).

26. Ingmar Bjorkman and Charles Galunic, *Lincoln Electric in China*, INSEAD, 1999, 11/2007-4850, 15.

27. Jordan Siegel and Barbara Zepp Larson, "Labor Market Institutions and Global Strategic Adaptation: Evidence from Lincoln Electric," *Management Science* (forthcoming).

CHAPTER FOUR

1. Don A. Seastone, "The History of Guaranteed Wages and Employment," *Journal of Economic History* 15 (1955): 134.

2. Jacoby, chap. 3 in *Modern Manors*, 57–94 (see chap. 1, n. 17).

3. Seastone, "History of Guaranteed Wages and Employment," 135.

4. Ibid., 141.

5. Ibid., 142.

6. Ibid., 136. I asked the firms why these policies had been terminated—the answers were, essentially, "Well, it was all a very long time ago."

7. "Bishop Sheil on Wages," *Muncie Post-Democrat*, December 1, 1944, 2, available at http://libx.bsu.edu/cgi-bin/showfile.exe?CISOROOT=/Post DemNews&CISOPTR=832&filename=835.pdf#search=%22sheil%22 (accessed April 16, 2009).

8. Quoted in Seastone, "History of Guaranteed Wages and Employment," 144.

9. Abraham Weiss, *Guaranteed-Employment and Annual Wage Provisions in Union Agreements*, Bulletin 828 (Washington, DC: Bureau of Labor Statistics, U.S. Department of Labor, January 1945).

10. Unnamed, quoted in Jacoby, *Modern Manors*, 254.

11. Legally, Lincoln Electric retains the near-absolute right to terminate its employees "for good cause, bad cause, or no cause at all"—as do almost all employers in the United States except when constrained by collective agreements with their employees—under the deeply rooted doctrine of "employment-at-will."

12. J. F. Lincoln, *Lincoln's Incentive System*, 40 (see chap. 1, n. 27).

13. J. F. Lincoln, *New Approach to Industrial Economics*, 82 (see chap. 1, n. 16).

14. Ibid., 80, 86.

15. Letters from Lincoln Electric archives, courtesy of Dr. Virginia Dawson, Cleveland.

16. James F. Lincoln, "Incentive Program's Success Scrutinized," *Christian Science Monitor*, May 12, 1939, WRHS.

17. J. F. Lincoln, "Lincoln Electric Company Incentive Plan" (see chap. 2, n. 18).

18. From Lincoln Electric Archives, courtesy Dawson.

19. Richard Sennett, *The Corrosion of Character: The Personal Consequences of Work in the New Capitalism* (New York: W. W. Norton, 1998), 147, 31.

20. During a Web-streamed conference call with investment analysts on April 28, 2009, senior vice president Vincent Petrella said, "The flexibility that you have in the U.S. in managing workforce relations including Lincoln's unique guaranteed employment program gives us much more flexible

and rapid ability to right-size, in particular our productive labor force, to existing business levels. Those types of tools are not available, and particularly in western Europe and other parts of the world. So there are much more limited capabilities for temporary reductions in compensation levels that can be done on the North American continent. So that is the fundamental difference between managing the U.S. business and businesses in other parts of the world, the flexibility that we have with workforce relations."

21. Frank Levy and Peter Temin, *Inequality and Institutions in 20th Century America*, Working Paper 07-17 (Cambridge: Massachusetts Institute of Technology Department of Economics, May 1, 2007).

22. H. W. Anderson, "Management's Responsibility for Discipline," *Engineering and Science Monthly* 19, no. 2 (February 1947): 4; unnamed, quoted in David Jenkins, *Job Power: Blue and White Collar Democracy* (Garden City, NY: Doubleday, 1973), 317.

23. Jacoby, *Modern Manors*, 238.

24. Sumner H. Slichter, "Are We Becoming a 'Laboristic' State?" *New York Times*, May 16, 1948.

25. Arthur M. Ross, "Do We Have a New Industrial Feudalism?" *American Economic Review* (December 1958): 903–920.

26. Clark Kerr, "Whatever Became of the Independent Spirit?" *Fortune* (July 1953).

27. Quoted in David E. Sanger, "News Analysis: A New Fear of Japan," *New York Times*, July 31, 1990.

28. Dick Sabo, interview with author, Chagrin Falls, OH, June 17, 2008.

29. William Ouchi, *Theory Z: How American Business Can Meet the Japanese Challenge* (Reading, PA: Addison-Wesley, 1981).

30. Richard Pascale and Anthony G. Athos, *The Art of Japanese Management: Applications for American Executives* (New York: Simon and Schuster, 1981).

31. For a fascinating exploration of the vital relationship between the culture of a workplace and the quality of its production, see Alexandre Mas, "Labor Unrest and the Quality of Production: Evidence from the Construction Equipment Resale Market," *NBER Working Paper Series*, Working Paper 13138, July 2003. Mas chronicled how resale prices for construction equipment produced by Caterpillar during the 1990s—when the company experienced nearly a decade of serious labor strife—fell markedly when compared with prices for the same equipment produced when the company was not having labor problems. Mas's analysis demonstrates that customers clearly believed that the quality of machines produced in a factory plagued by strikes, walkouts, threats, and the use of nonunion replacement workers would be lower—and prices fell accordingly.

32. George Strauss and Tove Hammer, "Worker's Participation in the United States," Institute for Research on Labor and Employment Working Paper Series iirwps-002-87 (University of California–Berkeley) (1987): 8–11.

33. Sidney Harman quoted in Barnaby J. Feder, "The Little Project That Couldn't: Others Learn from a Failed Test in Worker Democracy," *New York Times*, February 21, 1998.

34. Thomas A. Kochan, "Back to Basics: Creating the Analytical Foundations for the Next Industrial Relations System," *Proceedings of the 50th Annual Meeting of the Industrial Relations Research Association* (Chicago, 1998); Thomas A. Kochan, telephone interview with author, February 3, 2009.

35. Like most larger U.S. employers, Lincoln Electric opts out of its state-run workers' compensation program, preferring to self-finance a workers' injury and disability insurance plan. State officials, however, do track self-insured employers, and the Ohio Bureau of Worker's Compensation said there are no unusual incident reports in its files for Lincoln Electric that would indicate a safety record out of the ordinary for manufacturing companies of its size (telephone interview with author, August 13, 2008).

36. J. F. Lincoln, *New Approach to Industrial Economics*, 97.

37. Kate Bronfenbrenner, "No Holds Barred: The Intensification of Employer Opposition to Organizing," Briefing Paper no. 235, *Economic Policy Institute* (May 20, 2009): 1.

38. November 21, 1995. Courtesy of Donald Hastings.

39. Bill Burga, telephone interview with author, August 18, 2008.

CHAPTER FIVE

1. Bureau of Labor Statistics, http://data.bls.gov/cgi-bin/surveymost (accessed August 10, 2009). Every month, the U.S. Department of Labor issues a report on what it calls "mass layoffs," defined as a layoff where fifty or more people in a firm file a claim against their employer for unemployment insurance.

2. Quoted in Connie Guglielmo, "Hewlett-Packard Cuts 24,600 Jobs After EDS Purchase," http://www.bloomberg.com/apps/news?pid=20601087&sid=a.Aw8xiOfGgQ (accessed January 24, 2009).

3. Lincoln Electric 10-K 2009 and "Lincoln Electric Holdings, Inc.," http://www.reuters.com/finance/stocks/ratios?rpc=66&symbol=LECO.O (accessed August 10, 2009).

4. Bruce Cockburn, "The Trouble With Normal," written by Bruce Cockburn, © 1983 Golden Mountain Music Corp. Used with permission.

5. Edward P. Lazear and Michael Gibbs, *Personnel Economics in Practice*, 2nd ed. (New York: John Wiley and Sons, 2008), 103.

6. Bain and Company, *Winning in Turbulence: Strategies for Success in Tumultuous Times* (Boston: Bain and Company, 1999), 5.

7. Steven Greenhouse, *The Big Squeeze: Tough Times for the American Worker* (New York: Alfred A. Knopf, 2008); Katherine S. Newman, *Falling from Grace: Downward Mobility in the Age of Affluence*, paperback ed. (Berkeley and Los Angeles: University of California Press, 1999); Louis Uchitelle, *The Disposable American: Layoffs and Their Consequences* (New York: Alfred A. Knopf, 2006); Elizabeth Warren and Amelia Warren Tyagi, *The Two-Income Trap*, paperback ed. (New York: Basic Books, 2004).

8. Henry S. Farber, *Employment Insecurity: The Decline in Worker-Firm Attachment in the United States*, Working Paper no. 530 (Princeton: Industrial Relations Section, Princeton University, July 2008), 2.

9. Many academic researchers I interviewed bemoaned the lack of good statistical data for working women in the United States. As one woman researcher said, "We see the decline in earnings for men and then write about it for all. . . . I fall into the same trap. . . . Then we add something about how (we think) women's labor force commitments are changing . . . but we just can't see it."

10. Farber, "Employment Insecurity," 25.

11. Henry Farber, telephone interview with author, October 7, 2008.

12. In his 2008 paper cited above, Farber states that the proportion of men between thirty-five and sixty-four who have been with the same employer in the private sector for more than ten years dropped from 50 percent in 1975 to 35 percent in 2005. For those between forty-five and sixty-four, the proportion on the job for more than twenty years dropped from 35 percent to 20 percent. Tenure for women in the private sector has increased, but starting from a much lower level.

13. Farber, "Employment Insecurity," 25. See also Henry S. Farber, "Not So Fast: Long-Term Employment in the U.S., 1969–2004," in *Laid Off, Laid Low: Political and Economic Consequences of Employment Insecurity*, ed. Katherine S. Newman (New York: Columbia University Press, 2008).

14. Ann Huff Stevens, telephone interview with author, October 3, 2008.

15. Till von Wachter, Jae Song, and Joyce Manchester, *Long-Term Earnings Losses Due to Job Separations During the 1982 Recession*, Discussion Paper Series 0708-16 (New York: Columbia University Department of Economics, October 2007), 3.

16. Henry S. Farber, "What Do We Know About Job Loss in the United States? Evidence from the Displaced Workers Survey, 1984–2004," *Economics Perspectives*, 2Q/2005 (Federal Reserve Bank of Chicago) (2005): 23; Jacob Hacker, *The Great Risk Shift* (New York: Oxford University Press, 2006), 74.

17. Philip Oreopoulos, Marianne Page, and Ann Huff Stevens, "The Intergenerational Effects of Worker Displacement," *Journal of Labor Economics* 6, no. 3 (2008): 477.

18. Daniel Sullivan and Till von Wachter, "Mortality, Mass-Layoffs, and Career Outcomes: An Analysis Using Administrative Data," *NBER Working Paper Series* 13626, November 2007. The article received virtually no coverage in the mainstream media in North America.

19. Till von Wachter, interview with author, *World Report*, CBC Radio News, December 6, 2007. Because they were studying very large manufacturing firms, the authors' definition of a mass layoff—30 percent of a company's workforce—involved layoffs that affected many more workers at a time than the Department of Labor's "mass layoff" definition of just fifty workers or more.

20. Ibid.

21. Ibid. Since this research was published, some labor market experts have cautioned that the paper's disturbing findings should not be assumed to apply to the economy as a whole. See Steven J. Davis, "The Decline of Job Loss and Why It Matters" (paper presented at the American Social Science Association, New Orleans, January 2008).

22. Jussi Vahtera et al., "Organizational Downsizing, Sickness Absence, and Mortality," *British Medical Journal* (February 2004).

23. Interview with NewScientist.com, February 23, 2004, http://www .newscientist.com/article/dn4706-downsizing-raises-risk-of-death-in -workers.html (accessed June 12, 2009).

24. Von Wachter interview.

25. Kenneth de Meuse et al., "New Evidence Regarding Organizational Downsizing and a Firm's Financial Performance," *Journal of Managerial Issues* 16, no. 2 (Summer 2004): 173.

26. Henry S. Farber and Kevin F. Hallock, "The Changing Relationship Between Job Loss Announcements and Stock Prices, 1970–1999," Center for Advanced Human Resource Studies, School of Industrial and Labor Relations Working Paper 08-02 (Ithaca: Cornell University, December 17, 2007).

27. Darrell Rigby, "Look Before You Lay Off," *Harvard Business Review* (March 2002): 20; Gunther Capelle-Blancard and Nicolas Couderc, "How Do Shareholders Respond to Downsizing? A Meta Analysis," *University of Paris Pantheon-Sorbonne* (February 2007): 27.

28. De Meuse et al., "New Evidence Regarding Organizational Downsizing," 173.

29. Charles Trevor and Anthony Nyberg, "Keeping Your Headcount When All About You Are Losing Theirs," *Academy of Management Journal* 51, no. 2 (2008): 273.

30. Kevin F. Hallock, "Layoffs in Large U.S. Firms from the Perspective of Senior Managers," *Research in Personnel and Human Resources Management* 25 (2006): 137–179. See also Kevin Hallock, "A Descriptive Analysis of Layoffs in Large U.S. Firms Using Archival and Interview Data, 1970–2002,"

Institute of Labor and Industrial Relations (University of Illinois at Urbana-Champaign) (February 2003).

31. Kevin Hallock, telephone interview with author, October 6, 2008.

32. Sherrilyn M. Billger and Kevin Hallock, "Mass Layoffs and CEO Turnover," *Industrial Relations* 44, no. 3 (July 2005).

33. Jeffrey T. Brookman, Saeyung Chang, and Craig Rennie, "CEO Cash and Stock-Based Compensation Changes, Layoff Decisions, and Shareholder Value," forthcoming in *The Financial Review* (Iowa State University), 15.

34. Craig Rennie, telephone interview with author, October 6, 2008.

35. Robert D. Putnam, *Bowling Alone: The Collapse and Revival of American Community*, paperback ed. (New York: Simon and Schuster, 2000); Barbara Ehrenreich, *Nickled and Dimed: On (Not) Getting By in America*, paperback ed. (New York: Henry Holt); Sennett, *Corrosion of Character* (see chap. 4, n. 19); and Newman, *Falling from Grace*, 1999.

36. Jennie E. Brand and Sarah A. Burgard, "Effects of Job Displacement on Social Participation: Findings over the Life Course of a Cohort of Joiners," *Social Forces* 87, no. 1 (September 2008).

37. Jennie Brand, telephone interview with author, October 3, 2008.

38. Joe Latessa Jr., interview with author, Painesville, OH, September 6, 2008.

39. The full cost of each employee's private medical and hospital insurance is deducted, pretax, from the profit-sharing annual bonus before it is distributed in December. Employees can choose between a number of company-approved insurers; the resulting pooling of employees helps to reduce the cost of premiums.

40. Lincoln Electric began offering stock options to its employees in 1928. The company, which was privately held until 1995, now trades on the NASDAQ with the symbol LECO.

41. Peter Cappelli, telephone interview with author, October 6, 2008.

CHAPTER SIX

1. For an interesting exploration of path dependency, including the QWERTY keyboard debate and the similar battle between VHS and BETA in the videotape era, see Stan J. Liebowitz, and Stephen E. Margolis, *Winners, Losers, and Microsoft: Competition and Antitrust in High Technology* (Oakland: Independent Institute, 1999).

2. David Noble, *Forces of Production: A Social History of Industrial Automation*, paperback ed. (New York: Oxford University Press, 1986), 146.

3. Excerpt edited from Participant Centered Learning, "Harvard Business School: The Case Study Method," http://harvardbusinessonline.hbsp.harvard.edu/hbsp/case_method.jsp (accessed November 2008). For an

overview of MBA programs around the world and the prevalence of the case-study method, see the *Economist*, http://graphics.eiu.com/mba/docs/WMBA_08_Executive_summary_2.pdf (accessed June 12, 2009).

4. Norman Berg, radio interview with the author, CBC News, January 2006.

5. "Observations on the Lincoln Electric Company," EA-A 42, *Harvard Business School* (1947), out of print, WRHS.

6. Norman Berg and Norman Fast, *The Lincoln Electric Company*, HBS 376-028 (Cambridge: Harvard Business School, 1975). Norman Berg's 1975 case study is currently being taught, or has been, in universities as diverse as MIT's Sloan School of Management, the Stanford University Graduate School of Business, the University of Chicago School of Business, INSEAD, the University of Toronto/Rotman School of Management, Goethe University (Frankfurt), and the University of Hong Kong, among many others.

7. *The Lincoln Electric Company: Teaching Note*, HBS 5-395-230 (Cambridge: Harvard Business School, 1996), 2.

8. Thomas Kochan, telephone interview with author, October 23, 2008.

9. Jesper Sorensen, telephone interview with author, October 22, 2008.

10. Norman Berg, telephone interview with author, November 13, 2008.

11. George P. Baker, interview with author, Cambridge, MA, November 5, 2008. Professor Baker is not related to the library's namesake.

12. John Akers was CEO and chairman of IBM from 1986 until 1993.

13. Akers eventually did start large layoffs at IBM. His successor, Louis Gerstner, presided over layoffs totaling as many as 50,000 employees.

14. See Paul Milgrom and John Roberts, "Complementarities and Fit: Strategy, Structure, and Organizational Change in Manufacturing," *Journal of Accounting and Economics* 19 (1995): 179–208.

15. John Roberts, *The Modern Firm: Organizational Design for Performance and Growth* (New York: Oxford University Press, 2004).

16. Ibid., 46 (emphasis added).

17. Robert Gibbons, interview with author, Cambridge, MA, November 6, 2008.

18. James Rebitzer, interviews with author, August 12 (telephone) and September 10 (Cleveland), 2008.

19. John McCracken, telephone interview with author, October 24, 2008.

20. Corey Crowell, Jennifer Timmerman, and Giovanni Carraro, interviews with author, Cambridge, MA, November 5, 2008.

21. I had asked to sit at the back of the lecture hall when the Lincoln Electric case was taught, but school policy dictates that "what goes on in the classroom stays in the classroom" so that students are able to discuss, with complete candor, how they might make difficult business decisions.

22. *60 Minutes*, November 8, 1992.

23. Dhruv Mehrotra, telephone interview with author, November 1, 2008.

24. Jordan Siegel, *Lincoln Electric*, HBS 9-707-445 (Cambridge: Harvard Business School, 2006). There are eight entries in total for Lincoln Electric in HBS's online catalog: Berg's original 1975 case, Siegel's 2006 update, another by Professor Christopher Bartlett from 1998, a fascinating near–mea culpa by former CEO Don Hastings from 1999 detailing Lincoln's expansion mistakes in the late 1980s and early 1990s, a 1977 report from a Harvard MBA who was hired by Lincoln Electric, two Spanish translations, and a video lecture by former CEO George Willis, who visited Harvard in the 1980s.

25. Richard Freeman, interview with author, Cambridge, MA, November 6, 2008.

26. "The Cleveland, Ohio, area operations have a Guaranteed Continuous Employment Plan covering substantially all employees which, in general, provides that the Company will provide work for at least 75% of every standard work week (presently 40 hours). This plan does not guarantee employment when the Company's ability to continue normal operations is seriously restricted by events beyond the control of the Company. The Company has reserved the right to terminate this plan effective at the end of a calendar year by giving notice of such termination not less than six months prior to the end of such year" (Form 10-K, "Lincoln Electric Holdings Inc.–LECO," filed February 24, 2009).

27. Milton Friedman, "The Social Responsibility of Business Is to Increase Profits," edited from the *Sunday New York Times Magazine*, September 13, 1970.

28. J. F. Lincoln, *Lincoln's Incentive System*, 65 (see chap. 1, n. 27).

29. Jon Glick, telephone interview with author, October 24, 2008.

30. Sarah Anderson et al., *Executive Excess in 2008: 15th Annual CEO Compensation Survey* (Washington, DC: Institute for Policy Studies and United for a Fair Economy, 2008), 4.

31. Average total employee pay in 2007 was $68,000, according to data supplied by the company. Using the Department of Labor's inflation figure for 2008 of 3.8 percent yields just over $70,500.

32. Thomas Kochan, telephone interview with author, February 2, 2009; Douglas Kruse, telephone interview with author, May 5, 2009; David Wray, telephone interview with author, May 4, 2009.

33. See Simon Head, *The New Ruthless Economy: Work and Power in the Digital Age* (New York: Oxford University Press, 2003); David M. Gordon, *Fat and Mean: The Corporate Squeeze of Working Americans and the Myth of Managerial Downsizing* (New York: Free Press, 1996); and many others.

34. Hacker, *The Great Risk Shift* (see chap. 5, n. 16).

35. Blessingwhite, "2008 State of Employee Engagement" (April–May 2008): 2, available at http://www.blessingwhite.com/EEE_report.asp; Towers Perrin, "The Towers Perrin Global Workforce Study," October 22, 2007, avail-

able at http://www.towersperrin.com/tp/showhtml.jsp?url=global/publications/
gws/index.htm&country=global.

36. Jeffrey Pfeffer, *What Were They Thinking? Unconventional Wisdom About Management* (Boston: Harvard Business School Press, 2006); David I. Levine, *Reinventing the Workplace: How Business and Employees Can Both Win* (Washington, DC: Brookings Institution, 1995); Thomas Kochan et al., "What Works at Work: Overview and Assessment," February 1996, http://dspace.mit.edu/bitstream/handle/1721.1/2610/SWP-3886-34616085.pdf?sequence=1 (accessed June 12, 2009); Michael J. Handel and David I. Levine, *The Effect of New Work Practices on Workers*, Institute for Research on Labor and Employment Working Paper Series iirwps-131-06 (University of California–Berkeley, 2006); and Sabrina Deutsch-Salamon and Sandra L. Robinson, "Trust That Binds: The Impact of Collective Felt Trust on Organizational Performance," *Journal of Applied Psychology* 93, no. 3 (2008): 593–601.

37. John F. Helliwell and Haifang Huang, "Well Being and Trust in the Workplace," NBER Working Paper Series, Working Paper 14589 (December 2008).

38. Larry Christensen, telephone interview with author, April 27, 2009. See also http://www.labornotes.org/node/2218 (accessed April 26, 2009).

39. John Phillips Jr., telephone interview with author, April 21, 2009.

40. From letters written by Kindler and Immelt to Steven H. Korman, February 17 and February 12, 2009, and shared by Mr. Korman with the author. Korman, the founder and chairman of Korman Communities, a large commercial real estate company, had paid for an open letter to be published in the business sections of the *New York Times* and the *Philadelphia Inquirer* in which he appealed to his fellow American CEOs not to lay off their employees during the recession. Instead, he argued that a majority of shareholders like himself were quite prepared to accept smaller dividends and a lower share price until the economy recovered rather than see so many lives destroyed. Korman also wrote personally to Kindler, Immelt, and many others who had recently ordered huge layoffs. Only four replied.

CHAPTER SEVEN

1. John Stropki, telephone interview with author, May 18, 2009.

2. Mark Wells, telephone interview with author, May 22, 2009.

3. "Welding a New Career," http://www.thejobtrap.blogspot.com (accessed May 22, 2009).

4. Dawson, *Lincoln Electric: A History*, 139 (see chap. 1, n. 1).

5. For example, on May 23, 2008, according to Reuters, Lincoln Electric's long-term debt-to-equity ratio was 9.35 percent. For all industrial companies,

the ratio was 18.97 percent. For all manufacturing, it was 91.12 percent, and finally, for the S&P 500, it was 93.12 percent. See http://www.reuters.com/finance/stocks/ratios?rpc=66&symbol=LECO.O.

6. According to Lincoln Electric's quarterly reports to the SEC, from December 31, 2008, to June 30, 2009, the company's cash balance grew from $284 million to $406 million.

7. Dick Couch, interview with author, Hypertherm, Hanover, NH, October 28, 2008.

8. Dick Couch, telephone interview with author, May 5, 2009.

9. Skip Gould, interview with author, Hypertherm, October 29, 2008.

10. Melissa Carlson, interview with author, Hypertherm, October 28, 2008.

11. Melissa Carlson, telephone interview with author, April 22, 2009.

12. Wim Roelandts, telephone interview with author, October 17, 2008.

13. Wynn left Xilinx in 2005 to become vice president of HR for Adobe Systems. She is currently a senior vice president at California-based Granite Construction.

14. Figures taken from interviews cited and from Thomas Delong and Christina Darwell, *Xilinx, Inc. (A)*, HBS 9-403-136 (Cambridge: Harvard Business School, January 25, 2006).

15. Peg Wynn, telephone interview with author, November 13, 2008.

16. "Xilinx, a Chip Maker Pressed by a Rival, Will Cut 250 Jobs," *New York Times*, June 5, 2008.

17. Bizzia.com, http://www.bizzia.com/tag/xilinx-layoffs/ (accessed July 23, 2009).

18. Kathy Borneman, telephone interview with author, August 21, 2008.

19. Kathy Borneman, telephone interview with author, May 11, 2009.

20. Wim Roelandts, telephone interview with author, April 11, 2009.

21. Bruce Schlegel, telephone interview with author, May 6, 2009.

22. Richard B. Freeman and Joel Rogers, *What Workers Want*, updated ed. (New York: Russell Sage Foundation, 1999).

23. Richard Trumka, telephone interview with author, June 8, 2009.

24. See J. F. Lincoln, chap. 10 of *Lincoln's Incentive System*, 160–172 (see chap. 1, n. 27). See also James O'Toole and Edward E. Lawler III, *The New American Workplace* (New York: Palgrave Macmillan, 2006), 244.

25. Jeffrey Pfeffer, telephone interview with author, February 6, 2009. Pfeffer has explored this troubling issue with great insight in books such as *What Were They Thinking?* (see chap. 6, n. 36) and papers such as "Working Alone: Whatever Happened to the Idea of Organizations as Communities?" in *America at Work: Choices and Challenges*, edited by Edward E. Lawler III and James O'Toole (New York: Palgrave Macmillan, 2006), 3–21.

26. Jack Litzenberg, telephone interview with author, May 19, 2009.

27. Joe Keefe, telephone interview with author, May 13, 2009.

28. See the Department of Labor's fact sheet on WARN at http://www
.doleta.gov/programs/factsht/warn.htm (accessed June 16, 2009).

29. Thomas Kochan et al., "Workplace Innovation and Labor Policy Leadership: A Challenge to Business, Labor, and Government," March 14, 2009,
http://www.cepr.net/documents/publications/workplace-2009-04.pdf
(accessed June 18, 2009).

30. See http://www.whitehouse.gov/strongmiddleclass/ (accessed May 26,
2009).

31. The tone of potential controversy is apparent in a headline of a *New
York Times* story explaining Washington's impending takeover of the American automobile industry: "Highway to the Unknown," Business sec., May
20, 2009, B1.

32. Linda Barrington, telephone interview with author, May 20, 2009.

33. Rebecca M. Blank et al., *Working Nation: Workers, Work, and Government in the New Economy* (New York: Russell Sage Foundation, 2000).

34. U.S. Census, table 742, "Employer Firm Births and Deaths and Business Bankruptcies by State, 2005 to 2007," http://www.census.gov/
compendia/statab/tables/09s0742.pdf (accessed May 27, 2009).

35. Stropki interview, May 18, 2009.

36. Pew Research Center, "American Mobility: Who Moves? Who Stays
Put? Where's Home?" updated to December 29, 2008, http://pewsocial
trends.org/pubs/721/movers-and-stayers (accessed May 27, 2009). This figure
is actually the lowest in decades: Americans are moving less as the country
grows older.

37. Ohio Department of Development, "Cuyahoga County Profile,"
http://www.odod.state.oh.us/research/FILES/So/Cuyahoga.pdf (accessed August 4, 2009).

38. Paul Oyaski, telephone interview with author, April 1, 2009.

39. Raymond Hogler, telephone interview with author, August 22, 2008.

INDEX

COUVRETTE/OTTOWA

FRANK KOLLER is an economics journalist and former foreign correspondent for the Canadian Broadcasting Corporation. Over a twenty-seven-year career with CBC, he worked and lived around the world, including seven years in the United States. He holds a master's degree in engineering from the Massachusetts Institute of Technology. He lives in Ottawa.

www.frankkoller.com

PublicAffairs is a publishing house founded in 1997. It is a tribute to the standards, values, and flair of three persons who have served as mentors to countless reporters, writers, editors, and book people of all kinds, including me.

I. F. STONE, proprietor of *I. F. Stone's Weekly*, combined a commitment to the First Amendment with entrepreneurial zeal and reporting skill and became one of the great independent journalists in American history. At the age of eighty, Izzy published *The Trial of Socrates*, which was a national bestseller. He wrote the book after he taught himself ancient Greek.

BENJAMIN C. BRADLEE was for nearly thirty years the charismatic editorial leader of *The Washington Post*. It was Ben who gave the *Post* the range and courage to pursue such historic issues as Watergate. He supported his reporters with a tenacity that made them fearless and it is no accident that so many became authors of influential, best-selling books.

ROBERT L. BERNSTEIN, the chief executive of Random House for more than a quarter century, guided one of the nation's premier publishing houses. Bob was personally responsible for many books of political dissent and argument that challenged tyranny around the globe. He is also the founder and longtime chair of Human Rights Watch, one of the most respected human rights organizations in the world.

·   ·   ·

For fifty years, the banner of Public Affairs Press was carried by its owner Morris B. Schnapper, who published Gandhi, Nasser, Toynbee, Truman, and about 1,500 other authors. In 1983, Schnapper was described by *The Washington Post* as "a redoubtable gadfly." His legacy will endure in the books to come.

Peter Osnos, *Founder and Editor-at-Large*